Charlie Reed 3·21·97

Your Reading

NCTE Bibliography Series

Your Reading

A Booklist for Junior High
and Middle School

Ninth Edition

C. Anne Webb, Editor,
Paul Hirth, Associate Editor,
and the Committee on the Junior High
and Middle School Booklist
of the National Council of Teachers of English

National Council of Teachers of English
1111 W. Kenyon Road, Urbana, Illinois 61801-1096

NCTE Editorial Board: Keith Gilyard; Ronald Jobe; Joyce Kinkead; Louise Wetherbee Phelps; Gladys Veidemanis; Charles Suhor, Chair, *ex officio;* Michael Spooner, *ex officio*

Staff Editors: Michael G. Ryan and Rona S. Smith

Cover Design: R. Maul

Cover Illustration: Susan McGinnis

Interior Design: Tom Kovacs for TGK Graphics

NCTE Stock Number: 59427-3050

Library of Congress Cataloging-in-Publication Data
Your reading: a booklist for junior high and middle school /
   C. Anne Webb, editor, Paul Hirth, associate editor, and the
   Committee on the Junior High and Middle School Booklist of
   the National Council of Teachers of English. — 9th ed.
      p.   cm. — (NCTE bibliography series, ISSN 1051-4740)
   Includes bibliographical references and index.
   ISBN 0-8141-5942-7
   1. Children's literature—Bibliography.   2. Bibliography—Best
   books—Children's literature.   3. Junior high school libraries—
   United States—Book lists.   4. Middle school libraries—United
   States—Book lists.   I. Webb, C. Anne.   II. Hirth, Paul.
   III. National Council of Teachers of English. Committee
   on the Junior High and Middle School Booklist.   IV. Series.
   Z1037.Y68   1993
   [PN1009.A1]   93-8652
   011.62′5—dc20   CIP

Contents

III Exploring

IV Understanding

Acknowledgments

When I began attending NCTE conventions in 1972, my mentor was editing *Books for You.* It became my goal to serve on a booklist committee at some time before hanging up my American Express card. Thus, when Aileen Nielsen was named editor of the eighth edition of *Your Reading,* I offered myself for her committee. Two years later, with much amazement, I read the letter from NCTE's Executive Committee asking me to chair the committee for the ninth edition.

I considered all the pros and cons of taking on this responsibility and accepted because this list is for junior high/middle school teachers to use as a tool to inspire, intrigue, and motivate junior high/middle school kids, a difficult age group, but one I know something about, having been in the junior high classroom for twenty-six years.

I also accepted the challenge because of my twenty-plus-year love affair with YA literature. Through NCTE and ALAN (Assembly on Literature for Adolescents of NCTE) I have accumulated a storehouse of opinions about the body of literature published for young adults.

Therefore, I not only acknowledge the efforts of my committee, which were loyal and tremendous; the bullying which my associate editor, Paul Hirth, took from me; but I also acknowledge every teacher, author, publisher, librarian, editor, and NCTE staff member who has supported me all these years. You know who you are—I love you; I thank you.

C. Anne Webb
St. Louis, MO
January 1993

Charlie —
When you ask my advice and listened — it took me to a new level. Thanks for your friendship and support.
12/3/93   C. Anne

Foreword

The National Council of Teachers of English is proud to publish four different booklists, renewed on a regular rotation, in its bibliography series. The four are *Adventuring with Books* (pre-K through grade 6), *Your Reading* (middle school/junior high), *Books for You* (senior high), and *High Interest—Easy Reading* (junior/senior high reluctant readers). Conceived as resources for teachers and students alike, these volumes reference thousands of the most recent children's and young adults' trade books. The works listed cover a wide range of topics, from preschool ABC books to science fiction novels for high school seniors; from wordless picture books to nonfiction works on family stresses, computers, and mass media.

Each edition of an NCTE booklist is compiled by a group of teachers and librarians, under leadership appointed by the NCTE Executive Committee. Working for most of three or four years with new books submitted regularly by publishers, the committee members review, select, and annotate the hundreds of works to be listed in their new edition. The members of the committee that compiled this volume are listed on one of the first pages.

Of course, no single book is right for everyone or every purpose, so inclusion of a work in this booklist is not necessarily an endorsement from NCTE. However, it is an indication that, in the view of the professionals who make up the booklist committee, the work in question is worthy of teachers' and students' attention, perhaps for its informative, perhaps its aesthetic qualities. On the other hand, exclusion from an NCTE booklist is not necessarily a judgment on the quality of a given book or publisher. Many factors—space, time, availability of certain books, publisher participation—may influence the final shape of the list.

We hope that you will find this booklist useful and that you will collect the other booklists in the NCTE series. We feel that these volumes contribute substantially to our mission of helping to improve instruction in English and the language arts. We think you will agree.

Michael Spooner
NCTE Senior Editor for Publications

Introduction

Using This Book

This ninth edition of *Your Reading* covers books published primarily in 1991–1992 for the middle school/junior high audience. We have included a few 1990 titles which were published too late for inclusion in the eighth edition and a few early 1993 releases.

We have organized the book into four main sections: Imagining, Exploring, Learning, and Understanding. The Imagining and Understanding sections include both fiction and nonfiction within some chapters; the Learning section is entirely nonfiction, while the Exploring section is exclusively fiction.

Where series of books were selected, they will appear at the end of a section. Most series titles are given a general annotation with only the series' newest titles listed. However, in some cases, especially with nonfiction series, we did annotate each title separately; this was because we felt that nonfiction series books were less well known than fiction, as well as less self-promoting.

While the Contents will give you a general idea of the book's organization, the Subject Index will help you find individual books on a particular topic. An Author Index and a Title Index are also included. The Directory of Publishers rounds out the standard features of the booklist.

In a special appendix compiled by M. Jerry Weiss is a list of 150 "classics" of young adult literature from 1940 to 1990. We include this list as a guide for teachers who are new to the field of YA literature and may not have access to the earlier editions of *Your Reading*.

Further Sources for Keeping Up with New Titles

Some 5,000 titles are published yearly for the young adult market. It would be impossible to annotate them all. Accordingly, publishers were asked to send their best books for our consideration, and the readers of this committee, most of whom are classroom teachers or school librarians, were asked to screen the books further for literary merit, curriculum possibility, and age level suitability, while keeping in mind the likes, dislikes, and interests of their students.

Since this list covers only the publication years of 1991–92, we recommend that you refer to earlier editions of NCTE booklists for annotations of books published before 1990. Many older titles are still in print or are reprinted from time to time.

Because students in junior high/middle school cover a wide range of abilities and interests, it will help you to become acquainted with the other NCTE booklists: *Adventuring with Books,* the elementary list; *Books for You,* the senior high list; and *High Interest—Easy Reading,* for reluctant secondary school readers. The elementary and secondary section journals (*Language Arts* and *English Journal,* respectively) also offer regular features on young adult literature. And three times a year, NCTE's Assembly on Literature for Adolescents publishes a journal—*The ALAN Review*—devoted entirely to adolescent literature. A regular updating of new titles in *The ALAN Review* is the "Clip and File" section, which provides reviews of both hardback and paperback books.

Classroom Selection

We are a pluralistic society. Therefore, a book that plays well in Denver may not do so well in Peoria. You, the classroom teacher, know what is best for your classroom and what the individual needs of the students in your room are. Do not assume that because a book is listed in this collection, it will work in your particular situation. No book should be ordered for curricular use until it has been read cover to cover and a rationale written by the person(s) who will teach it. As recommended by NCTE's Standing Committee Against Censorship, it is always wise to have an alternative list available, regardless of the selection.

If you have questions about selection and/or rationale writing, NCTE staff can send you information on writing rationales for selections to be taught.

Recreational Reading in the Classroom

Encourage and model recreational reading. I recommend that you fit recreational reading into your plans as often as possible—one day a week for sustained silent reading is not too much. Talk about the new titles coming into the school library; have the kids talk about what they have just read. With your guidance, students can get as excited about a book as they do about the newest Batman movie or the latest Madonna release.

Give credit for reading and talking about books. Some kids will come alive with this opportunity to share an exciting reading experience. Teach the kids to conduct book talks and give points for doing them. Direct those chatty junior high kids into reading activities and provide a reason to channel all that energy into reading.

It's a good idea to start a class card file with annotations the kids themselves have written for the books they have read. Develop a class rating system for the readers themselves to code onto the annotation card. This will serve as a quick check for you to find out what happened while the books were read, and it will provide a recommendation for others to use in selecting books to read.

Read aloud to your classes; teachers from K–16 do it all over the country. Even reading just a chapter or two will catch your students' interest. One committee member could not get *Tom Sawyer* out of the library fast enough after her seventh-grade teacher read the chewing gum scene aloud to her. Teens today will have the same reaction with the newest Gary Paulsen or Walter Dean Myers book.

Keep books lying around the room and available to your students. Start a paperback library. Publishers' book clubs give bonus points for frequent buyers—use those points to stock the shelves in your room. Encourage students to donate paperbacks they have finished reading.

Finally, don't leave the selection for your library's collection entirely to the librarian. Make the wishes of your kids known. This would be a good place to show what extracurricular titles the students are carrying into your room. Make the library budget selection a collaborative effort of the entire staff. Suggest that the librarian try an experiment by buying a test number of paperbacks for general circulation. No, they won't hold up as well, but one paperback checked out may hook a lifetime reader. It is a small enough investment. Library budgets are limited, too, so the librarian will appreciate the suggestions to spend the funds most wisely.

Writing to the Authors

The most exciting aspect of young adult literature is that it dispels the old myth, "The only good author is a dead author." Readers like to question authors in person as to motives, reasons, and influences for their work. While questioning is not always possible in person, letter writing is. Authors are like anyone else in the arts—they need and encourage input from their fans.

The Directory of Publishers in the back of this edition lists all of the publishing companies contributing books to this list. Your students can write to authors in care of the publisher shown for their favorite book. The letter will be passed along to the author, and an answer will often be forthcoming.

One word of caution is to avoid sending a packet of letters by every member in a class. The author does not want to feel the letters being received have been "required." The class might have a contest to choose the best representative letter or might choose to put together a composite letter. Some teachers have even formed multiple groups to compose letters and then by some means chosen the best group letter. Answers to inquiries will be more likely if the author does not feel swamped.

I Imagining

I am giddy; expectation whirls me round;
The imaginary relish is so sweet
That it enchants my sense.

William Shakespeare
Troilus and Cressida
Act III, Scene 2, Line 17

1 Animal Stories

1.1 Beales, Valerie. **Emma and Freckles.** Illustrated by Jacqueline Rogers. Simon & Schuster, 1992. 195 pp. ISBN 0-671-74686-3.

Although Emma has taken riding lessons for several years, she has always wanted a horse of her own. Though her parents suspect that she is not mature enough to handle the responsibility, they give in to their daughter's pleading, but only with misgivings. Unfortunately, Emma's new pony, Freckles, is difficult to control. When he destroys Emma's father's vegetable garden, his pride and joy, Emma's parents sell the horse. Emma is heartbroken, especially when she begins to suspect that the owner of the riding school, who bought Freckles, mistreats his animals. Emma and her friends decide to rescue Freckles, even if they have to steal him!

1.2 Burgess, Melvin. **The Cry of the Wolf.** Tambourine Books, 1992. 128 pp. ISBN 0-688-11744-9.

The Hunter and the people of Surrey in England have discovered wolves, long thought to be extinct there, in the nearby countryside. The Tilleys and their young son Ben try to protect the animals, but the Hunter wants to kill all the wolves for sport. It takes a final confrontation between the Hunter and the last wolf, Graycub, to determine who is the predator and who is the prey.

1.3 Hall, Lynn. **The Soul of the Silver Dog.** Harcourt Brace Jovanovich, 1992. 128 pp. ISBN 0-15-277196-4.

Feeling rejected by her own family after her younger sister's death, fourteen-year-old Cory adopts a blind show dog and devotes herself to bringing back some of his championship glory by training him for agility competition.

1.4   Henry, Marguerite. **Stormy, Misty's Foal.** Illustrated by Wesley Dennis. Aladdin Books, 1991. 223 pp. ISBN 0-689-71487-4.

A hurricane destroys many of the wild ponies of Chincoteague and Assateague islands. Stormy, a horse born in the aftermath of the storm, and her famous mother, Misty, come to the rescue, though, by helping Paul and Maureen raise money to restore the herds. This sequel to *Misty of Chincoteague* is also based on a true story. Originally published in 1963.

1.5   Naylor, Phyllis Reynolds. **Shiloh.** A Yearling Book, 1992. 144 pp. ISBN 0-440-40752-4.

Marty Preston loves to roam the woods and hills surrounding his West Virginia home. One day, near the old Shiloh schoolhouse, a brown and white beagle begins to follow Marty; it follows him right home. But Marty's father says the dog belongs to Todd Travers, and Marty will have to return the animal to its rightful owner. Certain that Todd Travers abuses his dogs, Marty sets out to steal the dog, save it from abuse, and have it for his own. The dog Marty now calls Shiloh is eager to come with him, but Marty's theft is discovered. What follows teaches Todd Travers a lesson or two, and teaches Marty what love for animals can bring.

1.6   Sherlock, Patti. **Some Fine Dog.** Holiday House, 1992. 153 pp. ISBN 0-8234-0947-3.

This book tells the story of Terry, a twelve-year old gifted soloist in his church choir and his beloved border collie, Duffy. Terry may keep Duffy on two conditions: he must earn enough money to feed Duffy and continue to go to choir practice. But Terry dreams of training Duffy for a dog act to take on the road, an idea Terry's mother vehemently opposes. Will Terry ever reach his dreams?

1.7   Slade, Michael. **The Horses of Central Park.** Scholastic, 1992. 119 pp. ISBN 0-590-44659-2.

When Judith and Wendell decide to give the horses in Central Park their freedom for one night, their glorious adventure begins. With careful planning, the two children succeed, increasing the popularity of the horses and giving them their freedom, if only for a single night. Then the whole community becomes involved in the mysterious disappearance, leading to the return of the horses of Central Park.

2 Magic and Monsters: Fantasy

2.1 Banks, Lynne Reid. **The Farthest-Away Mountain.** Illustrated by Dave Henderson. Doubleday, 1991. 138 pp. ISBN 0-385-41534-6.

When the mountain nods, fourteen-year-old Dakin knows it is the signal for her to begin her quest: Before she marries, Dakin has vowed to visit the farthest-away mountain, meet a gargoyle, and find a prince for a husband. Her quest introduces her to an enchanted brass troll, his gargoyle brothers, and a two-hundred-year-old teacher who's been turned into a toad. Along the way, Dakin has a chance to bathe in bottomless magic ponds, to walk in bewitched multicolored snow, and to match wits with terrifying monsters. Determined and courageous, Dakin learns that the true hero is wise and brave, as well as good. Originally published in 1976.

2.2 Barron, T. A. **The Ancient One.** Philomel Books, 1992. 367 pp. ISBN 0-399-21899-8.

While helping her Great Aunt Melanie try to protect an Oregon redwood forest from loggers, thirteen-year-old Kate goes back five centuries through a time tunnel and faces the evil creature Gashra, who is bent on destroying the same forest. Companion book to *Heartlight*.

2.3 Bradshaw, Gillian. **The Dragon and the Thief.** Illustrated by Karen L. Baker. Greenwillow Books, 1991. 154 pp. ISBN 0-688-10575-0.

Prahotep, a young man living in ancient Egypt, seems to be unlucky at everything until he moves to Thebes and becomes a thief. But when Prahotep stumbles into a dragon's cave, his destiny becomes clear. Join him and Hathor the dragon as they undertake the dangerous but exciting task of transporting Hathor's treasure from Thebes to Nubia, where the dragon will rejoin her dragon kin.

2.4   Bradshaw, Gillian. **The Land of Gold.** Greenwillow Books, 1992. 154 pp. ISBN 0-688-10576-9.

Kandaki awakens one night in ancient Africa to find her parents, the king and queen of Nubia, murdered by guards. When Kandaki is suddenly taken to a lake to be a human sacrifice for a god, two Egyptians, Prahotep and Baki, along with Hathor, the last of the dragons, rescue her. From then on, the group of friends tries to return Kandaki to her rightful place as queen of Nubia and tries to find a mate for Hathor. Sequel to *The Dragon and the Thief.*

2.5   Brennan, J. H. **Shiva: An Adventure of the Ice Age.** J. B. Lippincott, 1989. 184 pp. ISBN 0-397-32453-7.

A "little ogre," separated from his family, saves young Shiva, a human girl, from a wolf. Shiva is grateful, even though her family's tribe is opposed to the Neanderthal tribe, from which the ogre comes. Meanwhile, Hiram, a young hunter from Shiva's tribe, has been captured by the Neanderthals. War between the two tribes seems inevitable. Can Shiva and her young ogre friend stop their families from killing each other?

2.6   Brittain, Bill. **Wings.** HarperCollins, 1991. 135 pp. ISBN 0-06-020648-9.

When twelve-year-old Ian grows an unsightly pair of wings, he becomes an embarrassment to his politically ambitious father and must look for help from class outcast Anita and her eccentric mother.

2.7   Coville, Bruce. **Jennifer Murdley's Toad.** Illustrated by Gary A. Lippincott. Jane Yolen Books, 1992. 160 pp. ISBN 0-15-200745-8.

Jennifer Murdley's life is ordinary and dull—until the day she purchases a toad from Mr. Elive's pet shop. The toad she picks is not just an ordinary toad—Bufo is a magic toad! He talks and reads, and Jennifer suddenly finds herself involved in a series of extraordinary adventures with her special new friend.

2.8   Coville, Bruce. **Jeremy Thatcher, Dragon Hatcher.** Illustrated by Gary A. Lippincott. Jane Yolen Books, 1991. 148 pp. ISBN 0-15-200748-2.

Dragons don't really exist, do they? Well, they do for Jeremy, who buys a dragon egg in a strange magic shop. As Jeremy watches in amazement, the egg begins to hatch, releasing a baby dragon into the world! Can Jeremy keep his dragon as it grows into full size?

2.9   Denzel, Justin. **Hunt for the Last Cat.** Philomel Books, 1991. 189 pp. ISBN 0-399-22101-8.

In prehistoric Florida, twelve-year-old Thorn feels conflicting loyalties when members of his clan blame his friend Fonn, a girl from a rival clan, for the marauding actions of a man-eating sabretooth cat. Thorn's tribal leaders insist that Fonn is an evil changeling, come to help the savage cat finish the work begun four years ago—when the cat killed Thorn's father. Who should Thorn believe? And what can he do to stop the killer cat?

2.10   Doyle, Debra and James D. Macdonald. **Knight's Wyrd.** Jane Yolen Books, 1992. 209 pp. ISBN 0-15-200764-4.

When Will Odosson receives his knighthood, he believes his future looks brighter. But a prophetic wizard doesn't agree; he predicts that Will will meet his death before a single year has passed. Undaunted, Sir Will sets out on a series of adventures, battling trolls, ogres, and ghosts, each day bringing him closer to his Wyrd, or fate.

2.11   Hersom, Kathleen. **The Half Child.** Simon & Schuster, 1991. 160 pp. ISBN 0-671-74225-6.

In the seventeenth century, Lucy Emerson cares for her younger sister Sarah, who is not normal and believed by some to be a changeling, a child left by the fairies. According to a popular belief of the time, a changeling could at any time be taken back to the land of fairies. When a new baby is born, Sarah suddenly disappears and Lucy, believing her sister to have been taken by the fairies, sets out on a quest to find Sarah.

2.12 Hildick, E. W. **The Case of the Dragon in Distress.** Macmillan, 1991. 153 pp. ISBN 0-02-743931-3.

The members of the McGurk Organization travel back in time to the Middle Ages, encountering an evil princess who tries to hold them captive. Dragons, dungeons, castles, knights, and kings combine to make this a rousing medieval adventure!

2.13 Hughes, Monica. **The Promise.** Simon & Schuster, 1992. 196 pp. ISBN 0-671-75033-X.

Princess Rania can't believe that her parents would just give her away to the Sandwriter, a strange and powerful woman who lives alone in the desert. The Sandwriter, using her power to protect the people of Roshan from storms, drought, and other hardships, chooses Rania as her successor. But Rania tries to escape the austere fate of a future Sandwriter, longing for the normal life she left behind. Yet she discovers that the skills the Sandwriter teaches will follow her everywhere, so that she is no longer fit for a "normal" life. Sequel to *Sandwriter.*

2.14 Jacques, Brian. **Mariel of Redwall.** Illustrated by Gary Chalk. Philomel Books, 1991. 387 pp. ISBN 0-399-22144-1.

Mousemaid Mariel achieves victory at sea for the animals of Redwall Abbey as she pursues her quest to avenge her father. The savage pirate rat Gabool the Wild, warlord of rodent corsairs, and his nasty allies want to possess Redwall Abbey, and they will stop at nothing to get it. Can the mice of the abbey hold off the evil rats? Mousemaid Mariel is sure they can!

2.15 James, Betsy. **Dark Heart.** Dutton Children's Books, 1992. 217 pp. ISBN 0-525-44951-5.

In this sequel to *Long Night Dance,* seventeen-year-old Kat's struggle to learn the ways of her dead mother's people in the hill country is complicated by her failure in the bear ceremony, a spiritual rite of passage. Her attraction to the blind outcast Raim only further confuses her, forcing her to choose between her society or her heart.

2.16   Jones, Diana Wynne. **Castle in the Air.** Greenwillow Books, 1990. 199 pp. ISBN 0-688-09686-7.

To escape an ordinary life as a carpet merchant, young Abdullah daydreams that he is really a long-lost prince with a beautiful princess. One day, after a stranger sells him a magic carpet, his dreams begin to become reality. Suddenly, encounters with a genie, a wild animal, an old soldier, and a beautiful princess make Abdullah's life more adventurous and dangerous than he had ever imagined!

2.17   Jones, Diana Wynne. **The Lives of Christopher Chant.** Bullseye Books, 1988. 230 pp. ISBN 0-394-82205-6.

In this prequel to *Charmed Life,* Christopher Chant is more interested in playing cricket than practicing sorcery. He's not very good at magic and can't even master the simplest spells, but his exciting Uncle Ralph convinces Christopher to use what abilities he has to enter the spirit worlds and do strange errands. On one of these adventures, Christopher is fatally injured but mysteriously comes back to life. When this happens a second time, a famous sorcerer determines that Christopher is a rare nine-lived enchanter, and Christopher is whisked off to be trained as the next Chrestomanci, the all-powerful guardian of the world's magic. Suddenly, he is in charge of powers and realms beyond anything he could have imagined. Can Christopher succeed as the Chrestomanci, even if he's a mediocre magician?

2.18   Kirwan-Vogel, Anna. **The Jewel of Life.** Illustrated by David Wilgus. Jane Yolen Books, 1991. 118 pp. ISBN 0-15-200750-4.

"Wherever you are at this moment, you are near a doorway into the most profound mysteries of the infinite worlds of wonder."

It is through one of these doorways that Duffy is lucky enough to be led when he is taken from the poorhouse and apprenticed to Master Crowe, an apothecary and alchemist. Duffy loves his master and teacher, but the rest of the village does not share Duffy's view of the old man, and both of their lives are threatened.

2.19 Luenn, Nancy. **Goldclimbers.** Atheneum, 1991. 184 pp. ISBN 0-689-31585-6.

In the Land of Caraccen, life revolves around gold, and status in the society is determined by the work done with this precious metal. Fifteen-year-old Aracco is expected to follow in his father's footsteps and become an expert goldsmith. But he dislikes the confinement of the casting room and wishes to do the more exciting job of the climbers, even if it means having to fight off the eirocs, giant birds of prey. Aracco sees no other future for himself until, when the supply of gold is threatened, he is chosen to find the legendary city where the streets are paved with gold.

2.20 McGowen, Tom. **A Trial of Magic.** Lodestar Books, 1992. 149 pp. ISBN 0-525-67376-8.

Earthdoom! The magicians of Atlan Domain have seen it in their annual ritual which reveals to them events of the coming year. This year, they have seen a threat to earth, a threat that will come from outer space. Having secured the aid of the wizards of the Dragons and the Little People in an effort to prevent Earthdoom, Mulng and his son Lithim and the other magicians of Atlan Domain must now face the fearsome opposition of a very powerful Alfar Master mage. Second book in the Age of Magic trilogy.

2.21 Pierce, Meredith Ann. **Dark Moon.** Little, Brown and Company, 1992. 238 pp. ISBN 0-316-70744-9.

Jan, a unicorn prince, is separated from his royal subjects during a battle with their enemies, the gryphons. His memory lost, Jan does not protest when a tribe of humans feed and stable him with ordinary horses. He doesn't even remember

Tek, the wife he chose just before the battle. Meanwhile, Tek, believing Jan is dead, is cast out of the unicorn community by Jan's grief-stricken father. Told alternately from Jan and Tek's points of view, this fantasy chronicles the eventual reunion between the two unicorns. Second book in the Firebringer trilogy.

2.22   Pratchett, Terry. **Diggers.** Delacorte Press, 1989. 185 pp. ISBN 0-385-30152-9.

In this second book of Bromeliad, tiny Nomes forced from the department store that has been their home for generations struggle to survive in an abandoned stone quarry. They face animals, cold, snow, and a generally argumentative population. Then, in case the lives of the Nomes aren't hard enough, humans appear and seem to be reopening the quarry. The Nomes vehemently disagree with each other about the best course of action: flee, fight, hide, negotiate, or try to contact the sky kingdom from which they originally descended. Sequel to *Truckers*.

2.23   Sherman, Josepha. **Child of Faerie, Child of Earth.** Walker and Company, 1992. 159 pp. ISBN 0-8027-8112-8.

Percinet, the only son of Queen of the Faeries, Rezaila, has fallen in love with a mortal. Percinet wants to romance the human Graciosa, the daughter of a medieval count, but she dreads anything or anyone magical. In twelfth-century France, even practicing a little magic could get Graciosa put to death. To make matters worse, Lady Eglantine, Graciosa's cruel stepmother who hides secret magic skills of her own, plots to send Percinet and Graciosa to their deaths.

2.24   Singer, Marilyn. **Charmed.** Atheneum, 1990. 219 pp. ISBN 0-689-31619-4.

Miranda's parents and friends criticize her for having an overactive imagination. But she knows her large, invisible catlike creature, Bastable, is real. When her Uncle Gerald gives her an old snake charmer's basket, she and Bastable accidentally end up inside the basket, where they find themselves in another time and world. There, the evil Charmer wants to conquer and control the universe. Can Miranda and Bastable find a way to stop the Charmer from ruling everything?

2.25   Stevenson, Laura C. **The Island and the Ring.** Houghton Mifflin Company, 1991. 275 pp. ISBN 0-395-56401-8.

The island of Elyssonne is Good, pure, peaceful and harmonious. But the mainland is Evil, controlled by a ruthless lord Prince Ascanet, who wants to claim Elyssonne for his own. And after treachery destroys her island kingdom, young Princess Tania finds herself caught in a battle between Good and Evil. Can she confront her destiny and save Elyssonne?

2.26   Strickland, Brad. **Dragon's Plunder.** Illustrated by Wayne D. Barlowe. Atheneum, 1992. 153 pp. ISBN 0-689-31573-2.

Jamie Falconer is willingly kidnapped from his life as an innkeeper's lackey to serve as cabinboy aboard the privateer *Betty* in an ancient mythical kingdom. The commander of the ship, Captain Deadmon, a living corpse who has been "dead" for twenty years, needs Jamie's ability to create favorable winds to reach the only remaining island which houses a dragon and its plunder. By stealing this plunder and dividing it among his crew, Deadmon can be released from an oath spoken at the time of his death. Can Jamie help Deadmon and his crew find the dragon of Windrose Island?

2.27   Thompson, Julian F. **Herb Seasoning.** Scholastic, 1990. 280 pp. ISBN 0-590-43023-8.

How will teenager Herb Hertzman ever find out what his life is all about? Well, he could search for answers his whole life—and maybe never learn anything—or he could travel to the Castles in the Air, a fantastical place where others have gone before him, searching for what would make them happy. Will his Alice-in-Wonderland-like adventure give him the answers he wants?

2.28   Turner, Ann. **Rosemary's Witch.** HarperCollins/Charlotte Zolotow Books, 1991. 164 pp. ISBN 0-06-026127-7.

The house nine-year-old Rosemary and her family move into has just enough room for everyone—except the 150-year-old witch living in the woods nearby! Mathilda, the witch, once lived in the old New England house, and she has every intention of taking it back. But Rosemary is the only one who knows there's a threat to the family's new home. Can she find some way to convince Mathilda to leave them be? Or will Mathilda take her house back by trickery?

2.29   Vande Velde, Vivian. **Dragon's Bait.** Jane Yolen Books, 1992. 131 pp. ISBN 0-15-200726-1.

After being accused of witchcraft by members of her village, fifteen-year-old Alys is tied to a stake as a sacrifice to the horrid dragon. When the dragon comes, however, instead of eating her, it agrees to help her take revenge on those who falsely accused her. But the methods Selendrile, the dragon, uses are not only unusual, they're also very dangerous, as Alys discovers as she tries to get even.

2.30   Vande Velde, Vivian. **User Unfriendly.** Jane Yolen Books, 1991. 256 pp. ISBN 0-15-200960-4.

Fourteen-year-old Arvin and his friends enter a dangerous computer game, a game in which they actually become fantasy characters in a magical world. It seems like fun as they quest for a king's daughter, but the computer program is a pirated one containing unpredictable errors. Suddenly, the fun turns to real danger!

2.31   Vande Velde, Vivian. **A Well-Timed Enchantment.** Crown, 1990. 184 pp. ISBN 0-517-57319-9.

Deanna's trip to France is boring. Of course, accidentally dropping her Mickey Mouse watch down a well couldn't change history. Or can it? Two Sidhe (elves) say it's not a simple well but instead a temporal loophole. With her intriguing cat-turned-human friend Oliver, Deanna has just twenty-four hours to find her watch in tenth-century France or history will be changed for the *much* worse.

2.32 Walker, Mary Alexander. **The Scathach and Maeve's Daughters.** Atheneum, 1990. 119 pp. ISBN 0-689-31638-0.

The Scathach is like a fairy godmother, a supernatural being that sometimes selects a special person to help with her magic. Maeve is the sixteen-year-old daughter of an eighth-century Celtic King, and her kindness and strength attract the Scathach to help her with a wish. But Maeve phrases her wish in such a way that the help continues through generations of Maeve's children, well into the 21st century. These vignettes are full of delightful surprises, humor, and magic as they describe the ongoing relationship of the Scathach with Maeve's descendants.

2.33 Woodruff, Elvira. **Back in Action.** Illustrated by Will Hillenbrand. Holiday House, 1991. 150 pp. ISBN 0-8234-0897-3.

Sneezing isn't dangerous. Or is it? Nate and Noah, two young friends, have found a magic powder. After Nate's untimely sneeze, the two boys are covered with the powder, and find themselves only four inches tall. What's it like to dwell in the world of Noah's plastic toy men? Just ask Noah and Nate!

2.34 Wrede, Patricia C. **Searching for Dragons.** Harcourt Brace Jovanovich, 1991. 242 pp. ISBN 0-15-200898-5.

Princess Cimorene is no helpless princess, waiting to be rescued from boredom by some handsome prince. In fact, Princess Cimorene can rescue not only herself, but dragons as well! With the aid of King Mandanbar, she saves the dragon Kazul *and* the Enchanted Forest from a band of wicked wizards! Book two of the *Enchanted Forest Chronicles*.

2.35 Yep, Laurence. **The Dragon Cauldron.** HarperCollins, 1991. 312 pp. ISBN 0-06-026753-4.

A dragon named Shimmer, a monkey wizard, a reformed witch, and two humans set out on a costly journey to find and repair a magic cauldron. Follow this unlikely team of heroes through their trials and triumphs as they seek the only solution that will mend the dragon's home.

2.36   Yolen, Jane. **Wizard's Hall.** Illustrated by Trina Schart Hyman. Harcourt Brace Jovanovich, 1991. 133 pp. ISBN 0-15-298132-2.

Henry is an apprentice wizard who is sent off to learn his trade at Wizard's Hall. But instead of learning more magic, Henry lets his homesickness cloud his judgment, making his spell-casting disastrous. Is Henry's future as a wizard ruined? Maybe not. When the evil wizard Nettle plots against the Wizard's Hall, Henry is forced to search inside himself for a way to save the hall from its enemy.

2.37   Zambreno, Mary Frances. **A Plague of Sorcerers.** Illustrated by Greg Tucker. Jane Yolen Books, 1991. 257 pp. ISBN 0-15-262430-9.

Jermyn, a wizard's apprentice, has difficulty making his magic work correctly, but his powers are challenged as, one by one, most of the wizards in his land succumb to a magic plague that puts them in a coma. Jermyn must use his powers to discover a way to reverse this threatening sickness. Accompanied by Delia, his skunk familiar, Jermyn sets out to stop the plague before it stops him!

3 Chills and Thrills: Mystery and the Supernatural

3.1 Alcock, Vivien. **A Kind of Thief.** Delacorte Press, 1991. ISBN 0-385-30564-8.

Elinor Forest is awakened early one morning to discover the police arresting her father! Before he is taken away, her father slips Elinor a railway locker receipt. She and her brother Matthew retrieve a satchel from the locker, a satchel Elinor is certain is filled with money her father stole. When Elinor's stepmother Sophia returns to her family in Italy, separating Elinor and Matthew, Elinor finds herself facing many unpleasant truths about her father and her family's way of life.

3.2 Bawden, Nina. **Humbug.** Clarion Books, 1992. 133 pp. ISBN 0-395-62149-6.

Cora hates staying next door with the seemingly pleasant woman called Aunt Sunday. But it isn't Aunt Sunday that's the problem; it's Aunt Sunday's mean-spirited, deceitful daughter Angelica. Angelica does nothing but torment Cora, and Cora desperately needs some help! She finds it in Aunt Sunday's elderly mother, Ma Potter, who tells Cora about "humbug," a magic ability that will help Cora through her trials with Angelica. When Cora learns to help herself a little more, the magic begins to take effect.

3.3 Bawden, Nina. **The White Horse Gang.** Clarion Books, 1992. 166 pp. ISBN 0-395-58709-3.

When Sam Peach, his cousin Rose, and lonely Abe Tanner become lost together while exploring the haunted Gibbet Wood, it will take all their strengths to find their way out again. Can they learn responsibility and rescue themselves? Originally published in 1966.

3.4   Bechard, Margaret. **Tory and Me and the Spirit of True Love.** Viking, 1992. 145 pp. ISBN 0-670-84688-0.

"I just don't think it was her fault," Aunt Fanny says of her late sister, Louisa, "falling in love with the wrong man." This declaration only makes eleven-year-old Tory and her cousin Emily more certain that there is a romantic story to be discovered here. Aunt Louisa's death and the arrival of her husband, Uncle Arthur, catapult the girls into discovering why Uncle Arthur was the "wrong man."

3.5   Bunting, Eve. **Coffin on a Case.** HarperCollins, 1992. 105 pp. ISBN 0-06-020273-4.

When Lily's mother is kidnapped, who can she call on for help? Henry Coffin, that's who! Henry, the twelve-year-old son of private investigator Coffin of Coffin and Pale Detective Agency, has some sleuthing skills on his own, and he puts those skills to the test as he follows the trail of the missing Mrs. Lawson. From jade statues to vicious mother-nappers, Henry finds himself up against some devilish adversaries as he closes in on the mystery surrounding the beautiful Lily's unusual case.

3.6   Cadnum, Michael. **Breaking the Fall.** Viking, 1992. 131 pp. ISBN 0-670-84687-2.

There's danger in the game that Stanley and Jared play, but that makes it even more fun. Late at night, alone, the high school students enter unlocked houses where unsuspecting owners are sleeping. Going into the bedroom, taking some insignificant item to prove they were there, and leaving without getting caught are part of the game. But then Stanley enters the house with the green shutters and takes the wrong item.

3.7   Christopher, Matt. **Skateboard Tough.** Illustrated by Paul Casale. Little, Brown and Company, 1991. 162 pp. ISBN 0-316-14247-6.

Brett Thyson wants to be an expert on the skateboard. Little does he know that his desire to challenge Kyle Robinson and actually best him at riding skateboards will be entirely dependent upon a "haunted skateboard" known as "The Lizard." But why was The Lizard buried in Brett's front yard? Where did it come from? And can it really help Brett beat Kyle Robinson?

3.8   Cormier, Robert. **We All Fall Down.** Delacorte Press, 1991. 193 pp. ISBN 0-385-30501-X.

When Buddy Walker and his friends break in to trash a stranger's house for fun, the repercussions are frightening. The Avenger is searching for the boys who vandalized a home in his neighborhood, and The Avenger wants revenge. Worse, Buddy increases his drinking in order to cope with his parents' separation and his obsession with the daughter of the owner of the vandalized house. Will The Avenger find Buddy? And if so, what will happen to Buddy?

3.9   Cusick, Richie Tankersley. **Teacher's Pet.** Scholastic, 1990. 214 pp. ISBN 0-590-43114-5.

Attending a writers' conference shouldn't scare you to death—should it? Kate loves to be scared, but she changes her mind during her attendance at a meeting in a secluded conference center. All Kate wants to do is get advice from a teacher about how to write and publish a professional horror novel. Suddenly, she finds herself in a real life horror story more terrifying than anything she could have imagined.

3.10   Davidson, Nicole. **Demon's Beach.** Avon, 1992. 154 pp. ISBN 0-380-76644-2.

When a group of high school students goes to the Florida Keys on an archeological expedition, students are warned by an old woman that a demon will destroy anyone trespassing on the site. The students laugh off the warning, but they are soon plagued by unexplainable changes in themselves—and the death of one of their friends. Only after tragedy strikes is the real demon discovered.

3.11   Dexter, Catherine. **The Gilded Cat.** William Morrow, 1992. 199 pp. ISBN 0-688-09425-2.

When Maggie buys the mummified remains of a cat at a yard sale, she suddenly finds herself drawn into the world of Egyptian magic. The mummified cat puts Maggie right in the middle of an ancient feud between twelve-year-old Pharaoh Thutmose and his greedy and ambitious Uncle Set, who carries his unscrupulous desires into the afterlife by using Maggie as his mediator.

3.12   Ferguson, Alane. **Overkill.** Bradbury Press, 1992. 168 pp. ISBN 0-02-734523-8.

Lacey Brighton has been having terrifyingly realistic nightmares. Suddenly, the seventeen-year-old's friend Celeste is murdered, and Lacey's nightmares become reality when she is accused of the crime. But Lacey thinks she can find the real criminal—by seeing the killer's face in her dreams. Can her therapist, Dr. Otkin, help her solve the murder and prove her innocence?

3.13   Fleischman, Sid. **Jim Ugly.** Illustrated by Jos. A. Smith. Greenwillow Books, 1992. 130 pp. ISBN 0-688-10886-5.

Upon the mysterious disappearance of his actor father, twelve-year-old Jake inherits his dad's pet, Jim Ugly, a mean, part-wolf, part-mongrel, one-man dog. But Jake doesn't believe that his father is dead. So, with Jim Ugly as a traveling companion, Jake sets off across the rugged terrain of the Old West to find out what really happened to his father.

3.14   Grant, Charles L. **Fire Mask.** Bantam Books, 1991. 202 pp. ISBN 0-553-29673-6.

Cliff and his friend Del become involved in a very mysterious adventure as they try to unravel the intrigue surrounding the man in the golden mask. Cliff's parents depend on him to be sensible, but getting shot at, being drugged, and becoming involved in one incredible predicament after another is anything but sensible! With the help of some of his friends, including his girlfriend Candy, Cliff manages to survive these adventures and unlock the mystery surrounding the fire mask.

3.15 Henry, Maeve. **A Gift for a Gift: A Ghost Story.** Delacorte Press, 1990. 104 pp. ISBN 0-385-30562-1.

After her father's desertion, Fran Kelly is overwhelmed by having to care for her mentally unstable mother, her two rebellious brothers, and their filthy house. When she runs away one day, she is drawn to a seemingly deserted house and there meets the mysterious Michael, a man who promises to solve all of her problems forever in return for one gift. But is it a gift Fran can afford to give? Mature language.

3.16 Hoh, Diane. **The Accident.** Scholastic, 1991. 165 pp. ISBN 0-590-44330-5.

She appears in Megan's mirror, little more than a wispy glow with a faint, hollow voice. But before Megan knows it, the ghost in her mirror has taken Megan's place in the real world! How can Megan return to where she belongs?

3.17 Inglehart, Donna Walsh. **Breaking the Ring.** Little, Brown and Company, 1991. ISBN 0-316-41867-6.

When Jessie, Emma, and Maggie go on vacation on the islands of the St. Lawrence River, they don't expect to find themselves embroiled in the world of drug dealers and cocaine, but that's what happens when they find a hidden stash of the drug! Spotted by the dealers who hid the drugs in the first place—dealers who are convinced that the three girls have stolen the cache—Jessie, Emma, and Maggie find themselves trying to escape the criminals while they avoid being suspected of dealing drugs themselves. And when Maggie suddenly disappears, what began as a simple summer vacation suddenly becomes a dangerous struggle to survive.

3.18 Johnston, Norma. **The Dragon's Eye.** Four Winds Press, 1990. 172 pp. ISBN 0-02-747701-0.

Who is "The Eye of the Dragon?" And why does "the eye" hate Doris Haywood? Graffiti on the walls of Crestwood High School torments poor Doris, scary poison-pen letters arrive through her computer mail system, and unexpected, hostile warnings are broadcast on the school's PA system. Sixteen-year-old Jenny Price is drawn into this disturbing sequence of events, and when tragedy strikes her cousin Michael, the school's star football player, she is determined to uncover the truth behind "the eye."

3.19   Kehret, Peg. **Terror at the Zoo.** Cobblehill Books, 1992. 131 pp. ISBN 0-525-65083-0.

Ellen and her little brother Corey can't wait for the campout that their grandparents have planned at the zoo. By an unlucky coincidence, however, an escaped convict has chosen that night of the campout to hide in the zoo. When Ellen and Corey catch him trying to kidnap a rare baby monkey, the convict takes Corey hostage. After Corey tries unsuccessfully to escape, Ellen remembers studies she has read on nonverbal communication with animals. Desperate, she sends silent S.O.S. messages to the elephants, who respond in ways she never would have expected.

3.20   Kerr, M. E. **Fell Down.** HarperCollins/Charlotte Zolotow Books, 1991. 191 pp. ISBN 0-06-021763-4.

Seventeen-year-old John Fell's determination to investigate his best friend's death in a car crash leads him to a ventriloquists' convention and an unsolved disappearance from almost twenty years ago. What secrets do the ventriloquists—and their dummies—know that might confirm Fell's suspicions that his friend's crash was no accident? Sequel to *Fell.*

3.21   Lasky, Kathryn. **Double Trouble Squared.** Harcourt Brace Jovanovich, 1991. 232 pp. ISBN 0-15-224127-2.

While in London with their family, telepathic twelve-year-old twins Liberty and July begin to receive strange emanations from an early residence of Arthur Conan Doyle and discover a literary ghost. Could it be the twin of Sherlock Holmes? The first of the Starbuck Family Adventure books.

3.22   Lasky, Kathryn. **Shadows in the Water.** Harcourt Brace Jovanovich, 1992. 211 pp. ISBN 0-15-273533-X.

Sea turtles, dolphins, and other creatures of the Florida Keys are threatened by a gang that is dumping toxic waste into the coastal waters. Liberty Starbuck and her twin brother, July, become involved with these toxic dangers when their father is hired to investigate the dumpings and to find the culprits responsible. The twins' ability to communicate telepathically has curious results as they try to help save this fragile environment. A Starbuck Family Adventure book.

3.23   Lehr, Norma. **The Shimmering Ghost of Riversend.** Lerner Publications Company, 1991. 168 pp. ISBN 0-8225-9589-3.

Strange things happen in the old family mansion when eleven-year-old Kathy Wicklow spends the summer with her Aunt Sharon. When Kathy is visited by the ghost of a woman who died in the nineteenth century, she learns of a family secret which dates back more than a hundred years.

3.24   Lindbergh, Anne. **Travel Far, Pay No Fare.** HarperCollins, 1992. 199 pp. ISBN 0-06-021775-8.

Twelve-year-old Owen has lived alone with his mother since his father walked out, remarking as he left, "Take care of your mother." And because Owen has taken such good care of his mother and prizes his independence, he finds it difficult to accept the wedding plans between his mother and his Uncle Owen, his father's brother. Once in his Uncle's Vermont home, Owen and his cousin, Parsley, plot to stop the forthcoming wedding with the aid of Parsley's magic bookmark, which allows the two children to actually enter different stories to search for an answer to their problem.

3.25   Mahy, Margaret. **Underrunners.** Viking, 1992. 169 pp. ISBN 0-670-84179-X.

Underrunners, vast networks of tunnels, run through the land around Tris Catt's house, and are Tris' secret places where he creates adventures with his imaginary friend. One day, however, he begins a real adventure when a mysterious man in a yellow sports car and a girl, Winola, come into his isolated life, turning the underrunners into dangerous places.

3.26 McGraw, Eloise Jarvis. **The Money Room.** Collier Books, 1991. 182 pp. ISBN 0-02-044484-2.

Is there really such a thing as a room full of money in the old Dover, Oregon, farmhouse? Most townspeople have heard rumors of it for years. So when Scotty, Lindy, and their mother move into the farmhouse to start a new life, the kids decide to search for the hidden room their great-grandfather had spoken of as the money room. But soon they realize that someone else is looking for the room, too! Originally published in 1981.

3.27 McHargue, Georgess. **Beastie.** Delacorte Press, 1992. 179 pp. ISBN 0-385-30589-3.

Does the Loch Ness Monster of Scotland really exist? A scientific expedition sets out to prove it does, trying to capture the "Beastie" on film—at least that's what the director of the expedition says. But Mary, Scott, and Theo, whose parents are working with the expedition, have reason to believe that the director might have different plans for the ultimate fate of the monster, so they begin their own research of the murky waters of the Loch Ness.

3.28 McMullan, Kate. **Under the Mummy's Spell.** Farrar, Straus and Giroux, 1992. 214 pp. ISBN 0-374-38033-3.

On a visit to the Egyptian exhibit at the Metropolitan Museum of Art, Harring the Daring's best friend Rodent dares Harring to kiss the mummy of Princess Nephia. Harring—who never passes up a dare—cannot resist sneaking one quick kiss, but that one kiss unleashes an ancient curse. Suddenly, Peter Harring finds himself caught between the forces of good and evil, and he must find the courage to right an ancient wrong.

3.29 McNamara, Brooks. **The Merry Muldoons and the Brighteyes Affair.** Orchard Books, 1992. 154 pp. ISBN 0-531-05454-3.

Pa, Vera, and Sam have been giving twelve shows a day at Sweeney's Dime Museum on the Bowery in 1893. But they are suddenly forced to abandon their vaudeville act when

Brighteyes, an acquaintance of Pa's, shows up to settle an old score—he wants the cache of diamonds he was forced to leave behind, diamonds Pa might have. Separated from their father as they flee across New York, Vera and Sam can barely stay one step ahead of the thugs who are after them. Can Uncle Mike in Poughkeepsie help them escape Brighteyes and his band of ruffians?

3.30   Monson, A. M. **The Secret of Sanctuary Island.** Lothrop, Lee & Shepard Books, 1991. 128 pp. ISBN 0-688-10111-9.

Todd and his friend, Kevin, witness a robbery and are chased by the burglars. After a narrow escape, they try to convince the police and their families about what they have witnessed. But no one believes that the burglary even took place! So, with only each other to rely on, the two boys set out to solve the mystery themselves.

3.31   Morgan, Helen. **The Witch Doll.** Viking, 1991. 143 pp. ISBN 0-670-84285-0.

At first, Linda likes the old doll she finds, but soon she begins to mistrust it. In fact, she is only somewhat surprised when brushing the doll's hair causes the doll first to grow, then to turn into a real little girl named Tilda. When she can't control Linda, Tilda turns to Linda's friend, Joanna, and soon Joanna is completely under Tilda's spell. Finally, an old woman visiting next door tells Linda a story about a possessed child she had once cared for. Amazingly, the child's wicked governess, a witch, looks just like Tilda! Can Linda save Joanna from the evil witch before it's too late?

3.32   Nixon, Joan Lowery. **A Candidate for Murder.** Delacorte Press, 1991. ISBN 0-385-30257-6.

Carry's life is perfect: her mother is a lawyer, her father is the successful owner of an oil company, and her boyfriend is a wonderful guy. But when Carry's father decides to run for governor of Texas, everything changes. Carry is thrust into a world of suspicion, treachery, and murder, where the volunteers for her father's campaign are not what they seem; Carry and her friends are arrested for possession of drugs, and she narrowly escapes several attempts on her life. When the police don't take Carry's suspicions seriously, she realizes she can only rely on herself to investigate the plot to sabotage her father's political campaign.

3.33   Nixon, Joan Lowery. **A Deadly Promise.** Bantam Books, 1992. ISBN 0-553-08054-7.

Sarah Lindley is certain that her late father was no murderer, and she vows to clear his name. From Leadville, Colorado, the place where her father was killed, Sarah sends for Susannah, her sister, asking Susannah to come to Leadville and help Sarah investigate the truth about their father. But when Susannah finally arrives, she is not the practical, sensible child Sarah left in Chicago. In fact, Susannah seems indifferent to their father's past and insists that Sarah return to Chicago! Worse, Sarah has uncovered a terrible secret that her father knew—a secret that can clear his name but hurt others. Sequel to *High Trail to Danger.*

3.34   Nixon, Joan Lowery. **High Trail to Danger.** Bantam Books, 1991. ISBN 0-553-07314-1.

When Sarah and Susannah's mother dies, the two sisters find themselves living with their aunt and uncle in a boarding house in Chicago during the late 1800s. Believing there can be a better life for them only if she could find their father, seventeen-year-old Sarah sets out for Leadville, Colorado, in search of the man who left his family behind so many years ago. But she soon finds that the mere mention of her father's name brings her strange looks and even an attempt on her life! What could be so awful about Sarah's father that people would want to hurt Sarah for it? Followed by *A Deadly Promise.*

3.35   Petersen, P. J. **Liars.** Simon & Schuster, 1992. 169 pp. ISBN 0-671-75035-6.

Life in Alder Creek is pretty boring for Sam and his friends until Uncle Gene, a local character, tells Sam that Sam has a special gift—by the twitch of his arm, Sam will be able to tell when people are telling the truth. When bad things suddenly begin to happen to Uncle Gene, Sam decides to put his newly discovered gift to work. Who in Alder Creek would want to hurt Uncle Gene? And why? Sam and his friends Carmen and Marty plan to find out!

3.36   Reiss, Kathryn. **The Glass House People.** Harcourt Brace Jovanovich, 1992. 277 pp. ISBN 0-15-231040-1.

Sixteen-year-old Beth, her brother Tom, and their mom return to the scene of their mother's youth, a suburb outside of Philadelphia. As they reconstruct the relationship between their mother and her sister, the two teens learn that their mother has been estranged from their Aunt Iris and the rest of the family because of the mysterious death of a man both sisters loved. Can Beth and Tom solve the mystery surrounding the man's death? If so, will it help patch things up between their mother and the rest of the family?

3.37   Reiss, Kathryn. **Time Windows.** Harcourt Brace Jovanovich, 1991. 260 pp. ISBN 0-15-288205-7.

When thirteen-year-old Miranda and her family move to a small Massachusetts town and a new house, Miranda discovers a mysterious dollhouse left behind in her new home. By looking through the windows of the dollhouse, Miranda is able to see the past, where she discovers her new home exerts an evil influence on the women of each generation of inhabitants—including Miranda's mother.

3.38   Rose, Malcolm. **The Highest Form of Killing.** Harcourt Brace Jovanovich, 1992. 226 pp. ISBN 0-15-234270-2.

Murder and danger surround Derek, Sylvia, and Mark, who become involved with a conspiracy at the Ministry of Defense security and laboratories. These labs test chemicals on animals and have developed a chemical called T42, one drop of which can destroy an entire city. Somehow, a vial of the deadly chemical has made it through security and into the town of Crookland Bay. Can the three friends do something to prevent a certain tragedy?

3.39   Ure, Jean. **Plague.** Harcourt Brace Jovanovich, 1991. 218 pp. ISBN 0-15-262429-5.

Fran and her friends go on a month-long camping trip, only to return home to find that the city in which they lived—London—is now a ghost town. Thousands of people are dead or dying as a devastating plague sweeps the city, throwing their civilized society into chaos. Can Fran and her friends survive on their own in the aftermath of such horror?

3.40   Westall, Robert. **Yaxley's Cat.** Scholastic, 1992. 147 pp. ISBN 0-590-45175-8.

Old Sipp Yaxley's cottage on the coast of Norfolk in England has been deserted for seven years. Then Rose and her two children, Timothy and Jane, stumble upon the old place. It's so quaint, so primitive, so remote. What a wonderful place to spend a holiday! But even as the family moves in, the eyes of the village are upon them, as well as upon Yaxley's cat. What does the cat know? What is it trying to show the newly arrived family? Does Yaxley's ugly old cat know the secret that the people of the village are hiding?

4   Stories Bigger Than Life: Myths, Legends, and Folklore

4.1   Bach, Alice, and J. Cheryl Exum. **Miriam's Well: Stories about Women in the Bible.** Illustrated by Leo and Diane Dillon. Delacorte Press, 1991. 168 pp. ISBN 0-385-30435-8.

Did you know that Moses, who brought the Ten Commandments down from the mountain, had a sister named Miriam? Did you know that Esther, wife of the Persian king Ahasuerus, saved her people from slaughter by Haman, a Persian schemer who sought the destruction of the Jews? These and other women of the Old Testament are given voices through scholarly details and powerful storytelling in this collection of enlightening anecdotes. Bibliographical references included.

4.2   Baker, Charlotte. **The Trail North: Stories of Texas' Yesterdays.** Illustrated by Mark Mitchell. Eakin Press, 1990. 135 pp. ISBN 0-89015-701-4.

A collection of folktales, this book traces the adventures of early Texas dwellers from over 200 years ago, through the Spaniards' days and the Civil War years, to the Texas of today. From a quest for the Snow Spirit to the raid of a Spanish mission, this look at yesteryear explores the history of the Lone Star state through a wealth of folklore, legend, and fact.

4.3   Bierhorst, John, editor. **Lightning Inside You and Other Native American Riddles.** Illustrated by Louise Brierley. William Morrow, 1992. 112 pp. ISBN 0-688-09582-8.

This collection of Native American riddles presents a brief study of part of the culture of many Native Americans. The introduction traces why the riddles were told and what various types of answers meant to Native Americans. Examples presented reveal riddles that were used for entertainment, initiation rites, a matching of wits, and a bit of folklore. These riddles also reveal the importance of subjects like nature and animals in Native American culture.

4.4   Gorog, Judith. **Winning Scheherazade.** Atheneum, 1991. 101 pp. ISBN 0-689-31648-8.

Because of her clever storytelling abilities, Scheherazade is released from her position as storyteller and doomed bride of the sultan. For some time, after ending her thousand and one Arabian nights, she settles into a life of security and serenity—until a mysterious but gracious stranger visits her palace and leads her on a dangerous adventure into the desert.

4.5   Liebman, Arthur. **The Ghosts, Witches and Vampires Quiz Book.** Illustrated by Jack Williams. Sterling Publishing, 1991. 127 pp. ISBN 0-8069-8408-2.

The word "Transylvania" means which of the following: (a) dark land, (b) land beyond the forest, (c) mountain home, or (d) rushing waters? This book contains over four hundred multiple choice questions exploring such categories as Dracula, Frankenstein, and Classic Movie Monsters; The Next Generation—Aliens, Demons, and Blobs; and Fact, Folklore and Fiction. The answers are provided and an index is included. By the way, Transylvania means "land beyond the forest."

4.6   Joseph, Lynn. **A Wave in Her Pocket: Stories from Trinidad.** Illustrated by Brian Pinkney. Clarion Books, 1991. 47 pp. ISBN 0-395-54432-7.

This collection contains six stories from Trinidad, as told by a tantie, or storyteller. Almost all families in Trinidad have tanties; they show up at all events and tell stories for different reasons: to give advice, to teach a lesson, or just to scare and entertain. Some of the stories originate in West Africa; others originate in Trinidad. And some originate solely in the mind of the tantie.

4.7   Price, Susan. **Ghost Song.** Farrar, Straus and Giroux, 1992. 148 pp. ISBN 0-374-32544-8.

Told by a cat tethered to an oak tree, this is the tale of Malyuta, a fur trapper for the czar, and Malyuta's son, Ambrosi. When Malyuta refuses to give his son to the evil Shaman Kuzma, Kuzma exacts revenge upon the fur trapper, making Malyuta's life miserable.

4.8   Tate, Eleanora E. **Front Porch Stories at the One-Room School.** Illustrated by Eric Velasquez. Skylark Books, 1992. 112 pp. ISBN 0-553-08384-8.

Take one front porch, any porch will do, but the one at the old one-room school is best; add one can to hold a rag fire to stave off mosquitoes in the summer time when the television reruns are at their worst, and you're ready to hear some stories about Missouri. Fact, fiction, myth, a little family history, and a whole bunch of folklore follow the rising smoke in this collection of stories. Tales about Eleanor Roosevelt, outlaws, cowboys, riverboat gamblers and pirates, pioneers, and Civil War soldiers from the North and the South make this a collection with true Midwestern appeal.

4.9   Yolen, Jane. **The Dragon's Boy.** Harper & Row, 1990. 120 pp. ISBN 0-06-026789-5.

Artos is tired of being picked on by the other boys at the castle. Sir Ector and Lady Marion took him in as a foundling, and they love and accept him; but Cai, Bedvere, and Lancot make fun of him and never ask him to join their games. One day while chasing a hound, Artos finds a hidden cave and a dragon inside who promises Artos wisdom. The dragon teaches him tales, songs, and how to read between the lines of both books and people, including the other boys who make fun of Artos. A surprise revelation about the dragon helps Artos to grow, giving him new understanding of his past and helping him step forward to meet his destiny. Based on the legends of King Arthur.

5   Rhythm and Rhyme: Poetry

5.1   Berry, James. **When I Dance.** Illustrated by Karen Barbour. Harcourt Brace Jovanovich, 1991. 128 pp. ISBN 0-15-296668-2.

Over sixty poems capture the joy of "And I celebrate all rhythms." This is the last line of "When I Dance," the title poem of the collection. Berry connects the cadence of city life in Great Britain with country life in the Caribbean. Concrete and kinetic imagery in "Seeing Granny," "Black Kid in a New Place," "Pair of Hands against Football," "The Barkday Party," "Riddle Poems," and "Sunny Market Song" mark the movement. The words invite vocal participation—solo, group, or call/response. Berry terms this, his first book of poetry for young people, a "special bagful of obsessions and celebrations."

5.2   Elledge, Scott, editor. **Wider than the Sky: Poems to Grow Up With.** HarperCollins, 1990. 358 pp. ISBN 0-06-021786-3.

Two hundred poems dot this collection, the title of which comes from Emily Dickinson's "The Brain—is wider than the Sky—." The reader will drift freely through poems of time, poems from authors like Shakespeare and Silverstein. Originally created for a ten-year-old niece, this collection includes poems of laughter, looking, longing, loathing, loving, and living; these poems are meant for growing with. Persona poems such as Williams' "This is Just to Say," Whittemore's "The Tarantula," X. J. Kennedy's "Mother's Nerves," Rieu's "Soliloquy of a Tortoise. . . ," and Clifton's "The 1st" mark the horizon. Explanatory notes follow this journey through the poetry from all times.

5.3   Gordon, Ruth, compiler. **Time Is the Longest Distance.** Har-
perCollins/Charlotte Zolotow Books, 1991. 74 pp. ISBN 0-06-
022297-2.

Gordon transports the reader to the past and present in this
offering of sixty poems. Moments of time—a day, a night, a
year, a life—stand still in this measurement. The reader lingers
in Lian Wu-ti's "From the Most Distant Time" or in the dream
time of the Pima in "Song of Creation." The ephemeral and
eternal tick are reflected in works from Emily Dickinson's
"There's a certain Slant of light" to Zack Rogow's "Monte,
Rio, California." In all, forty-one poets translate time's power
and wonder.

5.4   Harvey, Anne, compiler. **Shades of Green.** Illustrated by John
Lawrence. Greenwillow Books, 1992. 184 pp. ISBN 0-688-
10890-3.

Whether the color green reminds the reader of the color of
nature or the symbolic color of hope, this anthology of poems
arranged around green is a delightful collection of new and old
poems. These poems paint pictures, inspire ideas, and renew
the spirit. With categories like "The Grass is Green" and "Bird-
World, Leaf-Life," this collection enters the world of the color
of life with vigor.

5.5   Hearne, Betsy. **Polaroid and Other Poems of View.** Photographs by Peter Kiar. Margaret K. McElderry Books, 1991.
68 pp. ISBN 0-689-50530-2.

Percy Bysshe Shelley once said that poetry is looking at life
anew. Through clear images, contemporary metaphors, and
familiar sights, all with fresh perspectives, this collection of
poems by Betsy Hearne will entice readers to look at the world
from different points of view. *Polaroid* contains poems on such
topics as city sights, insights, and relationships.

5.6   Livingston, Myra Cohn, compiler. **A Time to Talk: Poems of
Friendship.** Margaret K. McElderry Books, 1992. 115 pp.
ISBN 0-689-50558-2.

Friends—those strange, false, lost, and remembered—come together in this gathering of eighty-two poems. Robert Frost's "A Time to Talk" initiates this sounding of voices on friendship, old and new, silly and serious. "Friendship" from the Aztec, translated by John Bierhorst, Langston Hughes' "Poem," John Kieran's "To Lou Gehrig," and Carl Sandburg's "One Parting" mark the time and talk. Sixty-eight poets give voice to the many wondrous facets of friendship.

5.7   Mitchell, Adrian, compiler. **Strawberry Drums.** Illustrated by Frances Lloyd. Delacorte Press, 1991. 40 pp. ISBN 0-385-30177-4.

Mitchell picked these thirty poems "because they are bright and sweet like strawberries. And all of them have a beat—like drums." The beat is heard from the ancient Navajo "Night Way" to the recent Lennon and McCartney "Yellow Submarine." It reverberates in McGough's "Hundreds and Thousands," Carroll's "Jabberwocky," Roethke's "Child on Top of a Greenhouse," and Agard's "Who is De Girl?" Such sounding lifts poems off the page and into the body and spirit. Biographical notes follow the drum rolls.

5.8   Nye, Naomi Shihab. **This Same Sky: A Collection of Poems from around the World.** Four Winds Press, 1992. 212 pp. ISBN 0-02-768440-7.

Nye introduces the reader to poets from all across our planet, one hundred twenty-nine voices from sixty-eight countries. From Tialvga Sunia Seloti in American Samoa who asks, "Friend, what's true?" to Vasko Popa in Yugoslavia, who longs to question his great-grandfather about wolf-ancestry, the faraway becomes the here-and-now. Poems in *Words and Silences, Dreams and Dreamers, Families, This Earth and Sky in Which We Live, Losses,* and *Human Mysteries* bring the reader closer to the blue expanse. Twentieth-century voices, both soft and forceful, show that all are connected by the same sky. An azure ribbon bookmark, a map, contributor notes, indices to countries and poets, and end papers with postage stamps and poets' signatures complete the connection.

6 Science Fiction

6.1 Baird, Thomas. **Smart Rats.** Harper & Row, 1990. 199 pp. ISBN 0-06-020364-1.

Laddie's 21st-century world is stark and dismal. Strict regulations on all facets of life are administered by Concilar Government; war and pollution have left only small parts of the country habitable. Though he could have gone on to Council School, seventeen-year-old Laddie chooses to stay with his family and try to help his sick mother, his weakling father, and his younger sister, whose behavior is becoming increasingly bizarre and dangerous. Then Laddie and his friends, the Smart Rats, are selected for "relocation" in a population reduction program, and he feels the power of the system closing in on them. It will take quick action if Laddie is to change his own fate and perhaps the future of others as well. RATPOWER!

6.2 Christopher, John. **When the Tripods Came.** Collier Books, 1990. 151 pp. ISBN 0-02-042575-9.

In this Tripods Trilogy prequel, Laurie, an English schoolboy, sights the horribly attractive alien tripod craft while on an orienteering weekend. Surprised by the growing popularity of the "Trippy Show," Laurie slowly realizes that the Tripods are deliberately mesmerizing the population into loyalty and servitude; cries of "Hail the Tripod!" spread from England and Europe to the rest of the world. The fragmented relationships between sibling and stepparent in Laurie's family begin to strengthen behind the common goal of avoiding the Tripods' dominance. This unified family goes on the run to find sanctuary and to plot the return of human freedom through the destruction of the Tripods.

6.3   Dickinson, Peter. **A Bone from a Dry Sea.** Delacorte Press, 1993. 199 pp. ISBN 0-385-30821-3.

In these two parallel tales of what is and what might have been, readers are introduced to the young sea-ape Li, who leads survivors of a tidal wave to safety, and to Vinney, who visits her father on an archeological dig in Africa. Through these two intertwining stories of prehistoric survival and modern science, readers are given the opportunity to consider the sea-ape theory as the missing link in hominid development, while examining the conflicts between people of science over what is truth and what is speculation.

6.4   Gilden, Mel. **The Planetoid of Amazement.** HarperCollins, 1991. 215 pp. ISBN 0-06-021713-8.

In a world of imagination, fourteen-year-old Rodney Congruent experiences an astonishing adventure on the Planetoid of Amazement, home to artifacts from across the galaxy. The adventure begins with strange instructions in Rodney's mail, and before he knows it, Rodney finds himself traveling via glitter dust and starship vehicles, and combatting evil space monsters as well as amusing alien shenanigans. Will Earth ever be the same after Rodney has seen the universe?

6.5   Griffin, Peni R. **A Dig in Time.** Margaret K. McElderry Books, 1991. 186 pp. ISBN 0-689-50525-6.

Staying with their grandmother, Nan and Tim discover artifacts buried in the yard that allow them to travel backwards in time. They see Grampa (who's been dead for several years) in his garden, participate in their parents' wedding, spend a wild, scary Halloween night with Gramma as a young girl, and help out during a flood that happened nearly eighty years ago. Nan and Tim never learn to control the time-traveling, which begins to seem random, but their adventures are exciting nonetheless as they visit significant moments in their family's history.

6.6   Haseley, Dennis. **Dr. Gravity.** Farrar, Straus and Giroux, 1992. 322 pp. ISBN 0-374-31842-5.

Meet Dr. Gravity, a one-time fledgling scientist whose innate clumsiness leads him to a lonely mountaintop where he and a faithful assistant create an anti-gravity potion. Dr. Gravity then returns to his hometown in Ohio to save it from the physical, emotional, and spiritual effects of gravity that have weighed down the lives of townspeople, including the mayor, the mayor's charming daughter, and an out-of-work actor. Add to this a trio of inept bank robbers, and you have a conclusion that even Dr. Gravity couldn't have predicted.

6.7 Heinlein, Robert A. **Time for the Stars.** Charles Scribner's Sons, 1990. 251 pp. ISBN 0-684-19211-X.

Project Lebensraum uses telepathic twins and other humans as instantaneous communicators on a one hundred-year Earth mission to locate colonization sites in the galaxy. Tom, one such twin, describes the routine and adventure of space travel to his earthbound sibling Rob, who sends back reports from home. As the mission proceeds, the widening distance between human transmitters becomes less a difficulty than the increasing time gap between Tom, travelling at light speed and Rob, whose time on Earth passes much differently than Tom's. Originally published in 1956.

6.8 Hoppe, Joanne. **Dream Spinner.** Morrow Junior Books, 1992. 228 pp. ISBN 0-688-08559-8.

After reading an article about dreaming for a class assignment, Mary experiments with her own dreams. Soon, her dreams of the Pinkhams, people who lived more than a hundred years ago, and their lavish balls and skating parties, are more appealing than her real life with her father, stepmother, and stepbrother. It takes an illness and a tragedy to force her to choose the world in which she wants to live.

6.9 Hughes, Dean. **Nutty Knows All.** Aladdin Books, 1991. 150 pp. ISBN 0-689-71470-X.

Fifth-grade Nutty wants to make an impression with his science project on subatomic particles of light. He does make an impression—but not the way he had planned! When his partner, William Bilks, transfers photons of light to Nutty's brain, all kinds of things begin to happen: Nutty develops a new personality, he begins to "hear" plants and animals, and his head glows in the dark! How will he ever get this mess straightened out?

6.10   Hughes, Monica. **Invitation to the Game.** Simon & Schuster, 1991. 183 pp. ISBN 0-671-74236-1.

In the year 2154, Lisse and her close friends have graduated from high school and find themselves with no hope of getting jobs. The government provides them with living quarters in an old abandoned warehouse, and they resign themselves to a boring existence in their "Designated Area." Then the day comes when the government invites them to play "The Game." Having faced difficult challenges during their stay in the warehouse, are Lisse and her friends adequately prepared to face the challenges of a game that takes them to a strange country— their future home?

6.11   Levin, Betty. **Mercy's Mill.** Greenwillow Books, 1992. 256 pp. ISBN 0-688-11122-X.

When Sarah moves to the country with her mother, stepfather, and foster sister, she feels cut off from the rest of the world. Then, as the restoration of the old mill proceeds, Sarah meets a strange boy named Jethro, who claims to have traveled forward in time from the nineteenth century. What do his odd riddles mean? And why does he hide from everyone but Sarah?

6.12   Lindbergh, Anne. **Three Lives to Live.** Little, Brown and Company, 1992. 183 pp. ISBN 0-316-52628-2.

Garret resents her "sister" Daisy, especially since Grandma insists the two girls are twins. If Garret didn't know better, she would suspect Grandma of favoring Daisy, who gets away with murder. Determined to find out the truth about Daisy's real identity, Garret is shocked to discover a secret connection between Daisy and Grandma. Garret's problems multiply when a homesick Daisy disappears, teachers demand Daisy's birth certificate, and a fingerprint test shows that Daisy and Grandma are, incredibly, the same person!

6.13 McKean, Thomas. **The Secret of the Seven Willows.** Simon & Schuster, 1991. 151 pp. ISBN 0-671-72997-7.

Magic, danger, and adventure are blended in this first book in the Doors Into Time trilogy. Ted Byram, his younger sister Martha, and their older brother Joe use the power of a magical ring to travel through time in hopes of preventing the sale of their ancestral home. But dark family secrets might make their mission through time impossible.

6.14 Peel, John. **Uptime, Downtime.** Simon & Schuster, 1992. 242 pp. ISBN 0-671-73274-9.

When Karyn and Mike hear their uncle admit that he never wanted to adopt them, they decide to run away. To their surprise, they find themselves suddenly able to travel through time. At first cautious, the two children grow more daring as their powers increase, visiting stone-age Britain, a deserted Pacific island, and turn-of-the-century America. But when Mike brings a dinosaur egg from one time to another, he changes the course of history, and the children lose control of their abilities, hurtling from time to time, not sure if they will ever manage to get home again.

6.15 Ryan, Mary C. **Me Two.** Illustrated by Rob Sauber. Little, Brown and Company, 1991. 179 pp. ISBN 0-316-76376-4.

"Raise Tiny Ocean Pups," says the ad. And twelve-year-old Wilf Farkus decides that sending away for this sea creatures kit as a science project will solve all his problems. He's grounded for low grades, feels lost at school, and is being railroaded into taking weird Heather Spears-Croxton to the school dance. Despite the fact that Wilf follows all of the kit directions exactly, what he ends up with is *not* an Ocean Pup. Instead, Wilf makes a full-size clone of himself! At first, he panics. Then he uses the situation to his advantage with exciting and surprising consequences.

6.16   Service, Pamela F. **Under Alien Stars.** Atheneum/Jean Karl
          Books, 1990. 214 pp. ISBN 0-689-31621-6.

Maroon-skinned, gray-haired, black-eyed aliens with claws for
hands have captured Earth and are using it as a military base.
Jason Sikes hates them and finds a way to join the Resisters, a
rebel group striving to break the aliens' control. Teenage Aryl,
an alien, hates Earth people, but her father, commander of the
alien group, wants her to be friendly, especially to Jason. When
another, much deadlier race invades the solar system, can Jason and Aryl put aside their differences to work together for
the good of both aliens and humans?

6.17   Silverberg, Robert. **Letters from Atlantis.** Illustrated by
          Robert Gould. Atheneum, 1990. 136 pp. ISBN 0-689-31570-8.

While his body remains in a deep sleep, Roy, a time observer,
travels to the year 18,862 B.C. and "borrows" the body of
Prince Ram, through whom Roy observes the legendary island
of Atlantis before it vanishes into the sea. By sending a series
of letters to a fellow time observer, Roy describes his adventures in the fascinating place and in the consciousness of the
future king of Atlantis.

6.18   Sirota, Mike. **The Ultimate Bike Path.** Ace Books, 1992.
          202 pp. ISBN 0-441-84391-3.

Jack Miller owns a 21-speed Nishiki Pinnacle mountain bike
with one special feature—it has twenty-two speeds! And that
twenty-second gear allows Jack to move through time and
space on the ultimate of all bike paths. On Jack's amazing
journeys, he visits a race of giant babies and their midget
parents, as well as a terrible house of horrors that might just
bring an end to his biking escapades.

6.19   Skinner, David. **You Must Kiss a Whale.** Simon & Schuster,
          1992. 94 pp. ISBN 0-671-74781-9.

Part science fiction, part surrealistic fantasy, this book covers
a few days during Evelyn's fifteenth summer, which she
spends in the desert with her mother and baby brother. During

the rainy season, violent thunderstorms tear pieces off their house, so that only the very center, where the family is forced to cluster, is safe. Resenting her mother (who is busy perfecting the ultimate raincoat), Evelyn halfheartedly cares for her baby brother. One day, however, she finds an unfinished short story in her mother's old trunk, a story written by her long-gone father. Soon, Evelyn is obsessed with deciphering the meaning of her father's words, hoping to discover why he left.

6.20 Stevermer, Caroline. **River Rats.** Jane Yolen Books, 1992. 214 pp. ISBN 0-15-200895-0.

It has been twenty years since the nuclear war that devastated the United States. Most of the cities are in ruin and are looted and plagued by gangs of wild young men. Tomcat and a group of other orphans pilot a steamboat, the last of its kind, over the toxic waters of the Mississippi River. These "River Rats" embark on one adventure after another as they struggle to cope with the destruction of the modern civilization they once knew.

6.21 Wilde, Nicholas. **Down Came a Blackbird.** Henry Holt, 1991. 182 pp. ISBN 0-8050-2001-2.

Thirteen-year-old James, a social case with a criminal record, is sent to live at his great-uncle's estate while James' mother is hospitalized for her alcoholism. Withdrawn, lonely, and uncertain about his future, James soon begins to experience strange dreams of a boy who once lived on the estate, a boy no one seems to know anything about. Determined to find an explanation for these dreams, James begins his search for answers about the estate, his family, and himself.

7 Quick Reads: Short Stories

7.1   Barry, Sheila Anne. **World's Most Spine-Tingling "True" Ghost Stories.** Illustrated by Jim Sharpe. Sterling Publishing, 1992. 96 pp. ISBN 0-8069-8686-7.

Legend says that if you see the friendly black dog of Hanging Hills three times, you will die. A certain ring brings bad luck to anyone who owns it, while a pair of earrings brings good luck to a family, luck that turns bad when they give the earrings away. Hauntings, poltergeists, dreams, and mysterious powers are all part of the true occurrences detailed in this collection of strange happenings from around the world. Index included.

7.2   Brooks, Bruce. **What Hearts.** HarperCollins/Laura Geringer Books, 1992. 194 pp. ISBN 0-06-021131-8.

The four separate stories in this novel focus on Asa at ages seven, nine, eleven, and twelve years old. In each episode, this bright, sensitive boy confronts serious problems—a new step-father, a friend's bad choice, a suicidal mother, and love. In each tale, Asa tries to cope with these problems as well as others, like attending new schools, playing baseball for a losing team, and being around adults who don't seem to understand him.

7.3   Carlson, Lori M., and Cynthia L. Ventura, editors. **Where Angels Glide at Dawn: New Stories from Latin America.** Illustrated by José Ortega. J. B. Lippincott, 1990. 114 pp. ISBN 0-397-32424-3.

Ranging in moods and characters, these ten short stories by various Latin American authors mix humor, politics, poetry, and imagination. The stories deftly illustrate the diversity of Latin America, while at the same time they entertain, amuse, and educate. Among the many interesting characters, readers will meet an eccentric millionaire, a musical elephant, a clown with nothing left but a smile, and magical, political rabbits.

7.4   Cohen, Daniel. **Ghostly Tales of Love and Revenge.** G. P. Putnam's Sons, 1992. 95 pp. ISBN 0-399-22117-4.

These eerie, supposedly true tales, collected by the author from a variety of times and places (ranging from Scotland to Japan) all deal with the dark side of romantic love. Abandoned lovers, betrayed lovers, even murdered lovers—all exact a terrifying revenge on their occasionally innocent victims. If you enjoy stories that cause you to glance nervously over your shoulder, shudder as you read, and sleep with the lights on, you will love this book!

7.5   Cohen, Daniel. **Phantom Animals.** G. P. Putnam's Sons, 1991. 111 pp. ISBN 0-399-22230-8.

Are there ghosts? If there are, then surely there are animal ghosts. People from all places and times have claimed to have seen spirits of animals, some of which have been spotted recently in the United States. One such ghost animal is DC— Demon Cat—glimpsed in the tunnels under the Capitol in Washington; DC is only seen when the person who sights him is alone. Folktales are filled with legends of animals, and the significance of spotting their spirits. Black dogs, white birds, or even steers, for example, may indicate that death is near. Are there ghosts? Read this book and decide.

7.6   Gale, David, editor. **Funny You Should Ask: The Delacorte Book of Original Humorous Short Stories.** Illustrated by Amy Schwart. Delacorte Press, 1992. 224 pp. ISBN 0-385-30535-4.

David Gale has collected sixteen original, humorous short stories, written for middle school students by a cross section of young adult authors, many of whom will be readily recognized by teachers, librarians, and students. Among the amusing new characters are fertile rabbits, a bat in the belfry, and one Aries Ape, while the readers will have met some characters before, such as Miriam Chafken's Jossi and Barbara Ann Porte's Taxi-cab Family. Constance Green assures readers that her character Virgil will be seen again. Other contributors known for their humorous writings are Jan Greenberg, M. E. Kerr, Walter Dean Myers, Gary Soto, and Zilpha Keatley Snyder.

7.7   Gallo, Donald R., editor. **Short Circuits: Thirteen Shocking Stories by Outstanding Writers for Young Adults.** Delacorte Press, 1992. 192 pp. ISBN 0-385-30785-3.

Ethan is locked in the school library after hours, and the spirits of literary characters begin to torment him! A dutiful brother, terrified of thunderstorms and snakes, is left alone on a rainy night with his sister's pet boa constrictor! These and other electrifying tales of terror are bound to jolt even the bravest of readers. Contributing authors include Joan Lowery Nixon, Vivien Alcock, Robert Westall, and Joan Aiken.

7.8   Gascoigne, Toss, Jo Goodman, and Margot Tyrrell, editors. **Dream Time: New Stories by Sixteen Award-Winning Authors.** Illustrated by Elizabeth Honey. Houghton Mifflin Company, 1991. 184 pp. ISBN 0-395-57434-X.

If you were asked to write a story based on the theme "Dream Time," what would you write about? Sixteen award-winning Australian authors were asked that same question, and their answers may surprise you! From aborigines to other worlds, these tales from Down Under offer a whole new perspective on dream time.

7.9   Griffiths, Barbara. **Frankenstein's Hamster: Ten Spine-Tin-gling Tales.** Illustrated by Barbara Griffiths. Dial Books, 1992. 113 pp. ISBN 0-8037-0952-8.

Do you own a cat? You may want to reconsider having your feline around after you read "The Takeover," a short story about cats that want revenge on all humans. Or have you told a secret that you promised not to tell? Luke has, and Franklyn, his friend, has an unusual way of getting even. From a school boy with a talent for taxidermy to a highwayman of death, the characters in these tales are sure to make your spine tingle!

7.10 Hollander, Phyllis, and Zander Hollander. **More Amazing but True Sport Stories.** Scholastic, 1990. 129 pp. ISBN 0-590-43876-X.

Even the casual sports fan will enjoy these entertaining stories about events in the wide world of sports. One unbelievable story tells about the welterweight match between Tony Wilson and Steve McCarthy: Minna Wilson, Tony's mom, climbed into the ring and beat her son's opponent over the head with her shoe. She cut Steve's head, and the decision was awarded to Tony!

7.11 Jacques, Brian. **Seven Strange and Ghostly Tales.** Philomel Books, 1991. 137 pp. ISBN 0-399-22103-4.

Brian Jacques likes to tell a story which twists and turns, arriving at a surprising, ghastly ending. Each of his seven stories in this collection begins with a poem which sets the stage and issues a warning for the strangeness to come. Malicious mischief, a badgering mother, lies, loneliness and pain, and bullies are just a few subjects for Jacques' creepy tales.

7.12 Nelson, Drew. **Wild Voices.** Illustrated by John Schoenherr. Philomel Books, 1991. 95 pp. ISBN 0-399-21798-3.

Life can by very difficult for animals in the wild, whether they are the predators or the prey. Each of these stories focuses on the winter hardships of an individual animal, from a fox to a wolf to a puma, as it searches for food and struggles to survive.

7.13 Schwartz, Alvin. **Scary Stories 3: More Tales to Chill Your Bones.** Illustrated by Stephen Gammell. HarperCollins, 1991. 115 pp. ISBN 0-06-021794-4.

In swamps and deserts, on farms and in deserted houses, the ghosts, goblins, spooks, and corpses from the stories in this book bring to mind tales told around campfires. Wild children raised by animals, nightmares, and an account of the eerie happenings in a haunted house are among the featured retellings of old folktales.

7.14   Schwartz, Howard, and Barbara Rush, editors. **The Diamond Tree: Jewish Tales from Around the World.** Illustrated by Uri Shulevitz. HarperCollins, 1991. 120 pp. ISBN 0-06-025239-1.

These fifteen Jewish folktales are a delightful mixture of Biblical stories and fairy tales, from Noah to the prophet Elijah to wise King Solomon. From some of these stories, it is easy to see how such tales as Little Red Riding Hood and Hansel and Gretel came to be. And each story contains a moral, with lessons for being honest, doing the right thing, and helping others.

7.15   Silver, Norman. **An Eye for Color.** Dutton Children's Books, 1991. 182 pp. ISBN 0-525-44859-4.

Eighteen-year-old Basil Kushenovitz narrates twelve short stories about his various experiences of growing up Jewish in South Africa. In his encounters, Basil begins to see the South Africa around him with double vision: a South Africa he has always taken for granted, and a South Africa whose government and policies he is beginning to question. From a fishing day shared with a Catholic priest to a classmate reclassified as "colored," Basil learns from his experiences and grows up to become an individual whose new awareness makes him a stranger in his own homeland. Glossary of Afrikaans words included.

7.16   Thomas, Joyce Carol, editor. **A Gathering of Flowers: Stories about Being Young in America.** HarperKeypoint, 1990. 232 pp. ISBN 0-06-447082-2.

Alfonso tries to look cool by slicking back his hair and pushing on his crooked teeth (since his parents can't afford braces). Reiko struggles to find a friend at her new school when her family is finally relocated from a Japanese internment camp after World War II. Zelma Lee Moses is called to preach from the time she is just a child in her small southern church, raising the spirits of everyone within the sound of her powerful voice. But can she use it to get Daniel to fall in love with her? These characters and others in this collection of short stories paint pictures of the growing-up experiences of American teenagers of many races and cultures.

7.17 Wilson, Budge. **The Leaving and Other Stories.** Philomel Books, 1992. 207 pp. ISBN 0-399-21878-5.

This collection of ten stories focuses on young girls and the events that shape their lives. In "The Metaphor," for instance, the narrator "outgrows" a favorite teacher who her mother despises, then is guilt-stricken when the teacher kills herself. In "Lysandra's Poem," Elaine wins a poetry contest but loses her best friend. In "The Leaving," a girl and her mother visit a city for the first time and return—after discovering museums, botanical gardens, and libraries—more confident and with a broader perspective on life. In each of these stories, the author illustrates how seemingly small incidents can change lives forever.

7.18 Yep, Laurence. **Tongues of Jade.** Illustrated by David Wiesner. HarperCollins, 1991. 191 pp. ISBN 0-06-022470-3.

In the nineteenth century, Chinese men were brought to the U.S. to perform heavy labor. The strict laws of immigration did not allow their wives to join these workers so, to keep alive the feelings of their homeland, the men told many stories which were eventually recorded in the late 1930s. Yep has selected seventeen stories for retelling under the headings "Roots," "Family Ties," "The Wild Heart," and "Beyond the Grave." The book's title comes from the funeral objects of jade which were placed in the mouth of a deceased person to insure everlasting life in the afterworld.

7.19 Yolen, Jane, editor. **2041: Twelve Short Stories about the Future by Top Science Fiction Writers.** Delacorte Press, 1991. 222 pp. ISBN 0-385-30445-5.

The twelve short stories contained in this collection reflect the possible future through the eyes of such noteworthy science fiction authors as Anne McCaffrey, Nancy Springer, and Joe Haldeman. What will school life be like in the year 2041?

What kinds of new inventions will exist? You can wait until you reach 2041, or you can read this book!

7.20   Yolen, Jane, and Martin H. Greenberg, editors. **Vampires: A Collection of Original Short Stories.** HarperCollins, 1991. 225 pp. ISBN 0-06-026800-X.

This collection contains thirteen original short stories about vampires, complete with sunlight (or the lack of it), garlic, and stakes through the heart. None of the stories are set in Transylvania or the other usual vampire haunts, and all but two of the selections have contemporary settings where vampires are least expected. With tales from "The Blood-Ghoul of Scarsdale" to "Aunt Horrible's Last Visit," this collection will thrill fans of bloodsucking creatures of the night.

8 Sports, Games, and Trivia

8.1 Aaseng, Nate. **A Decade of Champions: Super Bowls XV–XXIV.** Lerner Publications Company, 1991. 64 pp. ISBN 0-8225-1504-0.

True football fans will find this book fascinating. This is a history of the Super Bowl teams in the 1980s, a time when professional football was turned upside down. Teams that had dominated the sport at the beginning of the decade were struggling by its end, and this history examines how five key teams—the Redskins, the Raiders, the Bears, the Giants, and the 49ers—became winners.

8.2 Benson, Michael. **Dream Teams: The Best Teams of All Time!** A Sports Illustrated For Kids Book, 1991. 117 pp. ISBN 0-316-08993-1.

Using short chapters and black-and-white and color photographs, this book examines famous athletic teams, representing a variety of sports. A few examples of the teams discussed include the 1980 U.S. Olympic Hockey Team, the 1906–08 Chicago Cubs, the 1979 U.S. Davis Cup tennis team, and the 1969 New York Mets. The author describes particularly exciting plays, close matches, and personalities of the various players. Teams are chosen from baseball, basketball, hockey, football, tennis, track and field, golf, boxing, gymnastics, soccer, and even yachting.

8.3 Berler, Ron. **The Super Book of Baseball.** A Sports Illustrated For Kids Book, 1991. 129 pp. ISBN 0-316-09240-1.

This Sports Illustrated For Kids Book contains an interesting collection of baseball history, stories, records, facts, and trivia from the time the game began in 1889 to the latest World

Series. The book includes examinations of famous games, charts, records, and even a glossary of terms, exactly the kind of information young sports fans want to know.

8.4   Feldman, Jay. **Hitting.** Little Simon, 1991. 88 pp. ISBN 0-671-73318-4.

In this official major league baseball book, young athletes will learn the basic techniques of hitting successfully. The guide includes practice drills and exercises, as well as personal advice from such batting aces as Wade Boggs and Ryne Sandberg and from batting coach Dusty Baker.

8.5   Graham-Barber, Linda. **Mushy! The Complete Book of Valentine Words.** Illustrated by Betsy Lewin. Bradbury Press, 1991. 122 pp. ISBN 0-02-736941-2.

Definitions, histories, stories, and explanations for more than thirty-five words and ideas associated with Valentine's Day fill this book. The research in this book can both amuse and teach, as it explores the way words of romance have developed over time. For example, why is the word *love* used in tennis? Where did the word *romance* originate? Who was Cupid? These and other Valentine terms are defined and discussed.

8.6   King, Ron. **Rad Boards.** Illustrated by Jackie Aher. A Sports Illustrated For Kids Book, 1991. 83 pp. ISBN 0-316-49335-4.

For those interested in skateboarding, snowboarding, or bodyboarding, this book provides information on choosing the right board, acquiring the skill to perform tricks and stunts, and finding competitions. Safety equipment and habits are emphasized throughout, and diagrams and photographs bring the cutting edge to life.

8.7   McFarlan, Donald, Editor. **The Guinness Book of World Records 1991.** Bantam Books, 1991. 820 pp. ISBN 0-553-28954-3.

How big was the biggest snake? What's the tallest building in the world? What's the longest anyone has ever lived? What's the record for eating the most eggs at one time? These and other bizarre, amazing, and intriguing statistics make up the *Guinness Book of World Records,* a collection of all the astounding records set in our world every day. Who knows— maybe you'll find a record here that *you* can break!

8.8 Parietti, Jeff. **101 Wacky Sports Quotes.** Illustrated by Don Orehek. Scholastic, 1991. 94 pp. ISBN 0-590-44146-9.

The sports fan is sure to be entertained by this collection of sports puns, amusing comments from players in all branches of sports, and colorful descriptions of the accomplishments and errors of many sports heroes. From dugout and sideline comments to interview flubs, this book of wacky quotes is bound to make the sports fan chuckle!

8.9 Raber, Thomas R. **Wayne Gretzky; Hockey Great.** Lerner Publications Company, 1991. 64 pp. ISBN 0-8225-0539-8.

This biography of hockey great Wayne Gretzky traces his life and accomplishments from the time he was a young hockey player. Direct quotes from Wayne make the biography more personal as he comments on not only his professional career, but on what makes him happy in his personal life.

8.10 Schlossberg, Dan. **Pitching.** Little Simon, 1991. 86 pp. ISBN 0-671-73317-6.

This is an official major league baseball book aimed at the Little League pitcher. Through interviews with successful pitchers like Dwight Gooden, Nolan Ryan, and Warren Spahn, young pitchers are given hints for improving pitching skills and examples of successful techniques. The four areas of pitching are discussed: attitude, mechanics, strategy and regimen. Helpful photos demonstrate the correct procedures.

8.11 Sullivan, George. **All about Basketball.** G. P. Putnam's Sons, 1991. 160 pp. ISBN 0-399-61268-8.

This overview of the fast-paced game of basketball examines the history of the game, up-to-date rules and regulations for the game, and some of the famous players who have commanded the court. The book also discusses a variety of basketball techniques and plays, using detailed explanations of procedure so that even a novice to the game can understand it. Do you know what constitutes goal-tending? This is the place to find out!

8.12   White, Ellen Emerson. **Bo Jackson: Playing the Games.** Scholastic, 1990. 86 pp. ISBN 0-590-44075-6.

Bo Jackson is a star of both baseball and football, but his rise to the top was not easy. This book traces Bo's career and private life, from his days as a troublemaker to a sports legend. Emphasizing physical conditioning, motivation, and careful decision making, Bo Jackson overcame all the setbacks on his way to success, and readers will find his story inspirational.

Series

8.13   Bloom, Marc. **Know Your Game.** Illustrated by Joe Taylor. Scholastic.

The Know Your Game series explores some of today's most popular sports, offering advice on how to develop the skills required to play. Examining rules, equipment, and basics of the game, each book gives insight into the components that come together to form a winning team. Teamwork, patience, and self-confidence are particularly stressed.

8.14   Montgomery, Robert. **Gary Carter's Iron Mask.** Troll Associates.

Robbie Belmont is a talented high school baseball player who has to adjust to switching positions from pitcher to catcher as he pursues his dream of playing in the major leagues. This series traces Robbie's baseball career from high school through college to the minor leagues. But there's more to life than just baseball; Robbie confronts problems with his peers, romantic love, a sick father, and friendship in these stories of growing up. Titles include *Home Run, Grand Slam, Triple Play,* and three others.

8.15   Olympic Sports. Crestwood House.

The Olympic Sports series explores the history of a variety of sports in the Olympic program. In *Ball Sports,* readers will examine the six primary ball sports of tennis, soccer, hockey, handball, basketball, and volleyball; in *Ice Sports,* bobsledding, ice dancing, skating, and a number of other winter ice sports are explored. From combat sports like fencing and boxing to great moments in skiing, this series reviews the great history of the Olympics, one sport at a time.

II Learning

Let ignorance talk as it will, Learning has its value.

Jean de la Fontaine
Fables Book VIII
Fable 19

9   Arts, Crafts, and Skills

9.1   Greenberg, Jan, and Sandra Jordan. **The Painter's Eye: Learning to Look at Contemporary American Art.** Delacorte Press, 1991. 87 pp. ISBN 0-385-30319-X.

What do I see? What constitutes the work? How do I feel about this piece of art? Applying these three basic questions to thirty contemporary American paintings, Greenberg and Jordan introduce ways of seeing, experiencing, and appreciating art. The contemporary paintings are reproduced in color, and black-and-white photographs of the contributing artists at work in their studios are also included.

9.2   Longe, Bob. **World's Best Card Tricks.** Sterling Publishing, 1991. 128 pp. ISBN 0-8069-8232-2.

Have you ever wondered how magicians seem to know in advance which card a person will pick from a deck? This book tells you how it's done! With step-by-step instructions, this guide will teach you forty-one card tricks to amaze your friends with. From prediction tricks to mind-reading magic, this book examines and explains all aspects of the world of card tricks—including what to do if your trick doesn't work exactly as planned! Index included.

9.3   Longe, Bob. **World's Best Coin Tricks.** Sterling Publishing, 1992. 128 pp. ISBN 0-8069-8660-3.

Can anyone do magic, like making a coin vanish into thin air or passing a coin right through a solid table? The answer is yes with this comprehensive introduction to basic coin tricks. This book includes instructions for performing more than fifty coin tricks. Dozens of illustrations are used to clearly explain how the tricks are performed, and suggestions are given to help amaze and startle your audience.

9.4   Parnell, Helga, editor. **Cooking the South American Way.** Photographs by Robert L. and Diane Wolfe. Lerner Publications Company, 1991. 48 pp. ISBN 0-8225-0925-3.

How does almond meringue after a hearty meal sound? This book about South American cooking has more than just tasty recipes in it; it also includes a brief history of South America, a list of special ingredients, and even a key to pronouncing the more difficult names of the foods described. Besides detailing which dishes are appropriate for certain occasions, this book contains color photos of the finished dish, photos guaranteed to tantalize your tastebuds.

9.5   Sullivan, Charles, editor. **Children of Promise: African-American Literature and Art for Young People.** Harry N. Abrams, 1991. 126 pp. ISBN 0-8019-3170-2.

Words and images unite in this two-hundred-year celebration of African American literature and art; Galatians 4:28, "Now we, brethren, as Isaac was, are the children of promise," provides its vision. Poetry, prose, painting, and photography make real both voice and vision. Poets (Gwendolyn Brooks, Langston Hughes, Dudley Randall), presidents (Lincoln, Jefferson, Truman), leaders (Booker T. Washington, Frederick Douglass, Martin Luther King, Jr.), painters (Jacob Lawrence, Romare Bearden, Charles Searles), and photographers (Lewis W. Hine, Frances Benjamin Johnson) are among the over one hundred selected artists. Texts both common and distinct are included, from a bill of sale for a slave to an excerpt from Lorraine Hansberry's *A Raisin in the Sun.* Biographical notes accompany the collection.

9.6   Townsend, Charles Barry. **World's Best Magic Tricks.** Sterling Publishing, 1992. 128 pp. ISBN 0-8069-8582-8.

Detailed diagrams and easy-to-follow directions will help you amaze, confound, and entertain friends and family. Illusion and magic tricks include the balancing glass mystery, the heaven and hell paper trick, the impossible knot, and the dissolving coin. Hints are also included to help make your presentations smooth, effective, and entertaining.

9.7 Winget, Mary, editor. **Desserts around the World.** Photographs by Robert L. and Diane Wolfe. Lerner Publications Company, 1991. 56 pp. ISBN 0-8225-09261-1.

Who doesn't love dessert? This book contains recipes for making the favorite desserts of many countries, from Austria to New Zealand. Not only does the book give a brief history of desserts, but it also includes some cooking tips and a section on pronouncing the more difficult names. Color photos of many of the recipes help to make this recipe book an invaluable guide to cooking ethnic desserts.

10 History

10.1 Adler, Bill. **500 Great Facts about America.** Avon, 1992. 228 pp. ISBN 0-380-76787-2.

To celebrate the 500th anniversary of Columbus' discovery of America, the author has gathered together five hundred little-known facts about the New World. The book is divided into ten general categories, each arranged in chronological order to reflect the development of the United States. Among the five hundred great facts: No. 1: Columbus claimed the prize for himself, as he was the first to sight land. And No. 500: The Ninety-Niners, an international group of female aviators, planted trees in 1982 from each of the fifty states to memorialize Amelia Earhart.

10.2 Ashabranner, Brent. **A Memorial for Mr. Lincoln.** Photographs by Jennifer Ashabranner. G. P. Putnam's Sons, 1992. 113 pp. ISBN 0-399-22273-1.

In Washington, D.C., stands a simple but imposing memorial to one of our most beloved presidents, Abraham Lincoln. This book details the conception of that memorial, the efforts to find an architect and sculptor to design it, and its actual construction and dedication. Through words, pictures, and details of Lincoln's life and the lives of his descendants, we see the memorial rise from the marshy land near the Potomac to become one of the most visited tourist sites in Washington. Bibliography and index included.

10.3 Ballard, Robert D. **Exploring the Titanic.** Illustrated by Ken Marschall. Scholastic, 1988. 63 pp. ISBN 0-590-41953-6.

Robert Ballard tells of his journey to explore the remains of the supership *Titanic* in such detail that it's as if the reader is accompanying Ballard to the murky bottom of the sea. In a step-by-step narrative explanation, the author describes the tragic night in 1912 when the "unsinkable" *Titanic* sank, launching itself into the history books as one of the worst sea disasters ever. Using before and after illustrations to highlight the changes done to the luxury liner after eighty years underwater, Ballard charts his discovery and exploration of the world's most famous wreckage.

10.4   Chaikin, Miriam. **Menorahs, Mezuzas, and Other Jewish Symbols.** Illustrated by Erica Weihs. Clarion Books, 1990. 102 pp. ISBN 0-89919-856-2.

This book examines the history and significance of many Jewish symbols, such as the Shield of David and the menorah. Many of the customs and practices of Judaism are explained as well, as is much of the culture of Israel, the Jewish homeland. Bibliography included.

10.5   Fisher, Leonard Everett. **Tracks across America: The Story of the American Railroad, 1825–1900.** Holiday House, 1992. 192 pp. ISBN 0-8234-0945-7.

During the nineteenth century, the American railroad became the fastest and most efficient means of transportation ever invented. From the completion of the first railroad to the railroad's effects in the Civil War, this book provides details on seventy-five years of growth in the railroad industry, including examinations of train robberies, disasters, and hostile encounters with Native Americans, who resisted the extension of railways into their homelands. Photographs and bibliography included.

10.6   Giblin, James Cross. **The Riddle of the Rosetta Stone: Key to Ancient Egypt.** Thomas Y. Crowell, 1990. 77 pp. ISBN 0-690-04797-5.

This book details how the discovery and deciphering of the Rosetta Stone unlocked the secret of Egyptian hieroglyphs. Author James Giblin explains how Napoleon's army secured the stone, and how men like Thomas Young and Jean Francois

Champollion struggled to decipher the Egyptian writings. Once the stone's writings were translated, the world had the key to more than 3,000 years of Egyptian civilization. Excerpts from the Stone's hieroglyphs highlight the many photographs, prints, and drawings.

10.7   Jacobs, Francine. **The Tainos: The People Who Welcomed Columbus.** Illustrated by Patrick Collins. G. P. Putnam's Sons, 1992. 92 pp. ISBN 0-399-22116-6.

This book examines a little-known period in the development of the New World. The Tainos were the first Native Americans who welcomed Columbus in 1492. The book describes the history, the culture, and the mysterious fate of these people. It also discusses how the "gold fever" of the Spaniards affected their treatment of the Tainos and how this treatment virtually destroyed the Tainos and their culture.

10.8   Levine, Ellen. **Freedom's Children: Young Civil Rights Activists Tell Their Own Stories.** G. P. Putnam's Sons, 1993. 156 pp. ISBN 0-399-21893-9.

In conversations about civil rights and the 1960s, one hears many names: Rosa Parks, Medgar Evers, Martin Luther King, Jr., Emmitt Till, and even "Bull" Connor. These were the names in the headlines and on the evening news, but who were the people in the back row? Most were young blacks from the targeted areas. With, and more often without, their parents' approval, young people, most between the ages of four and seventeen, risked all for the right to be free. In their own words, these children of the Sixties tell their stories of the major events in the civil rights movement—the Montgomery Bus Boycott, sit ins, Freedom Summer, and Bloody Sunday. Photographs, bibliography, and index included.

10.9   Lynch, Amy. **Nashville.** Dillon Press, 1991. 59 pp. ISBN 0-87518-453-7.

In *Nashville,* author Amy Lynch describes the history, setting, and people of Nashville, a city known by many names—Music City, Athens of the South, or Buckle of the Bible Belt. The city's history dates back to more than 500 years before the arrival in America of Christopher Columbus, to a time when the first people settled where Nashville now stands. Yet Nashville has remained a big city in the country over all those years, allowing its people to enjoy a mix of both urban and rural lifestyles. Lynch enhances her description of Nashville with an historical time line and a directory of interesting sites. A Downtown America book.

10.10 St. George, Judith. **Mason and Dixon's Line of Fire.** G. P. Putnam's Sons, 1991. 128 pp. ISBN 0-399-22240-5.

The Mason-Dixon Line is perhaps history's most famous and violent boundary dispute. This book explores the roots of the line, recalling the clashes between colonial Maryland and Pennsylvania over land rights. It took two surveyors to establish the line that finally brought about peace, but the line ended up serving as another divisive boundary—when it came to represent the boundary between North and South during the Civil War. Bibliography and index included.

10.11 Schwabach, Karen. **Thailand: Land of Smiles.** Dillon Press, 1991. 127 pp. ISBN 0-87518-454-5.

Exploring the past and present of Thailand, the author focuses on the ethnic groups as well as the heritage, economy, politics and culture of the people of Thailand. The book also provides a handy section of fast facts, a map of Thailand, and a listing of consulates and embassies serving Thailand in the United States and Canada.

10.12 Walter, Mildred Pitts. **Mississippi Challenge.** Bradbury Press, 1992. 183 pp. ISBN 0-02-0792301-0.

In order to understand the challenge made by the members of the Mississippi Free Democratic Party (MFDP) at the 1964 Democratic National Convention in Atlanta, one must understand the history of race relations in Mississippi. From the time of slavery to the signing of the Voting Rights Act in 1965, this book examines the struggle for civil rights for African Americans in Mississippi. For many years, the state resisted the

extension of basic rights to blacks; its white-controlled government refused to accept the 13th and 14th amendments to the
Constitution, and the state refused to abolish the poll tax and
voter testing. Many people gave their lives to give Mississip-
pians of all colors the basic constitutional rights of the United
States. Among them are such activists as Medgar Evers, Emmitt Till, James Chaney, Michael Schwerner, and Andrew
Goodman. Photographs, bibliography, and index included.

Series

10.13   Cities at War. New Discovery Books.

The Cities at War series describes the effects of World War II
on the daily lives of citizens of Berlin, Amsterdam, and London. Topics include food rationing, prejudice against Jews and
other minorities, the evacuation of children, and the aftermath
of war as cities attempted to rebuild. Many black-and-white
photographs enhance the text. In addition, each book in the
series includes source notes, a bibliography, and an index.

10.14   City! Macmillan.

The City! series explores the sights of major American cities
through photographs, maps, and detailed background information. From the Empire State Building in New York City to the
White House in Washington, D.C., these books provide a tourist's delight as the reader is guided from one historic site to
another. Each book also contains a list of things to see and do
in each city, for the traveler who can't wait to go from a book
about an amazing city to the real thing!

10.15   Great Battles and Sieges. New Discovery Books.

From ancient times to World War II, this series explores some
of the great battles in history. Do you know the story of the
Trojan Horse? The giant wooden horse that the Greeks used to
breach the walls of Troy is included in this series, as is the great
desert battle of El Alamein, a battle between Allied Forces and
Axis powers in North Africa in 1942. Each book in this series

includes battle plans and maps, photographs, a bibliography, and an index.

10.16 **Hello U.S.A.** Lerner Publications Company.

Each state has its own unique history, and the Hello U.S.A. series brings that history to life. Each book in the series focuses on one particular state, emphasizing its geography, history, industries, and people. Do you know which state was named for the Virgin Queen of England, Elizabeth I? Do you know which state gave us President Jimmy Carter? These books are filled with fun facts and entertaining trivia about the states that make up the U.S.A. Each book contains a facts-at-a-glance listing, as well as a pronunciation guide.

10.17 **In America.** Lerner Publications Company.

The In America series provides a fact-filled source of a particular country's people in America from earliest explorations through the American Revolution to modern times. The states are divided into geographical regions, and the narration tells how immigrants from one particular country have been involved in that area's development. A list of immigrants who have made outstanding contributions to the nation is included in each volume.

10.18 **Places in the News.** Crestwood House.

The Places in the News series explores countries of the world where headline-making events are currently taking place. Tracing many current incidents to earlier events in history, these books examine the politics, cultures, and futures of many of today's world-shaping countries. From the rise of Saddam Hussein in Iraq and Fidel Castro in Cuba to the downfall of Ferdinand Marcos in the Phillipines and Nicolae Ceausescu in Romania, these books provide detailed accounts of the rapidly changing countries around us. Each volume contains a glossary and pertinent facts list.

10.19 **Portraits of the Nations.** HarperCollins.

The Portraits of the Nations series introduces readers to the culture, geography, people, and history of some of the world's most fascinating countries. Did you know that, despite its relatively small size, Pakistan is one of the ten most populous countries in the world? Did you know that the Vatican City in Italy has a different government than the rest of Italy? From the mountains of Spain to the ruins of ancient Rome, this series provides readers with a complete tour of some of the great nations of the world. Each book includes photographs, maps, a bibliography, and an index.

10.20   Visual Geography. Lerner Publications Company.

Each volume in the Visual Geography series provides a tour-through-photos of various countries of the world with text reflecting the topographical, historical, social, economic, and political backgrounds of each country, but it is the photography that makes this series unique. From the coast of Denmark to a lonely farmhouse in Scotland, these books offer a visual guide to the far corners of the earth. Each book includes an index.

10.21   Worlds of the Past. New Discovery Books.

Each book in the Worlds of the Past series examines the lives of ancient people and the civilizations they constructed. The Greeks and Romans, for example, built their empires around an entire pantheon of gods, gods that were very similar between the two cultures. And the Vikings were great shipbuilders who sailed the world in their drakkars, or Viking Dragon Ships. Each book includes a glossary, time line, and index.

11 Natural Sciences

11.1 Aldis, Rodney. **Polar Lands.** Dillon Press, 1992. 45 pp. ISBN 0-87518-494-4.

The plants, animals, and people that live in the polar regions survive entirely surrounded by ocean waters which have become polluted by pesticides, chemicals, and oil by-products. The survival of these life forms is threatened in three ways: by overhunting, by pollution, and by oil drilling. Organizations like Greenpeace and the World Wide Fund for Nature, as well as individuals, must work cooperatively to insure a safe future for the polar regions, or else these vast, natural wildernesses will be lost forever. An Ecology Watch book.

11.2 Alvin, Virginia, and Robert Silverstein. **Smell, The Subtle Sense.** Illustrated by Ann Neumann. Morrow Junior Books, 1992. 90 pp. ISBN 0-688-09396-5.

From types of smells (sweet, sour, or repulsive) to current research on artificial fragrances, this book discusses one of the most important of the five senses. Topics covered include noses, body odors, and the particular types of communication scent makes possible. The authors describe the dependence on smell experienced by all animals: moths, dogs, deer, cats, as well as humans. The book includes an index and a bibliography for readers who want more detailed information.

11.3 Batten, Mary. **Nature's Tricksters: Animals and Plants That Aren't What They Seem.** Illustrated by Lois Lovejoy. Sierra Club Books, 1992. 49 pp. ISBN 0-316-08371-2.

With detailed illustrations and explanations, this book explores the world of camouflage and trickery in nature, where animals and plants use many unusual means to protect themselves, to find food, and to attract mates.

11.4 Brooks, Bruce. **Nature by Design.** Farrar, Straus and Giroux, 1991. 69 pp. ISBN 0-374-30334-7.

Nature is filled with wondrous processes which seem mysterious to man. How does a spider spin its web? How do wasps construct huge paper nests? How do ants build massive colonies? How do birds weave and sew their nests? This book offers explanations for these and other processes of nature, explanations highlighted by photographs and easy-to-understand text. Index included.

11.5 Brooks, Bruce. **Predator!** Farrar, Straus and Giroux, 1991. 70 pp. ISBN 0-374-36111-8.

Hunger as the motivator of animals' behavior is explored in this look at how the food chain of predators and prey functions. When an animal hunts for food, it performs its best, for its survival hangs in the balance. An animal that is unable to track, lure, and bring down its prey is sure to die. Photographs punctuate the reader's understanding of the how and why animals such as the peregrine falcon, the crab spider, the shrike, the badger, or the poison arrow frog hunt, kill, and survive. A look at how humans fit into the predatory picture is also analyzed. Index included.

11.6 Burt, Denise. **Kangaroos.** Photographs by Neil McLeod. Houghton Mifflin Company, 1991. 40 pp. ISBN 0-395-55990-1.

From the different varieties to the factors threatening their existence, this book is all about kangaroos. The author describes the two main families of kangaroos—the Potoroidae and the Macropodidae—explaining how their tails, hind legs, teeth, and padded feet evolved to suit the environment. Readers will learn why some male kangaroos live in groups that do not include females, when kangaroos will attack and how (mostly with their forepaws), and how young kangaroos develop. Color photographs show kangaroos in poses both comic and lovely.

11.7 Cohen, Daniel, and Susan Cohen. **Where to Find Dinosaurs Today.** Cobblehill Books, 1992. 209 pp. ISBN 0-525-65098-9.

Where can you find dinosaurs today? All kinds of places! Science or history museums, Dinostores, state parks, and nature trails—many have displays, dioramas, or skeletal reconstructions of the great lizards that roamed the earth millions of years ago. This book offers a wealth of information about finding dinosaurs in your area. Arranged by state, this book lists locations, addresses, hours, applicable admission charges, and phone numbers for organizations and institutions with dinosaur displays. So where can you find dinosaurs today? Maybe in your own hometown! Photographs included.

11.8 Collinson, Alan. **Mountains.** Dillon Press, 1991. 45 pp. ISBN 0-87518-493-6.

European mountains differ from North American mountains, which are still different from low-latitude mountains. Mountain climates are affected by height, heat, light, rain, snow, ice, and the types of soils within each mountain range, and each range influences the weather and geography around it. This book offers explanations of mountain structures and explains in detail the various threats to the delicate mountain climates. An Ecology Watch book. Index included.

11.9 Cossi, Olga. **Harp Seals.** Carolrhoda Books, 1991. 47 pp. ISBN 0-87614-437-7.

Color photographs of desolate snow-covered landscapes, crystal-clear ice floes, and arctic seas provide the wintry background as harp seals are pictured swimming, mating, nursing, shedding their skins, and migrating. The author describes, in easy-to-understand words, every facet of the harp seal's existence, emphasizing their capacity for survival in a harsh environment. Glossary and index included.

11.10 Docekal, Eileen M. **Nature Detective: How to Solve Outdoor Mysteries.** Illustrated by David Eames. Sterling Publishing, 1989. 128 pp. ISBN 0-8069-6844-3.

For the would-be nature scientist, this handbook offers a unique presentation of clues to help identify wild animals, birds, snakes, trees, plants, and insects that live in the back yard, as well as in ponds and woods. Nature is filled with colors, shapes, tracks, sounds, and smells, each one a sign of the life around us. This book will help the reader decipher those mysterious signs.

11.11 Facklam, Margery. **Who Harnessed the Horse? The Story of Animal Domestication.** Illustrated by Steven Parton. Little, Brown and Company, 1992. 160 pp. ISBN 0-316-27381-3.

This book describes how humans began to think of wild animals as protectors, helpers, and companions. The many roles domesticated animals play are thoroughly discussed, from dogs as hunting companions to monkeys as aides to paralyzed humans. The author concludes by encouraging people to treat all animals with kindness and respect. Includes a glossary and an index.

11.12 Ganeri, Anita. **Rivers, Ponds, and Lakes.** Dillon Press, 1991. 45 pp. ISBN 0-87518-497-9.

Human water consumption has tripled in the last forty years; consequently, the natural water cycle and wetland habitats for many animals have become threatened. Photographs, maps, and illustrations point out how humans have placed our wetlands and our own fresh water supply in peril. The final chapter offers hopeful suggestions for solving our increasing water problems. An Ecology Watch book. Index included.

11.13 Goodman, Billy. **Animal Homes and Societies.** Little, Brown and Company, 1991. 96 pp. ISBN 0-316-32018-8.

This book examines how animals interact with each other and with their environments. Did you know that animals live in a variety of group sizes? Some animals live alone, like the tiger or the cobra; others live in closed families, like gibbons and beavers. Some animals live in extended families, like lions and elephants, while others live in extremely large groups of unrelated families, like bats, fish, and birds. A Planet Earth book. Index and photographs included.

11.14 Goodman, Billy. **Natural Wonders and Disasters.** Little, Brown and Company, 1991. 96 pp. ISBN 0-316-32016-1.

Why do earthquakes occur? Where do tornadoes come from? What causes floods? These and many other questions about the natural forces in the world around us are addressed in this book, which is highlighted by photographs of post-disaster devastation and box inserts charting record floods and earthquakes. A Planet Earth book.

11.15 Goodman, Billy. **The Rain Forest.** Tern Enterprise Books, 1991. 96 pp. ISBN 0-316-32019-6.

An amazing variety of plant and animal life exists in rain forests, but the activities of humans threaten these fragile ecosystems every day. Without the rain forests, the ozone layer around the earth would deteriorate, allowing dangerous rays from the sun to reach life on our planet. What can be done to protect these valuable forests? This book has some solutions. A Planet Earth book.

11.16 Hackwell, W. John. **Desert of Ice: Life and Work in Antarctica.** Charles Scribner's Sons, 1991. 40 pp. ISBN 0-684-19085-0.

Through the eyes of the archeologist/author, the reader will learn about many research projects being conducted in Antarctica, the icy continent, the continent least affected by industrialized society. The reader will experience a firsthand account of the work being done under subzero conditions and the research yielding a variety of unusual information on the "desert of ice." The history and geography of the sparsely populated Antarctica are also provided.

11.17 Herbst, Judith. **Animal Amazing.** Atheneum, 1991. 181 pp. ISBN 0-689-31556-2.

Does Nessie, the monster that allegedly dwells in the murky depths of Loch Ness in Scotland, really exist? Does Bigfoot really live in remote wildernesses of the world, including the United States? What happened to cause the dinosaurs to disappear? How do migrating birds and butterflies know exactly when to leave and how to get to the same place, thousands of miles away, year after year? These and other mysteries are explored in this book that examines the world of creatures both intriguing and baffling.

11.18   Hoff, Mary, and Mary M. Rodgers. **Groundwater.** Lerner Publications Company, 1991. 64 pp. ISBN 0-8225-2500-3.

The earth's primary element is water. Fresh water and salt water cover nearly three-fourths of our planet's surface. An additional supply of fresh water—called groundwater—lies underground, and in some regions, is the only fresh water available for drinking. The careless dumping of chemicals is endangering groundwater sources, thus endangering water supplies for humans and animals alike. Advanced technology is helping in the search for usable groundwater, one of the most valuable resources in the world. This book offers suggestions for preserving our groundwater supplies, and focuses on some of the abuses of this resource occurring right now. An Our Endangered Planet book.

11.19   Jedrosz, Aleksander. **Eyes.** Illustrated by Andrew Farmer and Robina Green. Troll Associates, 1992. 32 pp. ISBN 0-8167-2095-9.

Did you know that, like a camera, the human eye actually sees images upside down and backwards? Did you know that the eye is directly connected to the brain? These and other facts about the eye are examined in this book, which also offers technical terms and processes associated with vision and the visual organs. Also explored are a variety of problems which can afflict the eyes, causing blurry vision or even blindness.

11.20 Johnson, Rebecca L. **The Great Barrier Reef: A Living Laboratory.** Lerner Publications Company, 1991. 96 pp. ISBN 0-8225-1596-2.

One of the last unexplored frontiers in our world is the ocean, and the Great Barrier Reef is a beautiful, living coral reef in the shallow ocean waters along the northeast coast of Australia. This book describes the work of scientists who are studying the reef and the life around it, and how these things are affected by both natural disasters and humans.

11.21 Johnson, Sylvia A. **Roses Red, Violets Blue: Why Flowers Have Colors.** Photographs by Yuko Sato. Lerner Publications Company, 1991. 64 pp. ISBN 0-8225-1594-6.

In this detailed look at the functions of flowers and their colors, the author explains the pigments in plants and describes the ways colors attract bees and other insects that pollinate, helping flowering plants reproduce. The photographs, which enhance the text, give readers a much closer look at nature than can be seen by the human eye.

11.22 LaBonte, Gail. **The Tarantula.** Dillon Press, 1990. 58 pp. ISBN 0-87518-452-9.

Many people are terrified of tarantulas—the largest spider in existence—believing that the spiders are extremely poisonous as well as vicious. Although some of the largest species of tarantula—such as the Goliath Bird-Eater—will eat small mammals or birds, most species eat only insects. Moreover, while the tarantula's bite is fatal to small animals, it is merely painful to most humans. The author discusses many of the roles tarantulas have played throughout history: as food, as medicine, as "bodyguards" (in jewelry cases), and as objects of superstition. A glossary (with pronunciation guide) and an index are provided.

11.23 Langone, John. **Our Endangered Earth: What We Can Do to Save It.** Illustrated by Leslie Cober. Little, Brown and Company, 1992. 190 pp. ISBN 0-316-51415-2.

The earth is in danger—but we can help! This book examines the threats to our environment, threats such as pollution, global warming, and disappearing wildlife, and suggests some ways to improve life in the twenty-first century. All of us—even kids—can help to stop the deterioration of our planet, if we know where to begin.

11.24   Lauber, Patricia. **Living with Dinosaurs.** Illustrated by Douglas Henderson. Bradbury Press, 1991. 47 pp. ISBN 0-02-754521-0.

Could dinosaurs have lived in your back yard? Maybe! Seventy-five million years ago, dinosaurs and other strange creatures inhabited North America. The author and illustrator take the reader on a guided tour of the sea, forest, and nesting grounds of many prehistoric animals. The concluding chapter explains how fossils are formed and how archaeologists interpret scientific discoveries from the past.

11.25   Loewer, Peter. **The Inside-Out Stomach: An Introduction to Animals without Backbones.** Illustrated by Jean Jenkins. Atheneum, 1990. 55 pp. ISBN 0-689-31432-9.

Many different types of creatures fall into the category of invertebrates, which means "without a backbone." Inspecting pond water with a magnifying glass, we can see tiny protozoans such as the amoeba. With a snorkel and mask in the ocean, we might find saltwater sponges, sea anemones, or jellyfish. Spiders and earthworms, of course, are found almost anywhere. This book describes these unusual animals and more—all invertebrates—and provides detailed descriptions of each type, as well as where they might be found. A glossary, bibliography, and index are included.

11.26   McFall, Christie. **America Underground.** Cobblehill Books, 1992. 80 pp. ISBN 0-525-65079-2.

With the help of black-and-white photographs, line drawings, and maps, this book explores the many ways humans have found to use the space beneath the surface of the earth. The author explores topics as diverse as cave exploration, mining, subways, underground cities, and waste disposal. In addition, she discusses the catastrophic forces that cause earthquakes and volcano eruptions. An index is included.

11.27 McVey, Vicki. **The Sierra Club Wayfinding Book.** Illustrated by Martha Weston. Sierra Club Books, 1989. 88 pp. ISBN 0-316-56342-0.

Over thousands of years, humans have developed systems using their senses, landmarks, maps, navigation, and signs in the natural world to keep themselves from becoming lost. This book examines those systems by using games, activities, and experiments to illustrate the many ways people find their way around. A Sierra Club book.

11.28 McVey, Vicki. **The Sierra Club Book of Weatherwisdom.** Illustrated by Martha Weston. Sierra Club Books, 1991. 104 pp. ISBN 0-316-56341-2.

Inviting reader participation, this book relies on a combination of scientifically verified facts, folklore, and home projects to explain basic weather phenomena such as barometric pressure, rainfall, climate, winds, warm and cold fronts, and storms. While urging the reader to set up a weather station and journal, the book describes what it is that "real" meteorologists actually do and how they interpret their findings.

11.29 Patent, Dorothy Hinshaw. **Gray Wolf, Red Wolf.** Photographs by William Muñoz. Clarion Books, 1990. 64 pp. ISBN 0-89919-863-5.

This book provides an introduction to two species of wolves, with emphasis on their status as endangered species. The author stresses the essential wildness of wolves, noting that even when raised in captivity, wolves often never fully trust their human caretakers. Wolf packs and territories are described, along with attempts—some successful—to reintroduce wolves back into the wild. A list of addresses for those interested in further information is included.

11.30 Peters, David. **From the Beginning: The Story of Human Evolution.** Morrow Junior Books, 1991. 128 pp. ISBN 0-688-09476-7.

Rich with charts, diagrams, and illustrations, this book traces the evolution of man from bacteria to homo sapiens. Beginning with speculation on the origins of the universe via the "big bang" theory, the author continues with a discussion of DNA, cell evolution, flat worms to the first species of fish, the first land animals, various reptiles and amphibians, the first mammals, the primates, and finally describes "Lucy" the Australopithecine, homo erectus, and homo sapiens. The book concludes with speculation as to the future of humans, as well as a reminder that evolution is an ongoing process.

11.31 Pettit, Jayne. **Amazing Lizards.** Scholastic, 1990. 57 pp. ISBN 0-590-43682-1.

Lizards can be as small as just a few inches long (the gecko, for example) or as large as nine feet long (the komodo dragon). They live in swamps, rain forests, grasslands, and deserts—as far north as Norway and as far south as Argentina. Sixteen families of lizards are described in this book, with emphasis placed on the ability of all types of lizards to adapt to their environments. Much supplementary material is provided, including a "Geological Timeline," a center section of color photographs, a glossary, a bibliography, and an index.

11.32 Pringle, Laurence. **Batman: Exploring the World of Bats.** Photographs by Merlin D. Tuttle. Charles Scribner's Sons, 1991. 42 pp. ISBN 0-684-19232-2.

Batman, "the caped crusader?" No, this is not the story of a comic-book and movie hero. Instead, it is the true story of Merlin Tuttle's lifelong fascination with bats, animals he calls the "gentle friends" of humans. Despite his personal affection for them, Dr. Tuttle knows most people despise and fear bats, often slaughtering them in huge numbers for no reason. Chapters on "Getting to Know Real Bats" and "Gentle, Intelligent, and Endangered" introduce the reader to bats and how they are studied by scientists, providing many interesting facts about bats' habitats, species, and lifestyles. The final chapter asks us to "Meet the Challenge of Bat Conservation."

11.33   Reed, Don C. **Wild Lion of the Sea: The Steller Sea Lion That Refused to Be Tamed.** Illustrated by Norman Green. Little, Brown and Company, 1992. 115 pp. ISBN 0-316-73661-9.

When George, a Steller sea lion, is first brought to California's Marine World, he is only a pup. But as the years go by, George grows up to become a 2,000-pound problem for his trainers and keepers. This book describes the attempts to train George, examines the proper treatment of wild animals in captivity, and discusses the plight of the Steller sea lion, an animal that is now a threatened species.

11.34   Russo, Monica. **Insect Almanac: A Year-Round Activity Guide.** Photographs by Kevin Byron. Sterling Publishing, 1991. 126 pp. ISBN 0-8069-7454-0.

From Junebugs to beetles to butterflies, this book explores the wide variety of insects and the seasonal cycles in which they live. This book will guide the reader in finding, collecting, and keeping insects which thrive year-round or only seasonally. Organized by each of the four seasons, this book provides color photographs and illustrations to aid the budding collector in finding just the right bug! Index included.

11.35   Squire, Ann. **Understanding Man's Best Friend: Why Dogs Look and Act the Way They Do.** Macmillan, 1991. 119 pp. ISBN 0-02-786590-8.

Beginning with the history of dogs, this book tells of the selective breeding progression from wolves to domestic dogs. From this, humans have progressed to creating "customized" dogs to suit every need. Basic similarities between wolves and dogs are presented; knowing these similarities can help a pet owner better understand the pet's behavior. The book also provides help in choosing the right dog for you. Do you want a dog to work, to herd, to hunt, or to just be a friend? Lastly, dog problems are presented. Sometimes people have taken selective breeding too far, and the dogs have paid the price.

11.36   Stewart, Gail B. **Antarctica.** Crestwood House, 1991. 48 pp. ISBN 0-89686-656-4.

Antarctica is the lonely, frozen spot at the bottom of the world. Its hostile environment is unfriendly to people and most animals, but humans are destroying the delicate balance of nature by interfering in Antarctica's environment. Seals, whales, penguins, and krill who make their homes there are in danger of being destroyed as humans encroach on this untouched wilderness. The reader will learn this land's history and discover that the next few years are crucial for the continent's survival.

11.37   Stodart, Eleanor. **The Australian Echidna.** Houghton Mifflin Company, 1991. 40 pp. ISBN 0-395-55992-8.

Echidnas, also known as spiny anteaters, the only mammal other than the platypus to lay eggs and produce milk for its young, baffled scientists at first. This occurred, in part, because an echidna looks something like a porcupine. This book examines the echidna's habits—what it eats, how it manages to stay warm in the winter and cool in the summer, where it lives, and how it protects itself. Close-up photographs show the birthing process of the echidna step-by-step, and the author stresses the continuity in nature, describing how the baby echidna develops until ready to leave the pouch and fend for itself. An index and glossary are included.

11.38   Triggs, Barbara. **Wombats.** Houghton Mifflin Company, 1991. 39 pp. ISBN 0-395-55993-6.

Wombats—shy, furry animals native to Australia—are one of the world's largest burrowing mammals. They have pouches like kangaroos and live in tunnels more than 100 feet long. This examination of the wombat describes the animal's nocturnal habits and its tendency to avoid other animals, including other wombats; the color photographs included might be the only chance we have to see this fascinating creature in its natural habitat. Readers will learn how and what wombats eat, how they clean themselves, and how they mate, give birth, and take care of their young. The book concludes with a discussion of the dangers wombats face, from feral dogs to motorists.

11.39 Western, Joan, and Ronald Wilson. **The Human Body.** Illustrated by Michael Atkinson and Michael Saunders. Troll Associates, 1991. 91 pp. ISBN 0-8167-2235-8.

The human body is the most complex living organism in the world. This book offers information for understanding that organism, introducing the body's anatomical parts and systems, including tissue and cells, the skeleton, joints, muscles, blood, the heart, lungs, digestive and reproductive systems, the brain, and the senses. Also explored are commonly asked questions about the body, proper care and maintenance tips, and a section examining medical breakthroughs.

Series

11.40 **Creatures All around Us.** Carolrhoda Books.

From the lawn to the garden to the basement, insects are everywhere! In each book of the Creatures All around Us series, readers will meet a variety of flying, crawling, and hopping bugs, each insect highlighted by photographs and detailed explanations of what it is and what it does. Words such as larvae, which might be unfamiliar to readers, are carefully defined, and each book contains a classification chart and index to further clarify what each member of an insect family is. Moths, spiders, grasshoppers, and cockroaches—they're all here, ready to amaze you!

11.41 **Life Story.** Troll Associates.

Each book in the Life Story series focuses on the life cycle of an individual creature, from birth to death, and offers interesting details about the role that creature plays in its environment. Did you know that some species of frogs produce deadly poisons through their skin? Did you know that sharks frequently eat their own young? Did you know that ants sometimes capture ants from other colonies, forcing the prisoner ants to work in the captor ants' community? From spiders to snakes, this series offers rare insight into the amazing creatures that live all around us. Each book concludes with a section of "Fascinating Facts" about the topic creature. Index included.

11.42 **Repairing the Damage.** New Discovery Books.

Floods, famines, earthquakes, and pollution are just some of the natural and man-made disasters that threaten today's world. The Repairing the Damage series examines ways of predicting and preventing such disasters. Using eyewitness accounts, colorful photographs, diagrams, and charts, this series explains how and why these disasters occur, the impact they have on people's lives, and suggested ways for dealing with them.

11.43 **You and Your Body.** Troll Associates.

Each volume in the You and Your Body series begins by posing a question: How many times do we breathe in and out each day? How many muscles does the body have? These questions, as well as those relating to brain functions and hearing abilities, lead to fascinating looks at how the human body works. From a single cell to the entire skeletal structure, these books explain how the complex components of our bodies work together to make humans one of the most amazing creatures on the earth.

12 Physical Sciences and Technology

12.1 Berliner, Don. **Our Future in Space.** Lerner Publications Company, 1991. 72 pp. ISBN 0-8225-1592-X.

Is a trip to Mars possible? Will there ever be a base on the moon? Will humans someday travel to a space station in the sky? These and many other questions are considered in this book about the possibilities humans have as they reach for the stars. Current space research and future projects are also detailed. Bibliography and index included.

12.2 Darling, David. **Could You Ever Build a Time Machine?** Dillon Press, 1991. 59 pp. ISBN 0-87518-456-1.

In this book exploring the most fleeting of all subjects, the author examines the nature of time and time travel. Beginning with familiar "time machines" like camera and video recorders, which review events of the past, the author shows how we travel through time every moment. And through an examination of Albert Einstein's theory of relativity, the author considers the chances for the possibility of time travel. Additional discussion focuses on time tunnels and black holes in space, two other means that offer a chance for traveling through times past and future.

12.3 Darling, David. **Could You Ever Live Forever?** Dillon Press, 1991. 59 pp. ISBN 0-87518-457-X.

All living things eventually die. But will that *always* be true? New technology has allowed for the transplanting of old or failing organs and tissues, machines can be attached to the body to stimulate heartbeats and breathing, and advances in the field of medicine offer new drugs to help ward off disease. In this book, these and other life-prolonging techniques are examined and considered as part of the attempt to lengthen the human existence beyond the normal life expectancy.

12.4   Gallant, Roy A. **The Constellations: How They Came to Be.** Four Winds Press, 1991. 203 pp. ISBN 0-02-735776-7.

When you look up at the night sky, can you find the Big Dipper? Do you know which star is the North Star? Can you identify Leo the lion among the thousands of stars? This book details how certain stars came to be discovered and named, who discovered them, and what effect those stars had on cultures past and present. Readers will also discover a guide to the Zodiac and all of the animals and people that make up that mythological chart. Index included.

12.5   Gardner, Robert. **Investigate and Discover: Forces and Machines.** Julian Messner, 1991. 128 pp. ISBN 0-671-69046-9.

Scientists make discoveries by experimenting and observing— one of the best ways to learn and remember. Here are experiments to help readers learn the basics of physics, such as what happens when two objects push or pull on one another, or how air pressure can support a column of water. A variety of simple machines are also examined in this collection of hands-on activities. A Franklin Institute Science Museum book.

12.6   Liptak, Karen. **Dating Dinosaurs and Other Old Things.** Illustrated by David Prebenna. Millbrook Press, 1992. 72 pp. ISBN 1-56294-134-8.

This book demonstrates how scientists "date," or determine the age of, artifacts and relics, describing in detail the techniques used for and the purposes of dating things from the near and distant past. It discusses dinosaur bones, rocks, and famous works of art, most notably the Shroud of Turin, believed to be the burial shroud of Jesus. The book also projects the future for scientific dating.

12.7   Scott, Elaine. **Look Alive: Behind the Scenes of an Animated Film.** Photographs by Richard Hewett. Morrow Junior Books, 1992. 68 pp. ISBN 0-688-09936-X.

With the help of many photographs, this book illustrates the filming of Beverly Cleary's classic book *The Mouse and the Motorcycle*. First, artists formed the characters in the story from clay. Next, the props were designed, the artists combining everyday objects to create an impression of zany fantasy. Finally, the animated mice and human actors were filmed and the appropriate sound effects were added. The result: An award-winning video!

12.8 Skurzynski, Gloria. **Robots: Your High-Tech World.** Bradbury Press, 1990. 64 pp. ISBN 0-02-782917-0.

Beginning with Karel Capek's creation of the word robot for his play *R.R.R.,* this volume takes the reader through a brief history of the robotics field, providing definitions and descriptions, along with a number of color photographs. Computer advances have had a profound effect on the development of robots, and these effects in the fields of medicine, science, industry, and entertainment are examined. It concludes with a comparison between the human being and the robot, marveling at the complexity of the former and how far scientists and engineers will have to go in robotics to match the human brain.

12.9 Verba, Joan Marie. **Voyager: Exploring the Outer Planets.** Lerner Publications Company, 1991. 64 pp. ISBN 0-8225-1597-0.

In 1970, NASA began planning the Voyager 1 and 2 expeditions; Voyager 1 would leave the solar system after exploring Jupiter and Saturn, and Voyager 2 would explore Jupiter, Saturn, Uranus, and Neptune. This book chronicles the events of those two Voyager expeditions. Planet by planet, the book explains what scientists knew before the Voyager probes and shows photographs obtained and information learned after the probes.

Series

12.10   Scientific Magic. Franklin Watts.

Physics, the study of matter and energy and how they interact, is a part of our daily life. Riding a bicycle or even watching television involves physics. The Scientific Magic Series demonstrates how exciting physics can be. This series begins with the basic concepts of physics and progresses to the more complex. Hands-on activities, including experiments involving measurements and magic tricks to make water disappear, are used to explain the various principles of physics. From the amazing molecule to the earth's magnetic field, this series explores the hidden world of physics that is all around us.

13 Social Sciences and Contemporary Issues

13.1 Aitkens, Maggi. **Should We Have Gun Control?** Lerner Publications Company, 1992. 96 pp. ISBN 0-8225-2601-8.

The Second Amendment to the Constitution contains only twenty-seven words governing a citizen's right to bear arms. For more than 200 years, however, people have argued over the meaning of those words. Guns have been historically cursed for their roles in wars, gangster hits, and assassinations, and blessed for their uses in survival, hunting, and self-protection. Both sides of the gun control issue are objectively and factually presented in this book, which may help readers reach a decision of their own regarding gun control.

13.2 Alvin, Virginia, and Robert Silverstein. **Recycling: Meeting the Challenge of the Trash Crisis.** G. P. Putnam's Sons, 1992. 104 pp. ISBN 0-399-22190-5.

This book urges readers to consider the consequences of refusing to deal with our already overcrowded landfills. The authors discuss in both theoretical and practical terms possible solutions to the problem, with an emphasis on recycling. A final chapter details ways even very young citizens can help reduce the amount of trash sent to landfills, such as reusing packaging materials in creative ways and composting organic materials. The book includes many photographs that effectively illustrate the problem, a list of organizations readers can contact for more information, a glossary, bibliography, and index.

13.3 Ang, Susan G. **Invest Yourself: The Catalogue of Volunteer Opportunities.** The Commission on Voluntary Service and Action, 1991. 127 pp. ISBN 0-9629322-0-5.

This catalogue of volunteer opportunities provides names and addresses of organizations and programs that utilize volunteers. Each listing contains general information about the program, skills required of its volunteers, and the name of a person to contact for more information. Highlighted throughout the book are stories written by current or former volunteers involved with various projects, explaining the organization for which they worked and its goals.

13.4   Berck, Judith. **No Place to Be: Voices of Homeless Children.** Houghton Mifflin Company, 1992. 148 pp. ISBN 0-395-53350-3.

What is it like to be homeless? Omar knows: "I was living in the Bronx . . . One day the rent was low; the next day the landlord brought it up high. We couldn't pay. . . ." Maria knows what it's like, too: "When my father left my mother, he stopped supporting us. . . ." Through poems and stories, readers will get a glimpse of the lives of homeless children, many of whom are forced to live in shelters, welfare hotels, and even on the street. Bibliography included.

13.5   Bungum, Jane E. **Money and Financial Institutions.** Lerner Publications Company, 1991. 96 pp. ISBN 0-8225-1781-7.

This book is all about money—how it is made, where it is stored, and what it is used for. Full of interesting information about the difficulties in counterfeiting, the savings and loan fiasco, and much more, this book manages to painlessly introduce and define terms such as "collateral," "fractional reserve system," and legal tender." The author chronicles the history of banking from the fifteenth century to the present, emphasizing institutions such as the Bank of North America and the Federal Reserve. An index and glossary are included. An Economics for Today book.

13.6   Cohen, Daniel. **Prophets of Doom.** Millbrook Press, 1992. 139 pp. ISBN 1-56294-068-6.

This book examines all different kinds of prophecies, including end-of-the-world prophecies as predicted by many varied sources: the Bible, Greek oracles, Nostradamus, and Edgar Cayce. The book also discusses in detail some very specific prophecies, such as how the world was supposed to have ended in 1844. Exploring such diverse subjects as the pyramids and spaceships, dinosaurs and humans, signs in the sky and on the earth, and the four horsemen of the apocalypse, this book even examines predictions for the year 2000. Bibliography and index included.

13.7   Colligan, Louise. **Scholastic's A+ Junior Guide to Taking Tests.** Scholastic, 1990. 90 pp. ISBN 0-590-43148-X.

This "how to" book offers methods for taking notes, reading a textbook, creating study tools, and memorizing. Also included are hints for taking every type of test, from true-false to essay, and how to study for each type of test in each subject area. Such problems as nervousness, freezing up, and procrastination are also addressed, as are recommendations for dealing with poor test scores.

13.8   Emmens, Carol A. **The Abortion Controversy.** Julian Messner, 1991. 147 pp. ISBN 0-671-74967-6.

The Abortion Controversy provides updated information on birth control and abortion. Included is an explanation as to why so much emotion is involved in the abortion issue. The book also examines the legal, social, and medical aspects of abortion, as well as a range of opinions from anti-abortionists and pro-choice advocates.

13.9   Epler, Doris M. **The Berlin Wall: How It Rose and Why It Fell.** Millbrook Press, 1992. 128 pp. ISBN 1-56294-114-3.

For nearly thirty years, the German city of Berlin was divided by a much-hated wall which separated the East from the West, even separating parents from children and husbands from wives. Why was it ever constructed in the first place? And why did it take so many years for it to come down? This book explores these and many other questions about the Berlin Wall, the destruction of which represented the end of the Cold War between countries of the East and countries of the West. Photographs, bibliography, and index included.

13.10   Greenberg, Keith Elliot. **Erik is Homeless.** Photographs by Carol Halebain. Lerner Publications Company, 1992. 40 pp. ISBN 0-8225-2551-8.

Erik is a nine-year-old New Yorker who lives with his mother in a shelter for the homeless. Through Erik's story, the reader feels Erik's shame, helplessness and fear for the future. Erik's real-life story is portrayed not only in words but also through photographs which poignantly illustrate his desperate way of life.

13.11   Greenberg, Keith Elliot. **Out of the Gang.** Lerner Publications Company, 1992. 40 pp. ISBN 0-8225-2553-4.

Many young people join a gang for a sense of belonging and for protection from other gangs. However, as one gang member says, "The only direction a gang will take you is towards the jail or the cemetery." In this book, the reader will follow the sometimes shocking experiences of two Brooklyn boys, one who resisted joining gangs and one who escaped the gang lifestyle.

13.12   Harris, Jonathan. **Drugged America.** Four Winds Press, 1991. 200 pp. ISBN 0-02-742745-5.

Concentrating primarily on marijuana, heroin, and cocaine, this book describes the impact of drugs on contemporary American life. Everything from who makes big money by selling drugs and what they tend to do with the money to the causes and consequences of drug addiction are examined. In addition, the author discusses treatment, drug-related crime, and the pros and cons of legalization. The book offers a sadly realistic outlook for the future "war on drugs." An index and list of "suggested readings" are included.

13.13   Havens, Ami. **Now You're Talking: Winning with Words.** Troll Associates, 1991. 123 pp. ISBN 0-8167-2143-2.

Communication between teens and their parents can occasionally be difficult. Parents "just don't understand" at times; they say "no" too much and continue to treat teens as if they're children. This book presents basic rules about talking, like avoiding the "Dreadful Exaggerators" and the "I Factor." It presents quizzes and teaches communication skills so that teens can have a better relationship with their parents, thus becoming happier people. A Smart Talk book.

13.14 Hjelmeland, Andy. **Kids in Jail.** Photographs by Dennis Wolf. Lerner Publications Company, 1992. 39 pp. ISBN 0-8225-2552-6.

Photographs and the personal experiences of one juvenile delinquent provide a vivid picture of the stages of the juvenile justice system. The reader will follow John, a repeat offender, through his arrest, his time in jail, his court appearance, and his time spent in a correctional facility.

13.15 Hoig, Stan. **People of the Sacred Arrows: The Southern Cheyenne Today.** Cobblehill Books, 1992. 130 pp. ISBN 0-525-65088-1.

The Cheyenne, a strong, brave, gentle people, were massacred and moved onto a reservation by the soldiers and regiments who settled the West. In time, even their reservation was taken from them. Today, people like Joe Antelope, Lawrence Hart, Quentin Roman Nose, and others, are helping young Cheyenne rediscover the customs, languages, and ways of their Native American people; they are working to tell their tribal history not found in history books. Photographs, bibliography, and index included.

13.16 Jones, Jayne Clark. **The American Indians in America.** Lerner Publications Company, 1991. 72 pp. ISBN 0-8225-1037-5.

From the early expansion of the United States, when Native American tribes were forced to leave the land they had hunted for centuries, to the present, this book explores how the American Indians have gradually regained the land and rights they unjustly lost. The reader will learn about historical figures such as Sacajawea (who accompanied Lewis and Clark), Tecumseh (who founded an Indian confederation), and Geronimo (who was a notorious Apache Indian chieftain), and the more recent well-known Native Americans, Charles Curtis (who was vice president to Herbert Hoover), Jim Thorpe (who was a famed sports hero), and Will Rogers (who was a famed humorist), among others. The book includes an index, as well as numerous black-and-white photographs. Volume II in a two-volume series. Originally published in 1973.

13.17 Klausner, Janet. **Talk about English: How Words Travel and Change.** Illustrated by Nancy Doniger. Thomas Y. Crowell, 1990. 192 pp. ISBN 0-690-04833-5.

For those who are curious about the English language, this book traces it to its roots and shows how English has been influenced by borrowed words, altering words, and the creation of new words. For example, did you know that the word "secretary" came from a Latin word which referred to a hidden place where government officials could discuss affairs of state privately? Author Janet Klausner demonstrates these changes by providing examples of familiar words that have been reshaped through events in history and through everyday usage.

13.18 Kronenwetter, Michael. **United They Hate: White Supremacist Groups in America.** Walker and Company, 1992. 133 pp. ISBN 0-8027-8162-4.

Bigotry, hatred, and prejudice can be thinly disguised as religion, patriotism, or brotherhood, and there are many reasons why people might seek acceptance into a hate group. From the beginnings of the Ku Klux Klan through Adolf Hitler's Nazi Party to today's "skinheads," this book explores the history of white supremacy and the effects and consequences of its brand of hatred. The final chapters explore the penalties and the price members of hate groups must pay for their actions. Bibliography and index included.

13.19 Kuklin, Susan. **What Do I Do Now? Talking about Teenage Pregnancy.** G. P. Putnam's Sons, 1991. 179 pp. ISBN 0-399-21843-2.

This book examines teenage pregnancy from the unique perspective of first-person accounts. Teens discuss the difficult decisions they and their families had to face and what led them to the decisions they made. Psychological pressures, prenatal examinations and care, counseling, and even abortion are discussed frankly in this look at one of the most serious problems facing teenagers today.

13.20 Landau, Elaine. **Terrorism: America's Growing Threat.** Lodestar Books, 1992. 102 pp. ISBN 0-525-67382-2.

Terrorism. The word conjures up images of faceless people committing horrible crimes against innocent people and nations. For many years, the United States has been unaffected by terrorism, but recently, acts of terrorism have been committed against U.S. citizens and against the U.S. government on our own soil. Information in this book focuses on the beginnings of terrorism, the individuals responsible for many crimes, the types of weaponry used to commit terrorist acts, and the underlying causes and reasons for terrorist involvement, as well as counterterrorist measures being conducted by the U.S. government. Bibliography and index included.

13.21 O'Toole, Thomas. **Global Economics.** Lerner Publications Company, 1991. 72 pp. ISBN 0-8225-1782-5.

Why are some countries—such as the United States—affluent, while in others, most of the citizens can barely meet basic needs of food and shelter? How can overdeveloped countries help poorer countries improve living conditions? Why do people in many parts of the world take luxuries (such as televisions and cars) for granted, while elsewhere starvation is the rule rather than the exception? This book tries to answer these and other questions, citing the theories of both "modernization" and "dependency" economists. While no easy answers are provided, the author favors dependency theorists, believing that Third World countries should strive for economic independence. An Economics for Today book.

13.22 Parent/Teen Book Group, The. **Raising Each Other: A Book for Teens and Parents.** Hunter House, 1988. 147 pp. ISBN 0-89793-044-4.

Compiled by five eleventh-grade students and their English teacher, this book of essays—written by students and their parents—presents the problems that concern teenagers and their parents the most. Essays written by teens indicate that parents, school, and peer pressure are their primary concerns; parents write that money, teenagers, and jobs are what worry them most. This book also offers suggestions for rules to live by—rules governing privacy, responsibility, and curfews—that are fair to both parents and their teenage children.

13.23 Perl, Lila. **From Top Hats to Baseball Caps, from Bustles to Blue Jeans: Why We Dress the Way We Do.** Illustrated by Leslie Evans. Clarion Books, 1990. 111 pp. ISBN 0-89919-872-4.

This book is an historical survey of fashion, from the reasons people began to wear clothes to the changes of fashion that have occurred due to climate, status, or historical events. In addition to learning some cultural history and its influence on clothing style, readers will also be able to coordinate their choice of clothing to their lifestyles, thus presenting themselves the way they would like others to see them.

13.24 Pomeroy, Wardell B. **Boys and Sex.** Laurel-Leaf Books, 1991. 205 pp. ISBN 0-385-30250-9.

In direct, explicit language, the author examines all aspects of male sexuality, from how the sex organs work and how boys learn about sex with girls to the consequences of having sex and consideration of homosexuality. Well-known myths about sex are dispelled, and many questions male teens might have about sexually related topics like prostitution are also discussed. Contains mature language and themes.

13.25 Pomeroy, Wardell B. **Girls and Sex.** Laurel-Leaf Books, 1991. 207 pp. ISBN 0-385-30251-7.

This book presents an explicit discussion of everything from how reproductive organs of the female and male function to sexual aggressiveness in dating. The book also includes comments, actions, and reactions of boys during dating. Questions about masturbation, homosexual behavior, and other topics related to sex are included and discussed in a straight-forward manner. Contains mature language and themes.

13.26 Rogak, Lisa Angowski. **Steroids: Dangerous Game.** Lerner Publications Company, 1992. 64 pp. ISBN 0-8225-0048-5.

In this book, readers will find themselves immersed in the world of steroid use among athletes who desperately want to be stronger or faster or just physically better than the rest. The book explores the different types of steroids available and, through interviews with athletes, the devastating, negative effects the drugs can have on the human body. Index included.

13.27 Rosenberg, Maxine B. **Talking about Stepfamilies.** Bradbury Press, 1990. 133 pp. ISBN 0-02-777913-0.

Talking about Stepfamilies is a compilation of interviews with adults and children who are members of a stepfamily. Author Maxine Rosenberg has selected interviews that offer practical advice to stepparents and stepsiblings. These are frank expressions of family members' feelings about death, divorce, and remarriage. While those who were interviewed reveal their problems of adjustment, their predominant feelings about living in a stepfamily are optimistic.

13.28 Switzer, Ellen. **Anyplace But Here: Young, Alone, and Homeless: What to Do.** Photographs by Costas. Atheneum, 1992. 161 pp. ISBN 0-689-31694-1.

Their names and locations have been changed, but their reasons for running away from home and living on the streets have not. Physical and sexual abuse, alcoholism, and family problems cause children and teens to think that "anyplace but here" is better. The author describes individual cases of kids who have run away, examines people who try to help, and provides ways to cope with problems at home so that running away to live the dangerous street life can be avoided.

13.29 Terkel, Susan Neiburg. **Ethics.** Lodestar Books, 1992. 135 pp. ISBN 0-525-67371-7.

Ethics, or moral principles, affect all of our lives. This book explains what ethics are and how each of us determines right and wrong. Thought-provoking questions like, "What would you do if you found a wallet filled with cash?" are asked. Offering a balanced view of a very complex subject, this book aims to help young people evaluate themselves and judge what is right versus what is wrong.

13.30 Young, Robin R. **The Stock Market.** Lerner Publications Company, 1991. 80 pp. ISBN 0-8225-1780-9.

Do you know the difference between stocks and bonds? What causes interest rates to rise or fall? Is investing always risky? This book answers these questions and more, tracing the history of the stock market from its beginnings on Wall Street—under a buttonwood tree—in May of 1792. Learn the inside scoop on the stock market crash of 1929 that led to the Great Depression. If you would like to invest in a company, or merely want to understand the financial pages in your newspaper, this book can help. Look up an unfamiliar term in the glossary (just what is a *mutual fund,* anyway?) or check the handy index for a topic you're particularly interested in. An Economics for Today book.

Series

13.31 Our Endangered Planet. Lerner Publications Company.

The Our Endangered Planet series examines the escalating problems Earth faces as the twenty-first century approaches. Did you know that the earth's population of 5.3 billion people is expected to double by the year 2027. Where will those people live? Will there be enough water for them? With the rain forest vanishing at an alarming rate, will there even be enough air for all those people? Each book in this series considers a different aspect of the world's decline and offer suggestions to individuals on how to become involved in saving our planet.

13.32 Past and Present. New Discovery Books.

The Past and Present series examines such contemporary issues as censorship, terrorism, kidnapping, and refugees, and traces their history from ancient times to the present. Why is terrorism more commonplace now than it was earlier in this century? What kind of relationship exists between a kidnapper and a prisoner? Each book includes photographs, illustrations, and indexes.

III Exploring

The learn'd is happy Nature to explore,
The fool is happy that he knows no more;
The rich is happy in the plenty giv'n,
The poor contents him with the care of Heav'n.

Alexander Pope
An Essay on Man
Epistle II, Line 263

14 Accomplishments and Growing Up

14.1 Adler, C. S. **Mismatched Summer.** G. P. Putnam's Sons, 1991. 174 pp. ISBN 0-399-21776-2.

Opposites attract. Or do they? When circumstances throw together sophisticated Meg and Micale, the tomboy full of impish pranks, neither of the young teens is too happy. Meg lives on the Cape; she loves the serenity and natural beauty surrounding her. Unfortunately, Micale, shipped off to Meg's for the summer, sees the area quite differently. She misses the activity of the city and finds country living—and Meg—pretty boring. She finds ways to liven things up just a little bit, leading each girl to discover and to share her unique qualities.

14.2 Anderson, Mary. **The Unsinkable Molly Malone.** Harcourt Brace Jovanovich, 1991. 202 pp. ISBN 0-15-213801-3.

Molly Malone is a teenage artist who lives in New York and wants to positively affect society. As a community service, she teaches art to underprivileged children living in a welfare hotel. While undertaking this noble task, Molly learns to be more open-minded in her thinking and finds herself falling in love with a mysterious young man.

14.3 Auch, Mary Jane. **Out of Step.** Holiday House, 1992. 124 pp. ISBN 0-8234-0985-6.

Jeremy has lost his mother in a tragic car accident. Now, three years later, the twelve-year-old boy's father remarries, and Jeremy suddenly finds himself living in a house with two strangers: his stepmother (whom Jeremy's little brother calls Mom) and his super-athletic stepsister, Allison. To make matters worse, Jeremy's father seems to spend all of his free time with Allison. Can Jeremy overcome his feelings of isolation and regain the family he once knew?

14.4 Avi. **Windcatcher.** Bradbury Press, 1991. 124 pp. ISBN 0-02-707761-6.

All year, Tony Souza has delivered papers to earn money for a motorscooter. But when summer vacation begins, his father won't let him purchase one. Furthermore, he has to spend most of the summer at his grandmother's on the Connecticut shore. What begins as a bad summer changes when Tony buys a twelve-foot sailboat and learns a story about an old sailing ship believed to be sunk near Swallow Bay. What follows is an almost disastrous investigation as he begins to follow a strange couple who seem to be searching for something. But what?

14.5 Baehr, Patricia. **Summer of the Dodo.** Four Winds Press, 1990. 145 pp. ISBN 0-02-708135-4.

Dorothy Penny (or "Dodo," as her little brother calls her) tries desperately to fit in with the other girls by imitating their behavior. Her efforts are doomed to failure; Tamara, Gigi, and Barbie think she is stiff and unnatural. When "Dodo" finds a talking dodo bird in her aunt's bungalow and learns that the species became extinct many years ago, she decides to help the bird survive by teaching it to act like other birds. In this humorous tale of self-acceptance, Dodo the girl learns from dodo the bird that one might as well be extinct if change makes one beyond recognition.

14.6 Block, Francesca Lia. **Cherokee Bat and the Goat Guys.** HarperCollins/Charlotte Zolotow Books, 1992. 116 pp. ISBN 0-06-020269-6.

In this offbeat story of California teens, Cherokee Bat, her half-sister Witch Baby, and their friends Raphael and Angel Juan form a band called The Goat Guys. The excitement and energy they bring to the music and to each other lead to success, but also propel them further away from the basic purity, trust, and love that hold them together. Magical gifts unleash powers they're not sure they can understand or control. Sequel to *Weetzie Bat* and *Witch Baby.*

14.7 Bunting, Eve. **Such Nice Kids.** Clarion Books, 1990. 120 pp. ISBN 0-395-54998-1.

Jason and Meeker have always tried to protect their friend Pidge. That's why Jason loans Pidge his mom's car, with disastrous results. Big, slow Pidge wrecks the car, the start of a chain of events leading to his death. Jason then allows Meeker to talk him into one bad decision after another, from taking the mangled car to a shady repairman in the middle of the night, to unwittingly taking part in a robbery. Only when Pidge is shot and Meaker suggests they hide the body does Jason rebel.

14.8 Campbell, Eric. **The Place of the Lions.** Harcourt Brace Jovanovich, 1991. 183 pp. ISBN 0-15-262408-2.

In this story of survival on the immense Serengeti Plain, fourteen-year-old Chris is elated about living for the next three years with his dad in Africa. But a plane ride ends with disaster, and Chris is forced to assume the responsibility of saving his father and the pilot. A lion, dying of old age, takes responsibility for the boy, and they are bonded by a common need to survive.

14.9 DeFelice, Cynthia. **Devil's Bridge.** Macmillan, 1992. 95 pp. ISBN 0-02-726465-3.

Devil's Bridge is an exciting place to fish; the residents of Martha's Vineyard often choose it as the place to catch the "Big One." Twelve-year-old Ben Dagget, son of the island's record holder for catching the largest fish, is hoping to be the one to beat his late father's record in the annual Striped Bass Derby. But a local scoundrel is scheming to cheat in the contest and win the prize money himself. Can Ben handle the loss of his father, the overprotectiveness of his mother, and still win a fixed contest?

14.10 Ford, Barbara. **The Eagles' Child.** Macmillan, 1990. 146 pp. ISBN 0-02-735405-9.

With her parents settled happily into their lives after divorce, Amy Schultz gets an opportunity to observe the unpredictable, if not frustrating, world of adults. Amy's mother is off to Africa and arranges for Amy to stay in New York City with Liz, her godmother. Both Liz and Amy learn about adjustment, change, and patience from each other. Getting along is easier when Amy's wise new friend Matilda reminds her that it's fun to try new things, whether it's tap dancing, reading, or plotting a romance between your father and godmother.

14.11   Godden, Rumer. **Listen to the Nightingale.** Viking, 1992. 198 pp. ISBN 0-670-84517-5.

Lottie is an orphan whose lifelong dream is to be a ballerina. But when she is offered a scholarship to study at a famous ballet school, Lottie is torn between her love for dancing and her love for her newly adopted puppy named Prince.

14.12   Hamm, Diane Johnston. **Bunkhouse Journal.** Charles Scribner's Sons, 1990. 89 pp. ISBN 0-684-19206-3.

A Wyoming sheep farm in 1910 provides the backdrop for Sandy Mannix's journal of his sixteenth year. Sandy breaks away from his alcoholic father in Denver and heads for his cousin's ranch, where he quickly exchanges boyhood for manhood. Through his encounters with the lonely countryside, ranching, and the haunting feeling that he has abandoned his father, Sandy struggles with his dilemma: has he merely run away or has he struck out for something better? Finally, through the death of his father, the kindness of his dear cousin, and the affection of young Joanna on the neighboring farm, Sandy understands he must take steps toward his own future.

14.13   Hill, Elizabeth Starr. **Broadway Chances.** Viking, 1992. 152 pp. ISBN 0-670-84197-8.

Child actress Fitzi is taking a break from acting to pursue a normal life. She's enjoying her friendships, sleepovers, and regular classes at school. However, when her famous grandfather brings home news of auditions for a hit Broadway musical, Fitzi decides it is a chance she must not pass up. She tries out for the lead role against her long-time rival Tiffany. Fitzi finds that her chance at a lead on Broadway is fraught with risk and even danger, and she learns that even though she can depend on her parents when trouble arises, sometimes trouble has to be faced alone. A sequel to *Street Dancer.*

14.14 Hobbs, Will. **Downriver.** Atheneum, 1991. 204 pp. ISBN 0-689-31690-9.

"Hoods in the woods" is what they nicknamed it. But Discovery Unlimited is really an outdoor education program established to help troubled teenagers find a sense of self-esteem and accomplishment. Sixteen-year-old Jessie has been sent on this trip by her father to escape problems at home. She and her new friends execute a daring escape from the trip leader and, alone, tackle rafting the Colorado River through the Grand Canyon. Troy takes the lead, and Jessie is fascinated and a little frightened by his power and personality. As Star looks at the future in her tarot cards, Adam keeps a poisonous scorpion in a soap dish to lighten things up, and Freddy challenges Troy's authority, they all come to realize that the rapids might be the least of their worries. Excitement and exploration are part of the fun as Jessie learns she can trust her own strengths.

14.15 Marino, Jan. **Like Some Kind of Hero.** Little, Brown and Company, 1992. 216 pp. ISBN 0-316-54626-7.

Ted struggles to follow his dream instead of his parents' plan for him. He wants to be a lifeguard and hang out with the "in" crowd. In pursuit of his goal, Ted finds himself complicating his life by lying to his mother and neglecting his best friend. But a crisis in his friend's life helps Ted to discover what is important and who his real friends are.

14.16 Mazer, Norma Fox, and Harry Mazer. **Bright Days, Stupid Nights.** Bantam Books, 1992. 194 pp. ISBN 0-553-08126-8.

Four teenagers from very different backgrounds are selected for prestigious summer internships at a prize-winning Pennsylvania newspaper. Each brings enthusiasm and talent, but also a past filled with unresolved problems, pain, and secrets.

Christopher, Vicki, Elizabeth, and Faith must learn how to deal
with their expectations of each other—and of themselves.

14.17   Myers, Walter Dean. **The Righteous Revenge of Artemis
Bonner.** HarperCollins, 1992. 140 pp. ISBN 0-06-020844-9.

The year is 1882. Fifteen-year-old Artemis Bonner, the only
surviving male in his family, sets out to avenge the murder of
his rich Uncle Ugly by Catfish Grimes. Of course, finding
Uncle Ugly's treasure wouldn't be bad, either. But the tables
turn, and Catfish and his lady friend, Lucy Featherdip, pursue
Artemis on a stagecoach, which leads from New York City to
Tombstone, Arizona. On his journey, Artemis meets a half-
Cherokee lad by the name of Frolic, who becomes Artemis's
companion and advisor in the evil ways of the Wild West. Will
Catfish get the better of Artemis and Frolic before they find
Uncle Ugly's hidden treasure?

14.18   Nimmo, Jenny. **Ultramarine.** Dutton Children's Books, 1990.
199 pp. ISBN 0-525-44869-1.

Ned and Nell have always been different from other children.
Strangely drawn to the sea ever since nearly drowning as
infants, they live with, but rarely see, their mother, Leah. When
a mysterious man walks out of the sea and asks for their help
saving endangered birds, they readily agree. But can Nell cope
with what the strange man reveals to them about their pasts?
Perhaps not. Ned must try to talk his sister back to reality while
reconciling himself to the true identity of the mysterious
stranger.

14.19   Paterson, Katherine. **Lyddie.** Puffin Books, 1991. 192 pp.
ISBN 0-14-034981-2.

Impoverished Vermont farm girl Lyddie Worthen is determined
to gain her independence by becoming a factory worker in
Lowell, Massachusetts, in the 1840s. Can Lyddie overcome the
incredible odds stacked against her and save her farm and
family from poverty and separation?

14.20 Paulsen, Gary. **The Haymeadow.** Illustrated by Ruth Wright Paulsen. Delacorte Press, 1992. 195 pp. ISBN 0-385-30621-0.

Fourteen-year-old John Barron takes three months of canned food, two horses, four English border collies, and six thousand sheep to the summer pasture when Tink the hired man develops cancer and can't go. John is afraid of so much time alone and of the responsibility, but he takes consolation in the knowledge that his grandfather and father did the same thing at the same age. Using his wits and resolution, John survives rattlesnakes, coyote attacks, a bear, and a flash flood. Eventually, with his father's insight, he learns the difference between family myth and reality.

14.21 Paulsen, Gary. **The River.** Delacorte Press, 1991. 132 pp. ISBN 0-385-30388-2.

In this sequel to *Hatchet,* Brian is asked by the government to re-create the two months he managed to survive alone in the woods. This time, however, Brian is to have a companion, Derek, who plans to learn from Brian's expertise. At first, Brian considers their situation artificial, more like a camping trip than an actual survival experience. When Derek is struck by lightning and the radio no longer works, Brian once again must pit himself against nature, and somehow manage to find help for his companion.

14.22 Peck, Richard. **Unfinished Portrait of Jessica.** Delacorte Press, 1991. 162 pp. ISBN 0-385-30500-1.

Jessica's mother reluctantly sends her to Mexico to visit her father for Christmas. Her fourteen-year-old dreams of a remorseful father quickly fade as Jessica comes to understand the man he really is. Realizing the truth about her parents' divorce, she returns to Chicago to accept the life she left. Truth hurts, but life continues as Jessica becomes her own person.

14.23 Qualey, Marsha. **Everybody's Daughter.** Houghton Mifflin Company, 1991. 201 pp. ISBN 0-395-55870-0.

Where and how Merry Moonbeam Flynn grows up makes all the difference. The first child born in the Woodies' northern Minnesota commune, "Beamer" often feels more like a communal project than a near seventeen year old trying to sort out her philosophy of life. With the commune itself dissolving, Andy, her sensitive high school boyfriend, and Martin, a visiting college student, are ready to help her with the sorting. But Beamer finds she is better at keeping people at a distance than at expressing her inner feelings.

14.24   Radley, Gail. **The Golden Days.** Macmillan, 1991. 137 pp. ISBN 0-02-775652-1.

Dan and Michele Kapperman are Cory's third set of foster parents, and there is no way Cory will let them know how much he likes being with them. For eleven-year-old Cory, showing feelings means certain hurt. Then his social worker, Ms. Hanks, takes him to sing at Miss Sybil's, a retirement home, where he meets and befriends seventy-five-year-old Carlotta. Though crabby and feeble, she tells him stories of her exciting days with the circus. When Cory decides the Kappermans are going to reject him, he runs away and takes Carlotta with him. Life is hard for them, but together they discover what it means to be a family.

14.25   Rodowsky, Colby. **Lucy Peale.** Farrar, Straus and Giroux, 1992. 167 pp. ISBN 0-374-36381-1.

Rather than stand in front of her evangelist father's congregation and admit that she is pregnant out of wedlock, Lucy Peale runs away to Ocean City, Maryland, to escape her religious upbringing. Her restricted life has not prepared her for much of anything, let alone being a mother. But somehow she survives the first day and night, and she meets Jake, who insists on taking care of Lucy and the baby. Accepting Lucy for who she is, Jake brings her into his nonjudgmental family, where people accept life and love as it is.

14.26 Roper, Robert. **In Caverns of Blue Ice.** Illustrated by Roberta Ludlow. Little, Brown and Company, 1991. 188 pp. ISBN 0-316-75606-7.

Louise finds herself facing the greatest mountaineering challenge of her young life: scaling the legendary "blue ice" of the Himalayan Mountains. And if that isn't enough to make her heart race, there's the affection she has begun to feel for one of her fellow climbers. Can Louise have it all—fame *and* love?

14.27 Sherlock, Patti. **Four of a Kind.** Holiday House, 1991. 196 pp. ISBN 0-8234-0913-9.

After his parents divorce, Andy is sent to live with his grandpa. With his family split, Andy feels no one really wants him, and his only dream is to enter his draft horses, Maggie and Tom, in a pulling contest. Competition using his own horse team leads Andy to a startling conclusion about himself.

14.28 Smith, Doris Buchanan. **The Pennywhistle Tree.** G. P. Putnam's Sons, 1991. 175 pp. ISBN 0-399-21840-8.

When a new family, the Georges, moves into the neighborhood and takes over Jonathon's yard and favorite tree, the trouble begins. Everywhere Jonathon and his friends go, there are the Georges, especially Sanders, who shares his love of music with Jonathon and pleads for friendship. Jealousy, resentment, and guilt cloud Jonathon's compassion for a family in need, but his true character eventually begins to come forth.

14.29 Soto, Gary. **A Summer Life.** Laurel-Leaf Books, 1990. 150 pp. ISBN 0-440-21024-0.

In this collection of authentic essays, the reader witnesses life as seen through the eyes of an infant, a child, an adolescent, and an adult. The realistic experiences described can apply to anyone's life and the powerful sketches recall childhood with all its ups and downs: the sadness, the struggles, and the wonderful events that make life so interesting.

14.30   Spinelli, Jerry. **There's a Girl in My Hammerlock.** Simon & Schuster, 1991. 199 pp. ISBN 0-671-74684-7.

Disappointed when she can't impress Eric because she can't make the cheerleading squad, Maisie signs up for wrestling. What could get her closer to Eric than that? Maisie faces many obstacles in her search for acceptance by the team, including opposition from her best friend. Will she find enough confidence to last the season and still win Eric's attention?

14.31   Weaver, Lydia. **Child Star: When Talkies Came to Hollywood.** Illustrated by Michele Laporte. Viking, 1992. 52 pp. ISBN 0-670-84039-4.

Joey and his mother never seem to have enough money. Joey, growing up in glamorous Hollywood during the Depression, dreams of limitless wealth. Unlike most boys, however, Joey gets his wish. He is "discovered" by Fozzy, the famous actor of silent films. Joey is catapulted to instant fame and becomes rich beyond his wildest dreams. The stuttering, childish Fozzy becomes a close friend, sharing practical jokes as well as advice with Joey. Yet Joey still has problems: the director pretends that one of Joey's friends has died so that he will cry believably for the camera, Joey never has time to enjoy his wealth, and now "talkies" (films with sound) threaten to ruin Fozzy's career.

15 Family and Friends

15.1 Adler, C. S. **A Tribe for Lexi.** Macmillan, 1991. 158 pp. ISBN 0-02-700361-2.

Lexi, brought up in a variety of cultures, seems to fit in with no one. When she visits her cousin on summer vacation, she makes a friend of Jeb, who's a loner in his family. Together they find adventure, encounter misfortune, and come to the realization that being different isn't always a bad thing.

15.2 Adler, C. S. **Tuna Fish Thanksgiving.** Clarion Books, 1992. 165 pp. ISBN 0-395-58829-4.

Thirteen-year-old Gilda's parents are getting a divorce, in spite of Gilda's vigorous efforts to keep them together. Everyone expects the children to live with Mom, but Gilda, not wanting to leave her friends, secretly plans to move in with Dad and his girlfriend. At first, she wants her little brother and sister to follow her. When that doesn't work out, Gilda grows obsessed with a traditional Thanksgiving dinner. Will Gilda's efforts to retain a tradition succeed in bringing her family back together?

15.3 Ashley, Ellen. **Barri, Take Two.** Ballantine Books, 1991. 156 pp. ISBN 0-449-14584-0.

Barri and Melanie are best friends, but they often find themselves in friendly competition with one another. Both want to be actresses, and both try out for the same parts in school plays. When Barri's aunt, a soap opera star, invites them to New York City, sets up an audition for both of them for the same role, and introduces them to a new male soap opera star, they suddenly find themselves in competition that could ruin their friendship. A *Center Stage* book.

15.4   Benjamin, Carol Lea. **Nobody's Baby Now.** Bantam Books, 1991. 157 pp. ISBN 0-553-28896-2.

Olivia Singer's life is pretty good, most of the time; she likes Brian, her position as editor of a school magazine, and her friends. In fact, the one thing she doesn't like about her life is her weight problem. Then her grandmother must move in with the family, and Olivia must give up her room, as well as her freedom after school, to babysit her grandmother. She has always loved Grandma Minnie, who can no longer speak. Olivia begins reading and talking to her grandmother, and she begins running for herself. Results of both activities create astounding results that surprise Olivia and others in her life.

15.5   Bunting, Eve. **The Hideout.** Harcourt Brace Jovanovich, 1991. 144 pp. ISBN 0-15-233990-6.

Andy doesn't like his new stepfather and wants to go to England to see his dad. He runs away and finds the key to the elite Tower Suite of the luxurious San Francisco Countess International Hotel. It's a great place to hide until he can contact his dad, who is on an archeological dig somewhere in England. Andy decides to go overseas but needs money to do so—and that's where his "kidnapping" comes in. He learns about the love of his friends and family after getting caught in a terrifying experience.

15.6   Bunting, Eve. **Sharing Susan.** HarperCollins, 1991. 122 pp. ISBN 0-06-021693-X.

At twelve years of age, Susan discovers that she and another girl were mistakenly switched at birth. Her counterpart has died, and Susan's biological parents initiate action to claim her. Will she have to leave the people she's come to love as her parents, even if they're not?

15.7   Burgess, Barbara Hood. **Oren Bell.** Delacorte Press, 1991. 182 pp. ISBN 0-385-30325-4.

Competition comes in all sizes, shapes, and girls, such as Oren's twin sister, Latonya, his little sister, Brenda, and his band partner, Wesley. Oren is an underachiever, and he has to live under the same roof with a younger sister, who helps him with his math, and his twin, who orders him around. All of this in addition to the haunted house next door and the ceremony Oren must perform so the haunted house will not bring them bad luck. Oren wants to be the man of the house. To succeed, he must contend with a ghost, the treasure left behind by that ghost, and his mother's boyfriend—who could end up taking Oren's place as man of the house.

15.8 Byars, Betsy. **Coast to Coast.** Delacorte Press, 1992. 164 pp. ISBN 0-385-30787-X.

Thirteen-year-old Birch wants her grandfather to fly his Piper Cub plane one last time before he goes to the retirement home. And she wants him to fly it from South Carolina to California. And most important, Birch wants to come along! If her grandfather agrees to the flight, Birch is certain she can learn more about the poem by her later grandmother, the poem written on the day of Birch's birth: "The Baby took one fluttering gasp, Two . . . Three. . . ." Will grandfather shed some light on the mysterious poem's meaning?

15.9 Cannon, A. E. **Amazing Gracie.** Delacorte Press, 1991. 214 pp. ISBN 0-385-30487-0.

A remarkable girl, Gracie is in her sophomore year in school. Gracie has mixed family problems to deal with: a mother who suffers from depression, a newly acquired brother, and family moves. Through it all, Gracie learns of acceptance and of the resilience of love.

15.10 Cannon, Bettie. **Begin the World Again.** Charles Scribner's Sons, 1991. 181 pp. ISBN 0-684-19292-6.

Lake lives in a commune with her parents, Selene and Ty. She shares her parents' ideal of simple living, responsibility for the environment, and togetherness, yet sometimes she wishes she could have some space to herself. When Sun Dog joins the commune, Lake finds herself falling in love for the first time. Sun Dog's creativity and enthusiasm enhance the group, but eventually the troubled Sun Dog breaks down. Selene grows disillusioned with her husband's dream and leaves. Ultimately Lake, too, decides to leave the commune, carrying the values she has learned into her new life.

15.11 Clifford, Eth. **The Summer of the Dancing Horse.** Illustrated by Mary Beth Owens. Houghton Mifflin Company, 1991. 114 pp. ISBN 0-395-50066-4.

The summer of 1923, when Bessie is eight and her brother and friend are twelve, is a special one of sacrifices, fulfilled desires, and heartbreak. A town bully, an abusive father, a baby fox, and a special prancing palomino make this one summer in a small country town a special one for Bessie and her friends.

15.12 Crew, Linda. **Nekomah Creek.** Illustrated by Charles Robinson. Delacorte Press, 1991. 191 pp. ISBN 0-385-30442-0.

Robby's family is considered "weird" by the other kids at school because his father stays home with the two small children while his mother goes to work. This is Robby's "problem." His home life is unconventional in the eyes of everyone around him. And when one of his classmates whose home life is also a little different is sent to a foster home after talking to the school counselor, Robby is sure he will be next to go. Will he and his warm and wacky family survive?

15.13 Deaver, Julie Reece. **First Wedding, Once Removed.** Harper & Row, 1990. 216 pp. ISBN 0-06-021426-0.

Thirteen-year-old Pokie and her brother Gib love airplanes and flying. Their dream is to become pilots together. When Gib leaves for college and then falls in love with Nell, Pokie feels left behind and alone. Her friendship with Junior, a younger neighborhood boy, is strained when Pokie enters high school and Junior's antics and games seem babyish. Then when Gib brings Nell home over summer vacation, Pokie fears she will never regain his attention. This is a powerful tale of a young girl's pain as she deals with her own growth and the changes in her family.

15.14 Dunlop, Eileen. **Finn's Island.** Holiday House, 1991. 128 pp. ISBN 0-8234-0910-4.

Finn Lochlan dreams of someday visiting Hirsay, the island where his grandfather once lived. When Finn's dream finally comes true, the reality is far different from the idyllic isle he has imagined. After almost losing his life in a foolish venture on the cliffs, Finn comes to terms with and accepts reality over fantasy.

15.15 Ferguson, Alane. **The Practical Joke War.** Bradbury Press, 1991. 140 pp. ISBN 0-02-734526-2.

Taffy, Russell, and Eddy start summer vacation with a series of practical jokes. When these jokes get them grounded for a week, the children endure for two days before an all-out war ensues. In the end, family loyalties may be the only hope of ending the practical joke war.

15.16 Fine, Anne. **The Book of the Banshee.** Little, Brown and Company, 1992. 168 pp. ISBN 0-316-28315-0.

Will Flowers believes that his teenage sister has turned into a horrible banshee! By observing and recording his sister's behavior, as well as tracking his own reactions to her, Will comes to understand how changes in people's personalities can affect those around them, and in the case of his younger sister, how those changes can turn the family home into a veritable war zone!

15.17 Fleischman, Paul. **The Borning Room.** HarperCollins/Charlotte Zolotow Books, 1991. 101 pp. ISBN 0-06-023762-7.

Georgina's Ohio farm life is told through the events which occur in the borning room, the place in which Georgina was born many years ago and will likely soon die. Happy births, serious illnesses, and the sadness of death—each occurs in that special room set aside for these events. Georgina relates the events of her life, from her birth in the late 1850s to what seem to be her final days in the new twentieth century.

15.18 Geringer, Laura. **Silverpoint.** HarperCollins/Charlotte Zolotow Books, 1991. 153 pp. ISBN 0-06-023849-6.

Cora, who has just turned twelve, has convinced herself that she is about to meet her father face to face for the first time. And while she waits for her father to arrive, she discovers the importance of real friendship with her best friend, Charley. *Silverpoint* is an exploration into moments of loss and disappointment, giving first glimpses into the adult world and the longings of the heart.

15.19 Greenfield, Eloise. **Koya DeLaney and the Good Girl Blues.** Scholastic, 1992. 124 pp. ISBN 0-590-43300-8.

Two African American sisters, Koya and Loritha DeLaney, learn about growing up, sharing loyalty, and coping with challenges in school. When their famous cousin Del, a pop music star, comes to town, Koya finds herself with an opportunity to open up and express her frustrations with life.

15.20 Hadley, Irwin. **The Original Freddie Ackerman.** Margaret K. McElderry Books, 1992. 183 pp. ISBN 0-689-50562-0.

Twelve-year-old Trevor Frederick Ackerman refuses to spend another summer with his extended family of divorced parents, stepparents, and stepbrothers and stepsisters. So, much to his dismay, Freddie is sent to live with his great-aunts Cal and Lou, in their home in Maine. They don't even have a television set! But before he knows it, Freddie finds himself unexpectedly involved with his new friend Ariel in a mystery that will give him a summer to remember.

15.21 Hahn, Mary Downing. **The Spanish Kidnapping Disaster.** Clarion Books, 1991. 132 pp. ISBN 0-395-55696-1.

Two stepsisters are forced to be together because of their parents' marriage. During the honeymoon to Spain—which the "kids" are forced to join—the girls and their brother Felix are kidnapped after Felix boasts of the family's wealth to a stranger. Can the sisters put aside their differences long enough to escape their kidnapper?

15.22 Johnson, Emily Rhoads. **A House Full of Strangers.** Cobble-hill Books, 1992. 128 pp. ISBN 0-525-65091-1.

Twelve-year-old Flora can hardly stand it when her late mother's half-sister and family moves into Flora's house. According to Flora's grandmother's will, the Quiggs have been given the house and are to care for Flora until she is eighteen. Instant family is almost too much for Flora, who is accustomed to quiet, orderliness, and the peace of the woods nearby; the Quiggs, with four children and two television sets, have never heard of peace! Missy, the middle girl in the Quigg family, attaches herself to Flora, asking neverending questions. These questions make Flora realize that Missy may have a similar thirst for knowledge.

15.23 Johnson, Stacie. **Sort of Sisters.** Bantam Books, 1992. 160 pp. ISBN 0-553-29719-8.

Sarah Gordon is eager to receive her cousin, Tasha, from California, as part of the family. Tasha will be a built-in best friend and sister to share Sarah's junior year at Merphy High—or so Sarah thinks. Then Tasha arrives and takes opposite sides in almost everything Sarah does and becomes a rival for Sarah's place at school. The first in the *18 Pine St.* series created by Walter Dean Myers.

15.24 Joosse, Barbara M. **The Pitiful Life of Simon Schultz.** HarperCollins, 1991. 137 pp. ISBN 0-06-022486-X.

A young teen struggles with life as he grows up in a single-parent family. Simon learns to deal with his problems of youth, an overprotective mother, and his own shy demeanor. As he tries to understand and sort out his problems, he discovers the person he really is, not the person his mother thinks he should be.

15.25 Koertge, Ron. **The Boy in the Moon.** Avon, 1992. 166 pp. ISBN 0-380-71474-4.

When Kevin spends the summer before senior year in California with his mother, his friends Nick and Frieda can hardly wait for him to come home to Missouri. But the boy that returns is nothing like the Kevin who Nick and Frieda remember; this new Kevin is a blond, tan, hip Californian. Even as Frieda begins to indicate that she likes this new Kevin as more than just a friend, Nick realizes that his friend might not be as confident as he seems.

15.26   Koertge, Ron. **The Harmony Arms.** Little, Brown and Company, 1992. 177 pp. ISBN 0-316-50104-2.

Gabriel isn't looking forward to living in California with his teacher/writer father, but the apartment complex his father lives in is full of unusual characters who give him insight into himself and his father. Even the ninety-year-old nudist, Mr. Palmer, helps Gabriel to better appreciate his relationship with his father.

15.27   Koller, Jackie French. **If I Had One Wish. . .** Little, Brown and Company, 1991. 161 pp. ISBN 0-316-50150-6.

Alec only has one wish—that his little brother had never been born. But when Alec's wish comes true, his life is not changed for the better, as he had assumed it would be. As we learn what happens to Alec because of his wish, we learn that it may not be such a good idea to make wishes—they might come true.

15.28   Lowry, Lois. **Attaboy, Sam!** Illustrated by Diane de Groat. Houghton Mifflin, 1992. 116 pp. ISBN 0-395-61588-7.

Mrs. Krupnik's favorite kind of present is the homemade kind, so Sam and his sister Anastasia rush off to make their mother wonderful birthday presents. Anastasia's poem is going to be great, but what can Sam make? Then he overhears his father telling Sam's mother that her favorite perfume is no longer being manufactured, and suddenly Sam knows exactly what he's going to make. Making perfume, however, may be more than Sam can handle!

15.29   McEvoy, Seth and Laure Smith. **The New Kids on the Block: Block Party.** Pocket Books, 1991. 131 pp. ISBN 0-671-73321-4.

This fictional adventure of Donnie, Jordan, Danny, Jonathan, and Joseph—The New Kids on the Block—takes them back to their original neighborhood in Boston to perform a benefit concert at a block party. Conflicts arise as they try to avoid crowds of fans who surround their homes and who want to follow their every move; as they try to discover who has been ordering food and T-shirts in their names; and as they work with their friend, Calley, who has an alcohol abuse problem. Because of these difficulties, a normal concert becomes a challenge.

15.30 McKenna, Colleen O'Shaughnessy. **Mother Murphy.** Scholastic, 1992. 152 pp. ISBN 0-590-44820-X.

Excitement reigns in the Murphy family when Mrs. Murphy becomes pregnant again. Collette comes to the rescue to babysit the other kids when complications make it necessary for Mom to stay in bed for a few days, but babysitting and all the other responsibilities that go with it are an incredible challenge. But this doesn't stop Collette; she is determined to finish her job and succeed in helping her mother through this crisis.

15.31 McLaughlin, Frank. **Yukon Journey.** Scholastic, 1990. 99 pp. ISBN 0-590-43538-8.

This adventure story of fifteen-year-old Andy unfolds in the northwestern corner of Canada, bordering Alaska. Andy's mission is to rescue his father, whose plane has crashed in the sparsely populated Yukon Territory. Andy, who thinks of himself as a one-hundred-pound weakling, strives to fulfill his mission to save his dad from the wilderness.

15.32 Martin, Ann M. **Eleven Kids, One Summer.** Holiday House, 1991. 152 pp. ISBN 0-8234-0912-0.

When the whole family—both parents and all eleven kids—spend a summer vacation together on Fire Island, almost anything can happen. And in this adventure, which offers special insight into living with so many brothers and sisters, almost anything *does* happen!

15.33 Miller, Mary Jane. **Upside Down.** Viking, 1992. 151 pp. ISBN 0-670-83648-6.

When Sara's mother starts dating Dr. Quigley, the family dentist, Sara is horrified. Dr. Quigley's son, Adam, is one of the worst kids in the class. Sara hates the idea that anyone might find out that *his* father is dating *her* mother. Yet Mom seems happier lately; she doesn't get as many headaches, and for the first time since Sara's father died, she's starting to plan holiday celebrations. Just when Sara begins to accept the situation as inevitable, however, Adam's obnoxious older sister wants her help in breaking up the romance, and unlike Sara, Laurel doesn't intend to stop with whining. Sara doesn't want Dr. Quigley in her life, but she doesn't want to hurt her mother either.

15.34 Murphy, Claire Rudolf. **To the Summit.** Lodestar Books, 1992. 156 pp. ISBN 0-525-67383-0.

At seventeen, Sarah is the youngest person to ever climb Mount McKinley, but she's not after fame—she wants to strengthen the relationship with her father. On her expedition, Sarah changes as she learns to deal with being a child of divorced parents and as she becomes friends with her fellow mountaineers. She completes her journey with a different outlook on life and a deeper appreciation of her parents and of her friends.

15.35 Myers, Walter Dean. **Somewhere in the Darkness.** Scholastic, 1992. 168 pp. ISBN 0-590-42411-4.

Mama Jean and Harlem have been the two constants in Jimmy Little's life. Then one day a strange man announces, "Jimmy Little, I'm your father." Creb Little takes Jimmy from what he has known, which was honest and secure, on an odyssey of discovery to acquaint Jimmy with the past life of the convict father he has only heard about. Rather than being a joyous reunion, the father-and-son trip from New York to Chicago to rural Arkansas only brings forth more unanswered questions about Creb's past.

15.36 Naylor, Phyllis Reynolds. **Send No Blessings.** Atheneum, 1990. 231 pp. ISBN 0-689-31582-1.

Beth wonders how her mother can call all of her eight children "blessings." With the noise and mess and tumult of all of them crammed into their little trailer, there is no room, no money, no phone, and no car. Beth, fifteen and the oldest, is sure that what *she* wants is to get away from her small West Virginia town. As the best typist in her class, she feels she can make a better life for herself with a job in a big city office after she graduates. Then she meets Harless Prather. She can't believe love can be like this. Marrying him would take her out of the trailer—but only to move down the valley to a life just like her mother's. Then what could happen to her other dreams? Beth faces some hard choices as she discovers herself and learns to craft her own future.

15.37 Pearson, Kit. **Looking at the Moon.** Viking, 1991. 212 pp. ISBN 0-670-84097-1.

Norah and Gavin, sent from England to the Ogilvies' home for safety's sake, have lived for three years with Aunt Florence. Every summer, Aunt Flo and the rest of the Ogilvies meet at Gairloch, the family house that Norah has grown to love, where the girls and the boys have always slept in separate cabins. This summer, however, Norah is thirteen, and she finds herself caught between the adult world of the girls in her cabin and Gavin's younger world.

15.38 Pendergraft, Patricia. **As Far As Mill Springs.** Philomel Books, 1991. 151 pp. ISBN 0-399-22102-6.

It is during the Depression and things are pretty bleak for twelve-year-old Robert, who convinces his friend Abiah to go on a search for Robert's mother, a quest to end by Christmas. The orphans who have been in one foster home or another most of their lives have adventures that demand the courage to continue.

15.39 Pfeffer, Susan Beth. **Family of Strangers.** Bantam Books, 1992. 164 pp. ISBN 0-553-08364-3.

Through a series of letters to her sisters and her best friend, sixteen-year-old Abby Talbott reveals her fears, her insecurities, and her crush on a boy in history class. She feels invisible at home because her parents ignore her, and at one point, she is even suicidal, much like one of her two older sisters. The other, who has always seemed perfect, is as much a stranger to Abby as the rest of her family is—or as Abby is to herself.

15.40   Pfeffer, Susan Beth. **Most Precious Blood.** Bantam Books, 1991. 169 pp. ISBN 0-553-07109-2.

Valentina Castaldi attends an exclusive Catholic school, Most Precious Blood. Her life is complicated by her father's connection to the Mafia. One day, her cousin spills the beans, and Val finds out that she is adopted. She spends a great deal of time seeking the truth about her natural birth parents, and her difficulties with her relatives and friends are almost more than she can bear. Through all this conflict, Val tries to accept her father's love and his family name, while searching for the truth about herself.

15.41   Plummer, Louise. **My Name Is Sus5an Smith. The 5 Is Silent.** Delacorte Press, 1991. 217 pp. ISBN 0-385-30043-3.

Even though Susan wins first prize in an art contest for high school students, she still feels bored with her life in Utah. Her practical, unartistic parents don't understand her paintings. Susan clings to her memory of Uncle Willy, who long ago deserted both the Air Force and Aunt Marianne, but who made Susan feel special. Susan sets out to add excitement to her humdrum life: she moves to Boston, gets a job, shows her paintings to a gallery, and seeks and finds Uncle Willy. Will he be as she remembers him—or as the rest of the family has painted him, a selfish, unpleasant man?

15.42   Rosofsky, Iris. **My Aunt Ruth.** HarperCollins/Charlotte Zolotow Books, 1991. 215 pp. ISBN 0-06-025087-9.

Patty has always admired her Aunt Ruth, a beautiful, talented regular on a soap opera. Patty wants to act someday herself, and Aunt Ruth is willing to help her niece break into the field.

Patty begins to realize that her aunt's life is far from perfect when Aunt Ruth's husband leaves her, followed by the worsening of Ruth's diabetes, causing her to lose the use of both legs. Meanwhile, between a jealous best friend and insecurity about her acting, Patty has problems of her own. She and her aunt grow even closer, and Patty realizes there is far more to admire in the world than beauty and talent.

15.43   Ross, Rhea Beth. **Hillbilly Choir.** Houghton Mifflin Company, 1991. 166 pp. ISBN 0-395-53356-2.

When Laurie and her mother return to Guthrie, Arkansas, Laurie feels as though she'll never leave again—at first. But Mama is restless; if she can't get them out of Guthrie by her own acting, then she'll use Laurie's singing. Meanwhile, Laurie settles in happily with her grandmother, her grandmother's boarders, an aunt nearly her own age, and an old boyfriend. Everything changes, however, even Guthrie, and when Nathan acts more interested in the new girl all the time, Laurie finds herself as eager as Mama and Aunt Star to get away.

15.44   Sachs, Marilyn. **What My Sister Remembered.** Dutton Children's Books, 1992. 122 pp. ISBN 0-525-44953-1.

After their parents' deaths in a car accident, sisters Molly and Beth are separated. Molly grows up in New York with her working-class aunt and uncle and their two sons, while Beth, the older sister, lives in luxury in California with her adoptive parents, the Lattimores. When they are reunited after eight years, Molly is angered by Beth's vivid memories and hostile attitudes. When Beth hints at secrets from their past, Molly provokes a confrontation.

15.45   Seabrooke, Brenda. **The Bridges of Summer.** Cobblehill Books, 1992. 143 pp. ISBN 0-525-65094-6.

Zarah, city girl and ballet student, is sent one summer to live with her grandmother, Quanamina, on Domingo Island in South Carolina, where time has stopped—or so it seems to Zarah. It's "a black magic place," where the people speak

Gullah, an unusual English dialect, and many folk traditions are still a way of life. As the summer progresses, though, Zarah begins to make friends on the island, and to appreciate the Gullah traditions her grandmother lives by.

15.46 Shusterman, Neal. **What Daddy Did.** Little, Brown and Company, 1991. 230 pp. ISBN 0-316-78906-2.

Can Preston Scott ever really face what his father has done? It's unthinkable. Unimaginable. Can he ever forgive him? And now that his dad, the man who killed his mother, is coming home from prison, will life ever be normal again? In this novel based on a boy's real-life experiences, fourteen-year-old Preston and his younger brother try to ignore, forget, and finally confront the awful truth of their father's actions, and in the process, discover the power of love and the healing effects of time.

15.47 Steiber, Ellen. **Eighth Grade Changes Everything.** Troll Associates, 1992. 124 pp. ISBN 0-8167-2391-5.

Although Kerry and Kathy are identical twins, eighth grade provides different interests and opportunities for each of them. When Kathy becomes a cheerleader, Kerry decides to join the debate team. Each has her own special friends, including boys, but eventually both find that they are friends with each other, as well as sisters.

15.48 Thesman, Jean. **The Rain Catchers.** Houghton Mifflin Company, 1991. 182 pp. ISBN 0-395-55333-4.

Among the women of Grayling's house, stories are a way of life, a link between past and present. They all have a beginning, a middle, and an end. All, that is, except Grayling's story. Why did her mother abandon her in Seattle with her grandmother after her father's death and go to San Francisco alone? Until she knows this, Gray cannot join the circle of women at the tea table who care for and protect each other and who make sense of life through their stories. Grayling struggles to help her friend Colleen escape her angry father and obnoxious stepmother, to uncover a new relationship with Aaron, to deal with a dying aunt, and to find the answers to her past. Quite a summer for one fourteen-year-old girl!

15.49 Tomlinson, Theresa. **Summer Witches.** Macmillan, 1989. 83 pp. ISBN 0-02-789206-9.

When Sara and Susanna renovate an old World War II bomb shelter in Sara's back-yard into a clubhouse, they find strange paintings on the walls. They later find a link between the paintings and a fifty-year-old tragedy involving an elderly neighbor Sara thinks is a witch, an old woman who teaches them sign language and who needs their help to overcome her memories of World War II.

15.50 Twohill, Maggie. **Superbowl Upset.** Bradbury Press, 1991. 154 pp. ISBN 0-02-789691-9.

When Mrs. Bidwell wins a trip to the Superbowl in New Orleans, everyone is excited except her. It's one of the few things Lucas and Ginger, stepbrother and sister, can agree on—they both love football, and they're both excited about the trip to the game. The trip to New Orleans is not a dream vacation as planned, but it certainly has adventures, and Ginger and Lucas might actually become friends before the calamity-filled trip ends.

15.51 Walter, Mildred Pitts. **Mariah Keeps Cool.** Illustrated by Pat Cummings. Bradbury Press, 1990. 139 pp. ISBN 0-02-792295-2.

It's not a sunny summer for eleven-year-old Mariah. Her busy time is spent planning a surprise party for her sister, Lynn, and practicing her dives for her swim team. Complicating this hectic pace is the arrival of her half-sister, Denise. Angry at being rejected by her mother, Denise strikes out to destroy all that Mariah has worked for. As hard as it is for her, Mariah learns not only why Denise is as she is, but she also learns something about pride in who she is.

15.52 Wersba, Barbara. **You'll Never Guess the End.** HarperCollins/Charlotte Zolotow Books, 1992. 132 pp. ISBN 0-06-020448-6.

Fifteen-year-old Joel Greenberg has always been a good student, a person who cares about the homeless and is kind to animals. But no one seems to pay any attention to him, not even when he thinks he's having a nervous breakdown. When the brother he adores is arrested on drug charges, it throws Joel's world into turmoil. Even more confusing is that same, rehabilitated brother's sudden success as an author and celebrity. Joel finally begins to find direction for his problems when he and his dog Sherlock search for his brother's kidnapped girlfriend.

15.53 Willey, Margaret. **The Melinda Zone.** Bantam Books, 1993. 144 pp. ISBN 0-553-09215-4.

Mindy/Linda/Melinda has gone to spend the summer in Michigan with her uncle, aunt, and cousin Sharon. It is a summer she relishes from the beginning because she is rooted in one place. Her divorced parents are both caught up in activities over the summer which do not have a place for a teenager. Taking matters into her own hands, Melinda—the name she finally settles on—begins to plot an elaborate plan: she will get both of her parents to come to Michigan at the same time, neither of them aware that the other will be present! Then they can clear the air between them, and all three of them can be a family again. The question is: will it work?

15.54 Wright, Betty Ren. **The Scariest Night.** Holiday House, 1991. 166 pp. ISBN 0-8234-0904-X.

When her family decides to spend the summer in Milwaukee so that her adopted brother can perfect his genius at a special piano school, ordinary Erin finds herself consumed with jealousy and turns to a medium for help. What follows is a roller-coaster ride of conversations with the dead, creepy seances, talking dolls, and the death of an older friend.

15.55   Yektai, Niki. **The Secret Room.** Orchard Books, 1992. 181 pp. ISBN 0-531-05456-X.

New York City of 1903 is nothing like their farm near Albany, as Katharine and Freddie soon find out. And when their parents begin to climb the social ladder, things only get worse for the two children—their parents have hired a proper nurse to make proper children out of them! Desperate to be rid of Miss Pritt, Katharine and Freddie begin to plot a way to be free of the unpleasant new life they've been thrust into.

16 Exploring Diversity: Ethnic Relationships

16.1 Banks, Lynne Reid. **One More River.** Morrow Junior Books, 1992. 248 pp. ISBN 0-688-10893-8.

Fourteen-year-old Lesley is Jewish and lives a very comfortable life in Canada. But when her family suddenly moves to a kibbutz, or collective settlement, in Israel, Lesley finds, to her despair, that her well-to-do lifestyle is gone. As tensions with Israel's Arab neighbors build and men from her kibbutz are called to fight in the Six-Day War, Lesley comes to accept her Jewish heritage and to understand the need to be a citizen in her homeland. First published in 1973.

16.2 Berry, James. **Ajeemah and His Son.** HarperCollins/Willa Perlman Books, 1992. 83 pp. ISBN 0-06-021043-5.

In the early nineteenth century, at a time when slavery was still a way of life, Ajeemah and his son Atu are on their way to pay the bride price for Atu's chosen bride Sisi when they are suddenly captured by slave traders. Taken to the coast of Ghana and sold to a ship's captain, Ajeemah and Atu begin the six-week voyage to the sugar-cane fields of Jamaica. Upon arrival, they are sold to separate plantations, and both father and son plot and plan for escape and freedom with vastly different results.

16.3 Carkeet, David. **Quiver River.** HarperCollins/Laura Geringer Books, 1991. 236 pp. ISBN 0-06-022453-3.

Ricky Appleton is initiated into the adult world when he spends the summer after his junior year in high school working at a lake resort in the Sierra. He intends for this to be a summer of good times and girls. However, it becomes the summer of his growing up when he finds himself involved in a summer study of the early inhabitants of the area, the Miwok Indians, who had a strange initiation ritual for their teenage boys.

16.4 Garland, Sherry. **Song of the Buffalo Boy.** Harcourt Brace Jovanovich, 1992. 264 pp. ISBN 0-15-277107-7.

Loi is one of thousands of *con-lai* (children with one American and one Asian parent) left behind after Vietnam's long and bitter war. Living with scorn and ridicule every day of her life, she is happy in her love for Khai, a buffalo boy. They secretly plan to marry someday. But Loi's uncle has other plans. Officer Hiep has seen Loi and wants her to be his wife and mother to his five children. In Loi's eyes, death would be better. She runs away to Ho Chi Minh City where she meets Joe, another Amerasian, who teaches her how to survive and how to get started on her way to the United States. Khai can go with her as her husband, but do they want to leave everyone and everything they have always known behind?

16.5 Gogol, Sara. **Vatsana's Lucky New Year.** Lerner Publications Company, 1992. 156 pp. ISBN 0-8225-0734-X.

Although Vatsana was born in the United States and has experienced a conventional American life, she is, at times, uncomfortably aware of her Laotian heritage. When her aunt and cousin came from Laos to live with her family, a conflict with a prejudiced boy at school and a New Year's celebration help this typical American seventh grader accept her heritage.

16.6 Lipsyte, Robert. **The Brave.** HarperCollins/Charlotte Zolotow Books, 1991. 195 pp. ISBN 0-06-023915-8.

Sonny Bear from the Moscondagas Reservation runs away from the local toughs on the reservation to the streets of New York City. Easy prey to Doll and Strike, two streetwise troublemakers, Sonny is arrested by Alfred Brooks. Seeing some of himself in this seventeen year old, Brooks, a boxer turned cop, befriends and guides Sonny as Sonny tries to control the rage he feels inside. Sequel to *The Contender.*

16.7   Marino, Jan. **The Day That Elvis Came to Town.** Little, Brown and Company, 1991. 204 pp. ISBN 0-316-54618-6.

Wanda's house is different. Her parents have to take in boarders to make ends meet and there are often clashes among those boarders. Her father's mean sister April (one of the boarders), along with her father's drinking, uses up Wanda's mother's energy and patience. When things seem overwhelming, Wanda retreats to her Elvis Presley records and her daydreams. Into this tumultuous 1960s Southern family moves a new boarder, jazz singer Mercedes Washington. Wanda can't believe her good fortune! Mercedes is kind, beautiful, exciting, and once went to school with Elvis! Their friendship makes Wanda feel special and helps her cope with her parents. Then she discovers Mercedes's awful secrets. Will Wanda's life ever get any better?

16.8   Mayne, William. **Drift.** A Yearling Book, 1990. 166 pp. ISBN 0-440-40381-2.

This is a multicultural story about a boy, Rafe Considine, and a Native American girl, Tawena. All his life, Rafe has been taught that Indians are no good and he lets Tawena know that she is no exception. But when the two children are caught in the dangers of the wilderness, Rafe must learn to trust the Native American girl if either of them is to survive.

16.9   Means, Florence Crannell. **The Moved-Outers.** Walker and Company, 1992. 168 pp. ISBN 0-8027-7386-9.

First published in 1945, this story reveals one of the darker moments in American history. The Japanese American Ohara family lives in Cordova, California, and enjoys a typical American lifestyle. Then December 7, 1941, dawns with the attack on Pearl Harbor, and within days, the Ohara family is thrust into a nightmare. Taken from their home and business to the Santa Anita detention facility, they await their fate, which will be decided by those who see Japanese Americans as a threat to the United States.

16.10 Namioka, Lensey. **The Coming of the Bear.** HarperCollins, 1992. 230 pp. ISBN 0-06-020288-2.

Two disgraced samurai, Zenta and Matsuzo, find themselves on the island of the Ainus after a storm wrecks the boat of the two men. The Ainus, a primitive tribal people, care for the two samurai and even teach them some of the strange Ainu customs, including the bloody Bear Festival. The festival proves too much for Matsuzo, who persuades Zenta to travel with him to a nearby Japanese settlement. However, the Japanese are eagerly preparing to go to war against the Ainus, and Zenta soon realized that he and Matsuzo may soon be fighting against each other.

16.11 Neville, Emily Cheney. **The China Year.** HarperCollins, 1991. 244 pp. ISBN 0-06-024383-X.

Henrietta Rich's father is given a teaching position in China, and his family goes with him to experience the lifestyles and customs of the Chinese. Henrietta must study her eighth-grade work from packets sent to her by her American teacher, since there are no schools she can attend. She must also learn to deal with a land where traditions, values, and language are very different from those in America.

16.12 Orlev, Uri. **The Man from the Other Side.** Translated from Hebrew by Hillel Halkin. Houghton Mifflin Company, 1991. 186 pp. ISBN 0-395-53808-4.

Marek is a fourteen-year-old Christian living in Warsaw, Poland, during World War II. His country has been taken over by Germans, and most Jews are confined to a walled ghetto in the city. His stepfather smuggles food through the sewers to the Jews on the other side, and finally Marek is old enough to help. After a surprising revelation by his mother, Marek finds himself struggling to provide a hide-out to save a young Jew's life, even while risking his own. This is a true story told to the author by a Polish journalist in Israel.

16.13 Pettit, Jayne. **My Name Is San Ho.** Scholastic, 1992. 149 pp. ISBN 0-590-44172-8.

Coming to America from the war-torn country of Vietnam is a strange and frightening experience for San Ho. Getting used to a new country, new school, new friends, and a new way of life is sometimes more than he can handle. A teacher's patience, in addition to love and understanding from his parents, gradually gives San Ho the courage to try to forget some of the horrors of war and death he has left behind.

16.14 Rathe, Gustave. **The Wreck of the Barque Stefano Off the North West Cape of Australia in 1875.** Farrar, Straus and Giroux, 1992. 160 pp. ISBN 0-37438585-8.

When the *Stefano* sets sail from Dubrovnik in 1875, young Miho Baccich is ready for adventure. When the *Stefano* runs aground during a storm off the North West Cape of Australia, Miho and nine other survivors are washed to shore, and get more adventure than Miho had ever bargained for. When only Miho and Ivan survive the dangers of the island, they are taken in by Aborigines and wander the island for six months, until a pearling ship comes to their rescue. Gustave Rathe tells his grandfather's story as it was recorded by a Jesuit scholar.

16.15 Reaver, Chap. **A Little Bit Dead.** Delacorte Press, 1992. 230 pp. ISBN 0-385-30801-9.

In 1876, after interfering with the attempted lynching of a young Yahi Indian named Shanti, eighteen-year-old Reece finds his own life in danger and becomes intimately involved in the future of Shanti's people. Will good overcome for Reece, Shanti, and Shanti's people, even though the law is against them?

16.16 Roy, Jacqueline. **Soul Daddy.** Harcourt Brace Jovanovich, 1992. 235 pp. ISBN 0-15-277193-X.

Hannah and Rosie, who are twins, have problems adjusting when their father unexpectedly returns, bringing with him their half sister and a huge dog. Being children of a white mother and black father while growing up in predominantly white London, England, adds more complications to the girls' already challenging lives.

16.17   Shalant, Phyllis. **Shalom, Geneva Peace.** Dutton Children's Books, 1992. 182 pp. ISBN 0-525-44868-5.

Andi Applebaum is about as straight as a square can be. Not terribly popular at her private Jewish school, and lonely because her mother's rigid rules have caused her brother Mitchell to stay away, Andi is ready for the friendship of Geneva Peace. But is Geneva the right kind of friend for a lonely, unpopular girl? Geneva works hard at being rebellious, taking foolish risks like driving without a license and becoming infatuated with the handsome rabbinic intern at their school. Andi recognizes her friend's self-destructive nature and bows out of the rapidly disintegrating situation in time—the question is, will Geneva follow her lead?

16.18   Skurzynski, Gloria. **Good-bye, Billy Radish.** Bradbury Press, 1992. 137 pp. ISBN 0-02-782921-9.

In 1917, as the United States enters World War I, ten-year-old Hank sees changes all around him in his western Pennsylvania steel mill town and feels his older Ukrainian friend Billy drifting apart from him. Hank must make a great leap from childhood to adulthood as a world goes to war and even the simplest things in life become complicated.

16.19   Soto, Gary. **Pacific Crossing.** Harcourt Brace Jovanovich, 1992. 126 pp. ISBN 0-15-259188-5.

When fourteen-year-old Mexican American Lincoln Mendoza signed up to study Kempo, a type of Japanese martial arts, he had no idea that his decision to do so would lead him to become an exchange student in Japan. During his stay with the Ono family, Lincoln becomes friends and brothers with the Ono's son Mitsuo. Together, these two very different boys learn to appreciate each other's heritage and culture. Includes a glossary of Spanish and Japanese phrases.

16.20   Taylor, Theodore. **Maria: A Christmas Story.** Harcourt Brace Jovanovich, 1992. 84 pp. ISBN 0-15-217763-9.

Mexican American Maria Gonzaga feels left out when her friends talk about the floats their traditional American families are having built for the San Lazaro Christmas Parade. Unable to afford the entry fee for the parade, Maria creates a miracle in the traditional way of all Christmas miracles, and she and her family become the first Mexican Americans to enter a float in the annual parade. *Maria: A Christmas Story* puts a modern twist on the traditional tale of giving of one's self for the good of all.

16.21   Treseder, Terry Walton. **Hear O Israel: A Story of the Warsaw Ghetto.** Illustrated by Lloyd Bloom. Atheneum, 1990. 41 pp. ISBN 0-689-31456-6.

Isaac is a ten-year-old Jewish boy who once led a normal life. After the onset of World War II, he describes his life in the Warsaw Ghetto, a Nazi concentration camp. With faith and courage, he tells of his family's ultimate transfer to and decimation in the horrifying camp of Treblinka.

16.22   Vail, Rachel. **Do-Over.** Orchard Books, 1992. 143 pp. ISBN 0-531-05460-8.

Thirteen-year-old Whitman Levy's life is full of complications: his father is dating Whitman's drama coach, none of the girls around him seem even remotely interested in him, and his best friend Doug is acting strangely around Whitman's friend Andi—and Whitman thinks it's because Andi's black. It isn't until he tries out for the school play that Whitman is able to understand some of what's happening in the world around him, including the changes in his father's life since the separation from Whitman's mother.

16.23   Vos, Ida. **Hide and Seek.** Translated by Terese Edelstein and Inez Smidt. Houghton Mifflin Company, 1991. 132 pp. ISBN 0-395-56470-0.

Rachel, an eight-year-old Jewish girl living in Holland, tells of her experiences during the Nazi occupation of World War II, her years in hiding, and the aftershock when the war finally ends. What is it like to have your familiar world slowly taken away from you? And where can you find the courage to survive? Originally published in 1981.

16.24 Williams, Michael. **Crocodile Burning.** Lodestar Books, 1992. 198 pp. ISBN 0-525-67401-2.

Seraki Mandini's life among the crocodiles of Soweto, South Africa, is painful. School is senseless, his brother Phakane is in prison for anti-apartheid acts, his father drinks to forget, and his mother is always gone, working as a housekeeper for a white family. On impulse, Seraki auditions for *iSezela,* a musical about the oppressed lives of young blacks in the townships, written and directed by the great Mosake. When he lands a leading role, Seraki is sure he can conquer the crocodiles that surround him. But greed, anger, and old fears die hard. The successful show goes to Broadway, and Seraki sees a way to free his brother and his family. How can it be that the problems of his old life and homeland follow him to New York?

16.25 Woodson, Jacqueline. **Maizon at Blue Hill.** Delacorte Press, 1992. 131 pp. ISBN 0-385-30796-9.

Maizon is a smart, black orphan from Brooklyn. But that is her problem: she's too smart for the public schools, where the grades come to her easily. Maizon's grandmother wants Maizon to go to Blue Hill, where the classes are small and she will be intellectually challenged. But Blue Hill is for rich kids—*white* rich kids. The four blacks who already attend Blue Hill don't offer anything for Maizon, and she never feels comfortable around the whites. Realizing that Blue Hill isn't for her, Maizon wonders if there is any place where a smart black girl from Brooklyn can fit in. Sequel to *Last Summer with Maizon.*

16.26 Yep, Laurence. **The Star Fisher.** Puffin Books, 1991. 150 pp. ISBN 0-688-09365-5.

Joan Lee and her family, Chinese Americans, move to a small West Virginian town in the 1920s so that Papa can open a laundry. Only their landlady welcomes them. Bigots spray-paint insults on their fence, Papa has no customers, and Joan has trouble with the kids at school, who consider her a know-it-all. Fights with Mama, who never seems to appreciate how much Joan tries, make everything worse. Gradually, however, Joan's life improves; Mrs. Bradshaw teaches Mama to bake apple pie and does some advertising for Papa, and Joan makes a friend at school.

17 Love and Romance

17.1 Bauer, Joan. **Squashed.** Delacorte Press, 1992. 194 pp. ISBN 0-385-30793-4.

As sixteen-year-old Ellie Morgan pursues her two goals in life—to grow the biggest pumpkin in Iowa and to lose twenty pounds herself—she finds herself falling for Wes, a young man who grows champion corn. While Max, her prize pumpkin, is her first love, Wes is certainly second! And with Wes's support, Ellie begins to feel that both of her goals are just within her reach.

17.2 Conford, Ellen. **Loving Someone Else.** Bantam Books, 1991. 160 pp. ISBN 0-553-07353-2.

Holly must take a summer job to earn money for college when her family, once wealthy, comes upon hard times. Holly is cook, companion, and chauffeur for two eccentric, elderly sisters. She develops a crush on their rich nephew, hoping that he might be her way out of poverty, but the crush blinds her to the real affection of her friend Pete. More than one person comes to realize what it means to be loving someone else.

17.3 Geras, Adèle. **The Tower Room.** Harcourt Brace Jovanovich, 1992. 150 pp. ISBN 0-15-289627-9.

When her parents are killed while on a trip to Africa, Megan is sent to live with a foster mother. Dorothy, Megan's foster mother, is headmistress of a secluded girls' school, and while living at the school with Dorothy, Megan falls in love for the first time. But her affair with Simon Findlay poses a serious problem for young Megan—Dorothy has chosen Simon for herself. Contains adult themes and situations.

17.4   Hall, Lynn. **The Secret Life of Dagmar Schultz.** Aladdin
Books, 1991. 89 pp. ISBN 0-689-71446-7.

Dagmar is almost thirteen and lives in a small town where
everyone knows everyone else's business. To make life more
interesting, she creates an ideal, imaginary boyfriend. However, she finds it difficult to explain conversations with him to
her family. When her best friend plans a boy-girl party, Dagmar is expected to produce the idealized Doug.

17.5   Levoy, Myron. **Kelly 'n' Me.** HarperCollins/Charlotte Zolotow Books, 1992. 202 pp. ISBN 0-06-020838-4.

Anthony Milano is the son of divorced parents, an actress and
a director. While living with his emotionally wounded mother
in New York City, Anthony takes to playing guitar in Central
Park, where he meets Kelly, a beautiful, mysterious singer.
Together, they perform street music all over New York, but
their growing romance might be threatened by their very different backgrounds. Can they give each other what they
couldn't find in their families?

17.6   Lowry, Lois. **Anastasia at This Address.** Houghton Mifflin
Company, 1991. 129 pp. ISBN 0-395-56263-5.

Anastasia, thirteen, decides to answer an appealing ad she
finds in the back of a newspaper: "SWM (single white male),
28, . . . wealthy, looking for. . . ." With some stretching of
words, she fits his requirements, and since age wasn't men-
tioned, Anastasia sends off a letter to SWM. In fact, she sends
several, including in one a college picture of her mother. What
she doesn't count on is a series of circumstances that causes
her to meet SWM face to face.

17.7   Maguire, Jesse. **On the Edge.** Ivy Books, 1991. 180 pp. ISBN
0-8041-0447-6.

Caroline Buchanan is a loner. During her senior year in high
school, she finds a close group of friends but still can't confide
her problem: she's pregnant. A careless night spent with a boy
she cares nothing about puts her friendships and even her

future in jeopardy. Most of all, she could lose the love and respect of the boy whose love she wants the most.

17.8 Moulton, Deborah. **Summer Girl.** Dial Books, 1992. 133 pp. ISBN 0-8037-1153-0.

With her mother dying of cancer, Tommy is sent to live with the father she has never known. He is shy, old enough to be her grandfather, and his house is filthy. Tommy, doubting she can survive the summer, plans to run away. Gradually, however, she changes her mind. Her father might not talk much, Tommy realizes, but he is kind and well-intentioned, and most importantly, still seems to love her mother, who for years has regretted leaving him for a younger man. When her father finds Tommy a job, teaches her to sail, and even lets her dog live with them, she decides to stay. Meanwhile, through her mother's letters, Tommy grows to understand the shy man who had seemed so indifferent to his daughter.

17.9 Peck, Sylvia. **Kelsey's Raven.** Morrow Junior Books, 1992. 234 pp. ISBN 0-688-09583-6.

Kelsey Martine calls a chimneysweep when a raven falls down her New York City apartment chimney. Dustin, the chimneysweep, not only rescues the bird, but he knows a vet to fix its injured wing. Then Dustin becomes more than just a rescuer of birds; he becomes someone special to Kelsey's actress mother. And when Kelsey visits the Museum of Natural History to learn more about ravens, she meets Ned, who becomes special to her. But the raven might have been an omen of bad things to come. When Samantha, Kelsey's best friend, begins to fall for Ned, too.

17.10 Powell, Randy. **Is Kissing a Girl Who Smokes Like Licking an Ashtray?** Farrar, Straus and Giroux, 1992. 199 pp. ISBN 0-374-33632-6.

Heidi and Biff find themselves drawn to each other by their similar backgrounds; Heidi's mother died years ago, and so did Biff's brother. But Heidi is so unpredictable and impulsive; she smokes, visits Biff's friends unannounced, and hides things about her relationship with her father. Why does Heidi have a check for $10,000, payment never to see her father again?

17.11 Sonnenmark, Laura. **The Lie.** Scholastic, 1992. 181 pp. ISBN 0-590-44740-8.

Norrie has a crush on Mark, who hires her for a summer job. He doesn't notice her much until he thinks she is interested in an older man—even if it is a lie. It becomes difficult to tell the truth about her nonexistent "involvement," and it causes a strain in the relationship with Mark. The best laid plans sometimes don't work out, as Norrie discovers when she realizes that she's too embarrassed to tell the truth.

17.12 Sweeney, Joyce. **Piano Man.** Delacorte Press, 1992. ISBN 0-385-30534-6.

Fourteen-year-old Deidre learns the meaning of true love when she develops an enormous crush on Jeff, a twenty-six-year-old musician who lives upstairs from her. Mature in many ways, Deidre must deal with her feelings for Jeff, his feelings for her and for his lover Chrissie, and even her mother's feelings about her own relationships with men. Contains adult language.

17.13 Voigt, Cynthia. **Orfe.** Atheneum, 1992. 120 pp. ISBN 0-689-31771-9.

Emmy has known Orfe for many years; now Orfe is a street musician and a member of the band called the Three Graces, a band for which Emmy becomes business manager. But Emmy thinks Orfe might have a problem: she seems to be in love with Yuri, a recovering addict whom Emmy thinks is doomed. What can Emmy do to help her friend? Contains adult language.

17.14 Westall, Robert. **Stormsearch.** Farrar, Straus and Giroux, 1992. 124 pp. ISBN 0-374-37272-1.

Tim and Tracy Voux are spending the summer with their aunt and uncle on the coast of England. When a huge storm sweeps the sand from their cove, it reveals the wreck of a model ship. Uncle Geoff, who likes to fix and restore things, brings the model back to its former glory, but in doing so, raises some disturbing questions about his family and other families gone almost a century before.

18 Meeting Life's Challenges: Problems and Solutions

18.1 Arrick, Fran. **Where'd You Get the Gun, Billy?** Bantam Books, 1991. 104 pp. ISBN 0-553-07135-1.

The small town of Crestview, New York, is shaken when Billy, a high school senior, shoots and kills Lisa, his girlfriend. Although David Fuller wasn't especially close friends with either Billy or Lisa, he goes to the police station in an effort to make sense of this seemingly meaningless, tragic occurrence, and he tries to figure out where Billy could have gotten the gun. Lieutenant Wisnewski presents a series of hypothetical situations to explain to David and his new friend Liz how this might have happened and how life must go on.

18.2 Arter, Jim. **Gruel and Unusual Punishment.** Delacorte Press, 1991. 103 pp. ISBN 0-385-30298-3.

At home, Arnold Dinklighter faces an unbalanced mother and the emptiness left behind when his father walked out three years earlier. At school, his internal anger and external rebellion land him regularly in Mr. Applin's detention "gulag," where Arnold meets and befriends violent, psychotic Edward. It is Edward's misguided attempt to kill Mr. Applin that finally drives Arnold to get help for himself and for his mother.

18.3 Betancourt, Jeanne. **Kate's Turn.** Scholastic, 1992. 133 pp. ISBN 0-590-43103-X.

Kate has a chance to study with a national ballet company in New York. She loves it, makes many new friends, and is good enough to be advanced during her first year. However, the sacrifices she makes and her homesickness for Oregon give her second thoughts about continuing, and she must make a huge decision about her future as a dancer.

18.4   Brooks, Martha. **Two Moons in August.** Little, Brown and Company, 1991. 199 pp. ISBN 0-316-10979-7.

Sidonie, a fifteen-year-old girl, has lost her mother, and her father, her sister, and she have a difficult time adjusting to life without their wife and mother. Kieran, a new boy in town who is visiting for the summer, helps Sidonie and her family reunite and strengthen their love and happiness.

18.5   Bunting, Eve. **Jumping the Nail.** Harcourt Brace Jovanovich, 1991. 148 pp. ISBN 0-15-241357-X.

The Nail, a cliff where daredevils have made illegal and dangerous jumps into the ocean off the coast of California, is the symbol for choices and peer pressure for the local teens. Dru watches helplessly as her friend Elisa makes all the wrong decisions. Even after Elisa and Scooter jump the Nail and defy death, Dru knows that all the signs of Elisa's depression are returning, and Dru feels desperate as she and her boyfriend Mike try to ward off disaster.

18.6   Cooney, Caroline B. **Flight #116 Is Down.** Scholastic, 1992. 201 pp. ISBN 0-590-44465-4.

After a 747 plane crashes in her front yard, Heidi discovers talents and strengths she didn't know she had. Patrick, who is a junior member of the medic rescue team and who loves to save people's lives, learns to appreciate life, as well as Heidi, who is almost invisible in the eyes of her parents. In this tale of endurance, bravery, and human performance under incredibly dangerous circumstances, Heidi Landseth's life is changed forever.

18.7   Cooper, Ilene. **Mean Streak.** Morrow Junior Books, 1991. 190 pp. ISBN 0-688-08431-1.

Veronica has it all: she's the most popular and beautiful girl in the sixth grade. But at home, everything is a mess. Her parents are recently divorced, and now her dad is marrying a younger woman. To make herself feel better, Veronica hurts the less popular kids at school by pulling pranks on them. But when

Veronica plays a mean trick on Gretchen "Hippopotamus," it winds up hurting Veronica, too, teaching her a valuable lesson. A *Kids from Kennedy Middle School* book.

18.8   Covington, Dennis. **Lizard.** Delacorte Press, 1991. 198 pp. ISBN 0-385-30307-6.

Ugly, deformed Lizard is placed by Miss Cooley—a mysterious guardian not much older than Lizard—in a home for retarded boys. Lizard's appearance keeps the psychologists and social workers from realizing the truth—that he is actually quite intelligent. Unhappy in the home, Lizard jumps at the chance to run away with Callahan (who wants him to act in *The Tempest*), though he doesn't believe for one minute that Callahan is actually his father, as Callahan suggests. On the road, Lizard has many adventures, from skinny-dipping in a pond in the woods to acting successfully in *The Tempest*. He makes and loses friends, and although he ends up back with Miss Cooley, he will never be the same.

18.9   Fenner, Carol. **Randall's Wall.** Margaret K. McElderry Books, 1991. 85 pp. ISBN 0-689-50518-3.

Randall has built an invisible wall for protection around himself to shield him from the harsh circumstances of his life. Only his secret drawings help him deal with life's realities. Jean, a fellow classmate, is able to penetrate his wall. In fact, she literally "washes away the wall." Through his new friend, Randall's gift for drawing is revealed, and a new world outside his wall begins to open up, for him and for Jean.

18.10   George, Jean Craighead. **Who Really Killed Cock Robin?** HarperCollins, 1991. 159 pp. ISBN 0-06-021981-5.

Each year, the town of Saddleboro celebrates the arrival of Cock Robin as the sign of spring. This particular year, Cock Robin dies, and one of his chicks is born without the ability to make a sound. Eighth-grader Tony Isidoro collects clues and explores all the ecological data to discover who killed Cock Robin and what is happening to the environment around Saddleboro.

18.11 Getz, David. **Almost Famous.** Henry Holt, 1992. 182 pp. ISBN 0-8050-1940-5.

Ten-year-old Maxine wants more than anything to become a famous inventor so she can take care of her brother Wat's heart condition. When an invitation for an invention contest arrives in the mail, Maxine recruits a troubled classmate, Toni, to help her prepare her entry. But asking for Toni's help might be Maxine's biggest mistake!

18.12 Greene, Bette. **The Drowning of Stephan Jones.** Bantam Books, 1991. 217 pp. ISBN 0-553-07437-7.

In this tale of a different kind of prejudice, Carla, daughter of the liberal-minded town librarian, is thrilled to be noticed by Andy, son of the Bible-quoting first family in fundamentalist Rachetville, Arkansas. When two businessmen move their business from New York to Rachetville for a slower-paced life, Andy and his father become vocal in their scorn as it becomes apparent that the two businessmen are also a couple. Andy's outrage leads to vandalism and mailed threats until prom night, when things get tragically out of hand.

18.13 Haas, Jessie. **Skipping School.** Greenwillow Books, 1992. 181 pp. ISBN 0-688-10179-8.

Phillip Johnson doesn't like living in the city; he liked living in the country, but his father's illness made it necessary to move. Phillip's life is filled with unpleasant circumstances: he hates his job, school is awful, and, of course, his dad is terribly sick. When Phillip's sister needs their mother to come to her college, Phillip and his father are left alone together. As a result, a line of communication opens between them which proves to be therapeutic for them both.

18.14 Hall, Lynn. **Flying Changes.** Harcourt Brace Jovanovich, 1991. 175 pp. ISBN 0-15-228790-6.

Denny is trying to deal with the many changes that occur in her life when her father is injured on the rodeo circuit. She is struggling to keep her family's household running smoothly when her mother, after many years of absence, suddenly shows up to "help out" and take over, making Denny feel unimportant. And while her Gramma's love eases some of her pain, Denny moves out anyway, hoping to prevent conflict in her reunited family. Will her family ever need her again?

18.15 Henkes, Kevin. **Words of Stone.** Greenwillow Books, 1992. 152 pp. ISBN 0-688-11356-7.

Blaze Werla is an undersized, freckle-faced redhead who has known much sorrow. His mother has died after being burned in a fire at a Fourth of July celebration, and he has no friends. Enter Joselle, the equally lonely but sardonic girl who gets Blaze's attention by spelling out his dead mother's name with white rocks. Join Blaze and Joselle, two troubled children as they search for their places in an increasingly unkind world.

18.16 Hermes, Patricia. **Mama, Let's Dance.** Little, Brown and Company, 1991. 168 pp. ISBN 0-316-35861-4.

Daddy is long gone, and when Mama leaves one day and doesn't come home, eleven-year-old Mary Belle takes charge, working hard to keep the family together. Her older brother Ariel works harder, and seven-year-old Callie, though sick, spends the days dancing with her dolls to bring Mama back. But Callie's precarious health grows worse, until the day tragedy strikes. Then Mary Belle and Ariel learn to hope and trust again, thanks to two good neighbors, Amarius and Miss Dearly.

18.17 Herzig, Alison Cragin, and Jane Laurence Mali. **Sam and the Moon Queen.** Illustrated by Diane de Groat. Clarion Books, 1990. 168 pp. ISBN 0-395-53342-2.

Sam, a thirteen-year-old boy who lives with his widowed mother in lower New York, misses his sister and father, who were killed in an automobile accident. Then he finds a young girl and her little dog hiding in the basement of his apartment building. A runaway from many foster homes, December has to learn trust from Sam, a difficult process for one whose only teacher has been the streets and its people. In turn, Sam must learn to let December fill the emptiness left in the wake of the loss of his family.

18.18 Karl, Herb. **The Toom County Mud Race.** Delacorte Press, 1992. 152 pp. ISBN 0-385-30540-0.

Jackie Lee Crockett has every intention of winning the annual mud race through Black Cypress Swamp; if he wins, he'll prove that his '69 pickup is the best in the country. But Jackie Lee and his friends, Snake and Bonnie, hadn't planned on matching wits with the mean and nasty Slocum boys, who try to sabotage Jackie's efforts to win the race.

18.19 Karr, Kathleen. **Oh, Those Harper Girls!** Farrar, Straus and Giroux, 1992. 182 pp. ISBN 0-374-35609-2.

Lily Harper and her five older sisters live on a cattle ranch in West Texas in 1869. In order to keep their father from losing the ranch, the sisters take to highway robbery. Their attempt is unsuccessful, but a newspaper man's dispatches in a New York City paper convince a theater manager that the girls have a career on his stage.

18.20 Killien, Christi. **The Daffodils.** Scholastic, 1992. 129 pp. ISBN 0-590-44241-4.

Nicole is as shocked as everyone when she is no longer captain of the softball team. When the new girl Caitlin becomes the captain and things aren't going right, Nicole realizes that she must do something. The team isn't the same anymore and even her friends seem to be turning against her. Nicole will have to prove herself a winner both on and off the field if she wants to keep her friends.

18.21 Paulsen, Gary. **The Monument.** Delacorte Press, 1991. 149 pp. ISBN 0-385-30518-4.

Rocky, a racially mixed girl with a fused knee, is adopted by grain elevator owners in small Bolton, Kansas (population 2,000). Left mostly to her own devices, she becomes friends with Mick, an artist who has been commissioned by the citizens of Bolton to design a monument to Bolton's seventeen war heroes from the Civil War to Vietnam. Rocky's life is changed and her eyes are opened as Mick designs the memorial to those seventeen heroes, giving Rocky a perspective on herself which she never had before.

18.22   Shriver, Jean Adair. **Mayflower Man.** Delacorte Press, 1991. 198 pp. ISBN 0-385-30295-9.

After the sudden death of his beloved grandmother, thirteen-year-old Caleb, the last of the Brewsters, is stunned. His grandmother leaves no money, and the traditional family homestead is sold to modern Californians Mike Kelso, his wife Honey, and her wild daughter Mose. Caleb and his mother are forced to move into a modern apartment and leave the farm where Brewsters have lived since they first came to Massachusetts in the 1600s. How can Caleb reclaim his home and a place in his town? An unlikely friendship with Mose gives him a new understanding about himself, his mother, and his heritage.

18.23   Stiles, Martha Bennett. **Kate of Still Waters.** Macmillan, 1990. 232 pp. ISBN 0-02-788395-7.

Thirteen-year-old Kate loves her life on the family's Kentucky farm. Her father intends that someday it will be hers, and she works hard to learn all he teaches her about shearing sheep, raising lambs, and all of the other important farm chores. But there are problems—a terrible drought, a tornado, and endlessly increasing loan payments to the bank. Several of her friends' parents lose their farms to foreclosure. And after wild dogs attack the family's sheep, threatening this year's only income, Kate's not sure there will be any farm left for her to inherit. She wonders if she can ever be as "brave and tough" as her parents as they struggle to hold on to both their family and their farm.

18.24   Tamar, Erika. **The Truth about Kim O'Hara.** Atheneum, 1992. 187 pp. ISBN 0-689-31789-1.

Andy's new and perfect girlfriend is Kim O'Hara. But is she too perfect? She makes perfect grades and tries very hard to be the ideal daughter for her Vietnam vet father, but is something actually very wrong with her life? When Kim suddenly runs away, and Andy finds her in the last place anyone would think to look, Kim's tragic past is revealed. A sequel to *It Happened at Cecilia's*.

18.25 Towne, Mary. **Their House.** Atheneum, 1990. 198 pp. ISBN 0-689-31562-7.

Molly Jackson's parents are determined to live in the country, so they move into a big rural house owned by the Warrens, an elderly couple. While her parents are renovating, Molly gets to know the Warrens and is impressed by their different lifestyle and values, their sense of history, and their commitment to the disappearing traditions of country gentlemen and ladies. Molly wonders where they'll go when they move out. But soon, Molly and her parents aren't sure they ever *will* move out. When the Warrens finally choose a drastic course of action to resolve their problems, Molly stumbles on their plan in a touching conclusion to this story of the past making way for the future.

18.26 White, Ruth. **Weeping Willow.** Farrar, Straus and Giroux, 1992. 246 pp. ISBN 0-374-38255-7.

Tiny is poor, illegitimate, and lives in a "holler" in Virginia. In spite of all this, Tiny is able to make a life for herself in high school. Unable to understand why her mother married Vern, a coal miner who drinks too much, Tiny struggles to keep things together at home. When Vern shows too much interest in her developing body, Tiny lives in fear of being around him. Then he rapes Tiny, warning that he will kill her dog if she tells. With effort, she is able to live with her fear and even carry on a normal social life, but when she begins to notice changes in half-sister Phyllis, Tiny understands that Vern has changed his focus. This is too much; Tiny knows she's going to have to tell someone, or Vern will never stop his horrible abuse.

18.27 Whittaker, Dorothy Raymond. **Angels of the Swamp.** Walker and Company, 1992. 209 pp. ISBN 0-8027-8129-2.

When Taffy's grandfather dies in the summer of 1932, Taffy knows that soon Miss Bessie, the welfare agent, will come to get her. So Taffy decides to hide out in Cranes Bog, where a fourteen-hour rainstorm brings rattlesnakes floating into the swamp. Taffy is rescued by young Jody, who is trying to escape his alcoholic uncle. Together, they soon meet Jeff, another troubled teen, and the three of them discover that even the worst problems can be overcome with the help of friends.

18.28 Woodson, Jacqueline. **The Dear One.** Delacorte Press, 1991. 145 pp. ISBN 0-385-30416-1.

Rebecca, a streetwise fifteen year old from Harlem, comes to live with Feni and Feni's mom when Rebecca becomes pregnant. At first, Feni thinks that by doing a favor for "a dear friend from the past," her mother is infringing on her family time. Yet Rebecca needs a quiet place to have her baby. In time, the girls come to carry on the tradition of their mothers: to be there for each other. Contains adult themes and language.

19 School and Community Relationships

19.1 Amis, Kingsley. **We Are All Guilty.** Viking/Reinhardt Books, 1991. 93 pp. ISBN 0-670-84268-0.

Slow-witted Clive lies, steals petty amounts of cash from his mother's purse, and spends aimless hours with friends he doesn't even like. One night, looking for excitement, he breaks into a warehouse, inadvertently causing the accident that puts an innocent man in the hospital. At first relieved that no one seems to blame him, Clive feels increasingly guilty. He seeks forgiveness in vain from an assortment of well-meaning social workers, lawyers, and ministers, all of whom blame "society" rather than Clive. Even his pious stepfather eventually decides that Clive couldn't control his own actions. Clive feels gratitude only when a frustrated policeman holds him responsible for the tragedy.

19.2 Arrick, Fran. **What You Don't Know Can Kill You.** Bantam Books, 1992. 154 pp. ISBN 0-553-07471-7.

Ellen and Jack are the golden couple in Shelter Rock, New York, at least in the eyes of Debra, Ellen's younger sister. Then a tragic automobile accident has many people donating blood for the victims, and when Ellen tries to donate, she receives a shock—her blood test comes back positive for HIV, the AIDS virus. She cannot believe that she contracted the virus from Jack; she was his first and only sexual partner. Or was she? A romance, a family, and a community are torn apart by one night of booze and sex. Contains adult situations and language.

19.3 Baczewski, Paul. **Just for Kicks.** J. B. Lippincott, 1990. 182 pp. ISBN 0-397-32465-0.

Fifteen-year-old Brandon is the manager of the football team. His two "dumb-as-a-post" brothers are major players on the team, which desperately wants to win the state championship. But what they sorely need is a kicker. When Brandon "volunteers" his talented and smart sister Sarah, the consequences of putting her up against the team's prejudices, the ex-Marine coach, and their brothers may create more problems than the championship is worth.

19.4   Clark, Catherine. **What's So Funny about Ninth Grade?** Troll Associates, 1992. 125 pp. ISBN 0-8167-2397-4.

Sheila wants to be a famous actress someday, while her best friend Ellen is interested in sports. Ninth grade begins with a school talent show, and Sheila wants badly to impress a certain boy. When her performance doesn't turn out as well as she'd like, Sheila is ready to give up on everything, including trying out for the school play, *Grease*. Can Ellen help her find her self-confidence again?

19.5   Cleary, Beverly. **Strider.** Illustrated by Paul O. Zelinsky. Morrow Junior Books, 1991. 179 pp. ISBN 0-688-09900-9.

Leigh Botts is a mature fourteen-year-old boy who falls in love with a stray dog, Strider. Many things in life begin to matter to him after finding Strider, even the divorce of his parents and the hope of being a family again. Though joint ownership of Strider with his friend Barry almost costs Leigh and Barry their friendship, Strider comes to the rescue and makes a choice to the satisfaction of everyone. Sequel to *Dear Mr. Henshaw*.

19.6   Dygard, Thomas J. **Backfield Package.** Morrow Junior Books, 1992. 202 pp. ISBN 0-688-11471-7.

Joe, Tracy, Coley, and Lew make up the undefeated backfield of their high school football team. They work so smoothly together that these seniors have promised each other to go as a "package" to the same college to play football. When college scouts see Joe, the quarterback, as a more talented player, however, they make offers only to him, leaving the others to wonder what will become of their promise to stick together.

19.7   Geller, Mark. **The Strange Case of the Reluctant Partners.** HarperCollins/Charlotte Zolotow Books, 1990. 88 pp. ISBN 0-06-021972-6.

Mark Geller immerses his readers in an English class's collaborative learning project: writing a biography about your project partner. Thomas Trible is no more thrilled with the task of working with "weird" Elaine Moore than she is with being assigned to Thomas. But it doesn't take Thomas long to learn that a sensitive person lies behind her quiet face, the one she hides behind a big vocabulary and thick sarcasm. The two learn about sharing, honesty, and peer pressure as they transform from adversaries into friends.

19.8   Geras, Adèle. **Happy Endings.** Harcourt Brace Jovanovich, 1991. 173 pp. ISBN 0-15-233375-4.

Although Mel has never been particularly interested in show business, her mother persuades her to try out for a summer production of *Three Sisters*. Mel becomes immersed in the play, as well as in various complex relationships with and among the cast members. As soon as the play closes, Mel breaks her ankle; and as she writes about her memories of her summer, she searches for the happy ending.

19.9   Guy, Rosa. **The Music of Summer.** Delacorte Press, 1992. 180 pp. ISBN 0-385-30599-0.

Sarah accepts an invitation from her former best friend to spend part of her summer vacation at the beach, even though she and Cathy, her friend, no longer have much in common. In fact, Cathy alternately ignores and torments Sarah because of her dark skin, encouraging Cathy's friends to do the same. Sarah spends much of her time with Cathy's mother and grandmother, afraid to practice the piano lest she incite Cathy to further jealousy. Only a growing romance with Jean Pierre, a political activist quite a few years older than Sarah, means enough that she is willing to risk Cathy's disapproval. Her former best friend's revenge, however, is far worse than anything Sarah had bargained for.

19.10   Hall, Barbara. **Fool's Hill.** Bantam Books, 1992. 147 pp. ISBN
0-553-08993-5.

Libby Burke, fourteen, is used to slow, boring summers with
her friend Alice; their fun is in imagining what it would be like
to be part of the popular crowd. But the new girls in town,
Rosalyn and Linda, change Libby's boredom to excitement
when they get her involved with the fast-paced crowd she has
always imagined being in. There's a price to pay, however, for
being an insider, Libby discovers, as she struggles to find
where she really does belong.

19.11   Hart, Avery, and Paul Mantell. **Ninth Grade Outcast.** Troll
Associates, 1992. 125 pp. ISBN 0-8167-2393-1.

Megan's life changes dramatically when her father changes
jobs and she can no longer go to a private girls' school. At the
public junior high, she faces many awkward changes—larger
classes, boys, feeling left out, and choices of new, different
friends. Will her life ever be normal again?

19.12   Hayashi, Nancy. **The Fantastic Stay-Home-from-School
Day.** Dutton Children's Books, 1992. 106 pp. ISBN 0-525-
44864-0.

Leona and Eddie plot together to fool their mothers and to
spend the entire day playing instead of being in school. The
first hitch in their plans comes when Eddie's mother refuses to
believe that he is sick. A vacation from school, Leona finds, is
not nearly as much fun without Eddie. She sneaks over to his
house and is almost given away by his bratty little sister. After
hiding in the closet for what feels like *hours,* even school
appeals to Leona. The vacation gets even worse when she
breaks something that belongs to Eddie's big brother and then
loses her favorite rock—Esmerelda—in her haste to escape
without being caught.

19.13   Haynes, Mary. **The Great Pretenders.** Bradbury Press, 1990.
135 pp. ISBN 0-02-743452-4.

Being new in a small town proves tough for eleven-year-old Molly Hamilton, after she unwittingly insults a classmate who turns out to be the mayor's bossy daughter, Eloise Higgins. Eloise isn't about to let Molly fit in during that first hot summer in West Branch. However, resourceful, talented Molly—with the help of her little friend Henry; her new friend, the wealthy and once-famous actress, Mrs. Cora Knox Findley; and her baseball prowess—finds a Fourth of July way to call a truce with Eloise.

19.14 Henry, Marguerite. **Misty of Chincoteague.** Illustrated by Wesley Dennis. Aladdin Books, 1991. 173 pp. ISBN 0-689-71492-0.

What a wonderful place to live—Chincoteague Island, where Paul and Maureen live with their grandparents. When Paul can finally participate in Pony Penning Day and is allowed to help capture the wild horses to sell, he has his eye on one horse only—Phantom. Paul and Maureen have both saved to buy the Phantom, who has escaped capture for two years. Paul wants to catch her, bring her back, and try to win the big race the following year. Originally published in 1947.

19.15 Jones, Janice. **Secrets of a Summer Spy.** Bradbury Press, 1990. 175 pp. ISBN 0-02-747861-0.

Harbor Island, Michigan, becomes a haven for adventuresome antics for Ronnie Windslow as she teams up with Amy and Jimmy for another summer of fun. This June, however, brings changes: Amy's more interested in her nail polish and sees former playmate Jimmy as boyfriend "Jim," much to Ronnie's dismay. The trio's once-harmless child's game, spying on neighbors, leads Ronnie into the secret world of the old Cat-lady, Mrs. Peet, who helps bring out the best in thirteen-year-old Ronnie and her Clamdigger pals.

19.16 Mauser, Pat Rhoads. **Rip-Off.** Collier Books, 1990. 158 pp. ISBN 0-02-044471-0.

In spite of her protests, fourteen-year-old Ginger is transferred to a high school across town, away from her friends. Her locker partner, Doylita, happens to be one of the most popular girls in school, and she introduces Ginger to the "in" crowd. The group's favorite pastime is going to the mall after school and shoplifting items just for fun. Although her conscience bothers her, Ginger wants to be accepted, especially by handsome Rol. Shoplifting does have its consequences, she discovers, and so does trying to be in an "in" crowd just to be popular.

19.17 Mills, Claudia. **Hannah on Her Way.** Macmillan, 1991. 151 pp. ISBN 0-02-767011-2.

Ten-year-old Hannah is not like the other kids at her new school; she's shy, quiet, and introspective, and she much prefers dolls and drawing over make-up and boys. Then she becomes friends with Caitie Crystal, the popular new girl at school, and Caitie teaches Hannah a little something about growing up.

19.18 Morris, Winifred. **The Jell-O Syndrome.** Collier Books, 1990. 159 pp. ISBN 0-02-044712-4.

Stephanie, a senior in high school, tells her story about being immune to the "Jell-O syndrome." She is not a woman whose head is filled with thoughts of looking good, dating, and boys. She likes being smart and not drippy over some hunk at school. Then Keith, a new student, arrives on the scene and the Jell-O syndrome begins for Stephanie. She must resolve the conflict between her desire to be independent and her new-found affection for Keith.

19.19 Naylor, Phyllis Reynolds. **Reluctantly Alice.** Atheneum/Jean Karl Books, 1991. 182 pp. ISBN 0-689-31681-X.

Are there more positives or negatives about seventh grade? Alice isn't sure, but she is determined to make this school year a good one. She tries to be friends with everyone, but Denise Whitlock threatens to dunk her in a clogged toilet, make her sing in public, and generally make her life miserable. Getting advice from Alice's widowed father and older brother doesn't seem to help Alice at all because her family members are having enough social troubles of their own. And when her best friend gets angry with her, Alice isn't sure how to solve all these difficulties. Maybe she could go back to sixth grade. Sequel to *The Agony of Alice* and *Alice in Rapture, Sort of.*

19.20 Pinkwater, Jill. **Tails of the Bronx: A Tale of the Bronx.** Macmillan, 1991. 208 pp. ISBN 0-02-774652-6.

The kids of Burnridge Avenue are quite a diverse bunch. In solving the mysterious disappearance of the neighborhood cats, they become involved with the neighborhood "witch" and also experience the plight of homelessness firsthand.

19.21 Shreve, Susan. **The Gift of the Girl Who Couldn't Hear.** Tambourine Books, 1991. 80 pp. ISBN 0-688-10318-9.

Eliza Westfield enters the seventh grade and meets adolescence head-on. Everything bothers her. She is moody, grouchy, and even though she's waited since third grade to have the lead in the seventh-grade musical, she announces she will not try out for a part. Her lifelong friend, Lucy, doesn't get the part *she* wants because she is deaf and can't sing, but she gives Eliza a lesson in life and the gift of courage and understanding.

19.22 Thesman, Jean. **Triple Trouble.** Avon, 1992. 153 pp. ISBN 0-380-76464-4.

Heather and Erin are spending the summer in Fox Crossing, Washington, with the family of their cousin Amelia. Fox Crossing doesn't have much to offer; the big event of the summer is the centennial celebration which Amelia's stepfather, a professor at the local college, is overseeing. But the town's mayor is dead-set against the centennial and uses his office to put obstacles in the way of its success. Then Erin meets Toby, who just happens to be the mayor's son. Can she use her influence on Toby to make this all work out?

19.23 Weyn, Suzanne. **All Alone in the Eighth Grade.** Troll Associates, 1992. 126 pp. ISBN 0-8167-2395-8.

The sudden change in Chris, who has been Tracey's best friend since first grade, leaves Tracey wondering what to do. Tracey allows Chris to persuade her to dress as she does and become part of the "in" crowd. But Tracey doesn't like what is happening, and eventually she must make a decision between Chris's way and her own.

IV Understanding

I want, by understanding myself, to understand others.
I want to be all that I am capable of becoming . . .

Katherine Mansfield
Journal (1922)

20 Battles and Battlefields: Understanding Armed Conflicts

20.1 Bergman, Tamar. **Along the Tracks.** Translated from the Hebrew by Michael Swirsky. Houghton Mifflin Company, 1991. 245 pp. ISBN 0-395-55328-8.

When Yankele's papa joins the Russian Army to fight the Germans after the German invasion of Poland, Mama, Yankele, and little Sarele begin a long journey by train from Poland to Russia. Each day brings hunger, danger, and risk of detection. When an ambush forces the refugees to jump from the train and run for cover, Yankele is left behind when the train leaves again. So begins his solitary journey of survival and his search for his family.

20.2 Bosco, Peter I. **The War of 1812.** Millbrook Press, 1991. 128 pp. ISBN 1-56294-004-X.

The War of 1812 details the acts of heroism and victory—as well as the failures and defeats—of the famous "Old Ironsides" and the battle on the sea between America and Britain. We read of Tecumseh, the influential Shawnee Chief; of the burning of Washington, D.C.; and of the famous Battle of New Orleans, a battle ironically fought two weeks after the peace treaty ending the war had been signed, but before word had reached the soldiers. The War of 1812 brought no gains to either side, but it did free the United States for a long period of prosperity and expansion.

20.3 Cross, Gillian. **Wolf.** Holiday House, 1990. 140 pp. ISBN 0-8234-0870-1.

Two quick taps at the front door, a midnight visitor, and suddenly Granny Phelan sends Cassy away across Dublin to stay with her irresponsible mother, Goldie. With just a shopping bag and a small suitcase, Cassy tracks her wandering mother to a seemingly abandoned house. A multi-colored painted van outside advertises MOONGAZER. What can Goldie be up to now? Then Cassy discovers plastic explosives in the bottom of her shopping bag, and Granny won't take her phone calls. Her fears are compounded by a strange man she sees lurking around the house. Is he a terrorist, or Mick, her mysterious missing father? No one will give her explanations, and Cassy has to find out for herself how to "keep the wolf from the door."

20.4   Dickinson, Peter. **AK.** Delacorte Press, 1990. 229 pp. ISBN 0-385-30608-3.

They call him AK because of the gun he carries. His name is Paul; he is a warrior in the Fifth Commando. Twenty-three men and nine other warriors like Paul, commandos in training, are prepared to blow up a train when news comes that the war is over. Michael Kagomi, the unit leader, adopts Paul as his son. So Paul buries his AK, goes to school, and Michael becomes important in the new government. But peace in Nagala, a fictitious African nation, doesn't last. A military coup erupts, and Michael becomes a prisoner in the palace where he lived. It's up to Paul, his rifle, and his friend Jilli to do what they can to free Michael.

20.5   Marrin, Albert. **The Spanish-American War.** Atheneum, 1991. 182 pp. ISBN 0-689-31663-1.

History comes to life in this description of the United States' involvement in Cuba and the Phillipines. The text covers the role William Randolph Hearst and his newspaper played in tilting public opinion in favor of war, the complex—sometimes fierce, sometimes surprisingly humane—personalities of key figures such as Theodore Roosevelt, and the betrayal of the Phillipines. Neither the United States nor her enemy is tinted with rose-colored glasses. Photos of "heroes" and "villains" alike add to this exploration of America's recent history.

20.6   Murphy, Jim. **The Boys' War: Confederate and Union Soldiers Talk about the Civil War.** Clarion Books, 1990. 112 pp. ISBN 0-89919-893-7.

Elisha Stockwell describes his first taste of a Civil War battle as "foolishness for a boy of sixteen." Author Jim Murphy's account, combining firsthand narratives and photographs, takes the reader from the excitement and pride of enlistment to the sorrows, fears, and horrors of warfare as seen through the eyes of Elisha and other teenage boys. Through the words of those who fought and died, Murphy offers an insight into our nation's most divisive and bloody period.

20.7   Talbert, Marc. **The Purple Heart.** HarperCollins/Willa Perlman Books, 1992. 135 pp. ISBN 0-06-020428-1.

While Luke's father is in Vietnam, Luke and his best friend Mike watch the evening news for details about the war and play games in which fearless soldiers wage heroic battles. Luke's father brings a hero's medal home, but where is the fearless soldier in this tired, thin, haunted man? After Luke and Mike play a prank on old Mrs. Pederson, they learn how war really affects people and discover that being brave is sometimes terrifying.

20.8   Westall, Robert. **The Kingdom by the Sea.** Farrar, Straus and Giroux, 1990. 176 pp. ISBN 0-374-34205-9.

Harry Baguely, a twelve-year-old boy, survives a German air raid in northern England during World War II. He and his dog flee from their home and travel up the English coast, encountering helpful characters and engaging in suspenseful adventures as they learn to live on their own and to defend themselves from the hostile, war-torn world around them.

21 Biographies and Autobiographies

21.1 Aaseng, Nathan. **Robert E. Lee.** Lerner Publications Company, 1991. 107 pp. ISBN 0-8225-4909-3.

Robert E. Lee, the top Confederate General during the Civil War, was a peaceful man who many times regretted his choice of a military career. This book offers insight into Lee who is considered by many to be one of the most brilliant military strategists ever and who outsmarted one Union general after another during the Civil War. This man's life, symbol of integrity, loyalty, and courage, is examined chronologically from his early childhood, through the many campaigns in which he was involved, to his quiet, dignified surrender near the end of the war to General U. S. Grant of the Union Army. Lee's military strengths and weaknesses are also carefully reviewed.

21.2 Anderson, Catherine Corley. **John F. Kennedy: Young People's President.** Lerner Publications Company, 1991. 144 pp. ISBN 0-8225-4904-2.

John F. Kennedy believed that everyone could make a difference to society, and he lived his life according to this belief. Overcoming many childhood illnesses and family tragedies, he became the 35th President of the United States and made his mark in history. This book examines his war experiences, his marriage, his complex family relationships, and his tenure in office until that fateful November day in Dallas, Texas, when the young president was struck down by an assassin's bullet.

21.3 Anderson, William. **Laura Ingalls Wilder: A Biography.** HarperCollins, 1992. 240 pp. ISBN 0-06-020113-4.

Charles and Caroline Ingalls were true pioneers. With grit and determination, they homesteaded and raised four daughters. It was not until one daughter, Laura, began at age forty-four, to write for a Missouri farm newspaper the *Ruralist* that the family became special. At age sixty, Laura Ingalls Wilder was writing *Little House* books to capture the stories her father had told and to keep alive the saga that her family had lived. In the ninety years of Wilder's life, the United States went from a Civil War-scarred land to a world power, and Laura Ingalls Wilder defined children's literature. Black-and-white photographs and index are included.

21.4   Bauleke, Ann. **Rickey Henderson: Record Stealer.** Lerner Publications Company, 1991. 56 pp. ISBN 0-8225-0541-X.

Although as a child Rickey Henderson didn't even like sports, he went on to become one of the greatest baseball players of all time. Because he wanted someone to practice with, his brother pushed him into baseball, teaching Rickey to catch by throwing balls at him. By the end of high school, Rickey had talent scouts from both baseball and football after him. Even then, Rickey preferred football, and only chose baseball because his mother asked him to. Rickey went on to break Lou Brock's base-stealing record. Not content with that, however, Rickey improved his batting skills until he was voted Most Valuable Player of 1990. This book is enhanced by many photographs of Rickey at home and on the field.

21.5   Borland, Kathryn Kilby, and Helen Ross Speicher. **Harry Houdini: Young Magician.** Illustrated by Fred Irvin. Aladdin Books, 1991. 192 pp. ISBN 0689-71476-9.

Harry Houdini is considered to be one of the greatest magicians of all time, and this book recounts the early years of the escape master's career. A great deal of hard work and determination led to Houdini's name becoming synonymous with "escape," including life-threatening escapes from underwater and from dizzying heights. Some of the secrets behind his magic are even revealed in this book! A biography from the Childhood of Famous Americans series. Originally published in 1969.

21.6   Carpenter, Angelica Shirley, and Jean Shirley. **L. Frank Baum: Royal Historian of Oz.** Lerner Publications Company, 1992. 144 pp. ISBN 0-8225-4910-7.

Even as a child, L. Frank Baum showed signs of extraordinary creativity. Although a poor student, Frank invented numerous gadgets at home and published several newspapers. As an adult, he ricocheted from career to career, nearly always successfully. His pursuits included writing, theatrics, gardening, science, and business. Wildly impractical, he experienced affluence, bankruptcy, and then a return to affluence, all within a few years. Best known for creating the Wizard of Oz, Baum's famous series is still a bestseller, inspiring fan clubs, newsletters, and one of the most famous movies ever. Bibliography and index included.

21.7   Chaney, J. R. **Aleksandr Pushkin: Poet for the People.** Lerner Publications Company, 1992. 112 pp. ISBN 0-8225-4911-5.

Aleksandr Pushkin was often called the "Father of Russian Literature." He was the first Russian author to write in the Russian language, though his country was a turbulent nation during his lifetime; tsars kept close reign on popular expression such as his. This book makes use of many photographs in examining the life of the poet whose works are widely recognized as the origins of Russian classical literature.

21.8   Collins, David R. **J. R. R. Tolkien: Master of Fantasy.** Illustrated by William Heagy. Lerner Publications Company, 1992. 112 pp. ISBN 0-8225-4906-9.

This book describes the life, from childhood to adult, of the creator of the *Lord of the Rings* series. An orphan and brilliant student, Tolkien led an ordinary life in many respects, by marrying happily, having children, and teaching linguistics at a university for many years. Yet for more than ten years, he labored over his masterpiece whenever he had the chance, inventing an alternate world, complete with nonhuman creatures such as fairies, elves, hobbits, and orcs—it even had its

own geography and language! With the rare ability to successfully integrate reality and fantasy, Tolkien excelled in both
areas, proving that tormented isolation is not a prerequisite for
genius. Bibliography and index included.

21.9   Conklin, Thomas. **Muhammad Ali: The Fight for Respect.**
Millbrook Press, 1991. 101 pp. ISBN 1-56294-112-7.

The day young Cassius Clay had his bike stolen was a fortu-
nate day for the sports world, because that was the day he first
entered a boxing gym, a step that would change his life. Cassius Clay grew up in Louisville, Kentucky, during the 1950s.
In spite of many hardships caused by racial prejudice, Cassius
became one of the greatest boxers of all time, known to the
world as Muhammad Ali. Through informative text and many
black-and-white photographs, this biography recounts the
story of a man who showed the world how to "float like a
butterfly, and sting like a bee."

21.10   Dana, Barbara. **Young Joan.** HarperCollins/Charlotte Zolotow
Books, 1991. 371 pp. ISBN 0-06-021422-8.

How did Joan of Arc—a very young girl, uneducated, deeply
attached to peasant tradition—manage to lead a French army
into battle and to later find the courage to die for her beliefs?
This fictional book provides answers by depicting Joan as a
child, living and working with her family and friends. Although in many ways Joan seems no different from the other
girls, the author portrays her as unusually kind, gentle, contem-
plative, and religious. When Joan begins to have visions of her
favorite saints, she is astonished, frightened, and joyful, and
she finally accepts the mission she feels God has placed upon
her. Eventually, she leaves the countryside she loves, hoping to
convince the "Dauphin" to fight for his right to rule.

21.11   Devaney, John. **Bo Jackson: A Star for All Seasons.** Walker
and Company, 1992. 132 pp. ISBN 0-8027-8178-0.

Bo knows sports! Bo Jackson was the first person to play on
both a major league baseball team and a professional football
team. This biography tells how the superathlete, whose real

name is Vincent Jackson, grew up—how he was nicknamed Boar (which became Bo) before he was ten because of his wild behavior. Readers will learn how Bo overcame his aggressive nature and went on to become 1985 Heisman Trophy winner. Index included.

21.12   Faber, Doris. **Calamity Jane: Her Life and Her Legend.** Houghton Mifflin Company, 1992. 60 pp. ISBN 0-395-56396-8.

When Ned Wheeler began writing dime novels about a whip-cracking sharpshooter named Calamity Jane, he didn't have to make up the character! Calamity Jane—whose real name was Martha Jane Cannary—was born in 1852, and grew up to become a legend of the American West. From her days as a Pony Express rider to her romance with Wild Bill Hickcock, Calamity Jane came to epitomize the last great pioneers of the Wild West. Photographs and bibliography included.

21.13   Finkelstein, Norman H. **Captain of Innocence: France and the Dreyfus Affair.** G. P. Putnam's Sons, 1991. 156 pp. ISBN 0-399-22243-X.

In the 19th century, Alfred Dreyfus was a Jewish French army officer charged with spying for the Germans. Was he guilty? Or was he a victim of prejudice because he was Jewish? The mysteries surrounding the Dreyfus affair continue to demand attention because of the international focus placed on the captain's multiple trials; the issue of prejudice is as important to people today as it was to Dreyfus in the 1800s.

21.14   Finkelstein, Norman H. **Theodor Herzl: Architect of a Nation.** Lerner Publications Company, 1991. 128 pp. ISBN 0-8225-4913-1.

This biography of an Austrian journalist who became founder of the modern Zionist movement—a movement for the establishment of a Jewish state—tells of Theodor Herzl's belief that Jews should go back to Israel to escape the anti-Semitism that had tormented them for centuries. He set the stage for the creation of a Jewish nation in Israel; he became involved in the trial of Captain Alfred Dreyfus who was being charged as a spy, but who many believed was being persecuted for his religion. Herzl's contributions to the world were varied and widespread, but all contained one particular focus—to find one perfect land for his people, a place where they could live—and pray—in peace.

21.15 Freedman, Russell. **An Indian Winter.** Illustrated by Karl Bodmer. Holiday House, 1992. 96 pp. ISBN 0-8234-0930-9.

An Indian Winter details the true adventures of Alexander Philipp Maximillian, a German prince; and Karl Bodmer, a Swiss artist during their stay with the Mandan Indians in the winter of 1833-34. Maximillian kept journals of their adventures, while Bodner recorded in drawings and paintings the lives and ways of the Indian. The trip of these two men through the Missouri River Valley gave one of the first accurate accounts of the Mandan Indians. This book consists of the drawings and much of the actual journals of that adventure.

21.16 Freedman, Russell. **The Wright Brothers: How They Invented the Airplane.** Holiday House, 1991. 129 pp. ISBN 0-8234-0875-2.

Wilbur and Orville Wright are famous as the developers of the first airplane. But do you know *how* they did it? And did you know that they took numerous photographs as their work progressed? This book follows the lives and labors of America's famed inventors and includes many of those personal, amazing photos of an event that shaped the future.

21.17 Fritz, Jean. **Bully for You, Teddy Roosevelt!** Illustrated by Mike Wimmer. G. P. Putnam's Sons, 1991. 127 pp. ISBN 0-399-21769-X.

The almost childlike energy, enthusiasm, and *joie de vivre* of Teddy Roosevelt are well depicted in this biography. By examining Roosevelt's childhood in a large family, his love of reading, his growing enthusiasm for naturalism and contrasting interest in hunting, and his training in law and subsequent desire to become a politician, the author provides a rich background for Roosevelt's later accomplishments. Roosevelt is depicted as both human (his grief at his first wife's death) and heroic (the reforms he pursued in spite of the risks to his political career) and in the end as a very likeable man, flaws and all.

21.18   Goldstein, Margaret J. **Brett Hull: Hockey's Top Gun.** Lerner Publications Company, 1992. 48 pp. ISBN 0-8225-0599-0.

Brett Hull, one of the stars of the St. Louis Blues hockey team, hasn't always had the "star" mentality. Describing himself as "laid back," Brett drifted into playing hockey. Born in Canada, his father was a well-known hockey player and his mother a professional ice skater. Brett's obvious talent kept him prominent in the hockey arena, though his coaches worried that he would never achieve the dedication they believed necessary. As Brett matured, however, he developed his own style, and his increasing practice time and determination began to pay off.

21.19   Greenberg, Keith Elliot. **Magic Johnson: Champion with a Cause.** Lerner Publications Company, 1992. 64 pp. ISBN 0-8225-0546-0.

This brief biography of Magic Johnson, published since his public announcement that he was HIV-positive, deals primarily with how Johnson has reacted to the diagnosis. Emphasizing his positive attitude, ambition, and strong work ethic, the book details Johnson's childhood, his rise to stardom, his serious knee injury, and his subsequent comeback to achieve even greater fame. The book concludes with a page of basketball statistics. A book in The Achievers series.

21.20   Harrison, Barbara, and Daniel Terris. **A Twilight Struggle: The Life of John Fitzgerald Kennedy.** Lothrop, Lee & Shepard Books, 1992. 159 pp. ISBN 0-688-08830-9.

When President John F. Kennedy was assassinated in November of 1963, the nation lost a man who many considered to be one of the greatest leaders of all time. This book explores Kennedy's childhood, his family, and his political career from a senator for Massachusetts to the President of the United States. Kennedy's personal and political strengths and weaknesses are examined in relation to his decisions in dealing with the nation's problems of the early 1960s. Bibliography included.

21.21 Hildebrand, Lee. **Hammertime.** Avon, 1992. 162 pp. ISBN 0-380-76690-6.

M. C. Hammer is best known for refining rap music and bringing it into mainstream music. But Hammer wasn't always "Hammer"; he was once Stanley Kirk Burrell, a mascot for the Oakland A's baseball team. This biography examines M. C. Hammer's early days around the baseball stadium and explains how his music was destined to win out over baseball. Black-and-white photographs included.

21.22 Loeper, John J. **Crusade for Kindness: Henry Bergh and the ASPCA.** Atheneum, 1991. 98 pp. ISBN 0-689-31560-0.

Henry Bergh, founder of the ASPCA (American Society for the Prevention of Cruelty to Animals), changed the attitude of America toward animals. During his life in the 19th Century, he disrupted illegal dog fights, pigeon shoots, and the cruel drowning of animals in city pounds. He forced the owners of streetcars to treat their horses in a humane way. He attacked the slaughterhouses and forced them to kill the animals meant for food in a quick, painless manner. And by using the laws against cruelty to animals as his starting point, Bergh was able to bring about the first conviction in a case of child abuse. His tireless efforts to open Americans' eyes to the cruelty all about them has continued to benefit society, and his organization is now the leader in animal cruelty issues, such as the sale of animal furs for fashion and the unnecessary killing of dolphins at sea.

21.23 Lyons, Mary E. **Sorrow's Kitchen: The Life and Folklore of Zora Neale Hurston.** Charles Scribner's Sons, 1990. 144 pp. ISBN 0-684-19198-9.

Zora Neale Hurston was a writer of many talents, compiling black folklore while authoring stories, plays, essays, and articles. A participant in the Harlem Renaissance, Hurston helped pave the way for African American writers to join the established literary community, and this book examines that work through Hurston's own words, as well as those of her critics. Photographs, bibliography, and suggested reading list included.

21.24   Mason, Miriam E. **Mark Twain: Boy of Old Missouri.** Illustrated by Henry S. Gillette. Aladdin Books, 1991. 192 pp. ISBN 0-689-71480-7.

Samuel Clemens actually lived many of the adventures he wrote about as Mark Twain. From events in his life came the basis for the friendship between Tom Sawyer and Huck Finn, as well as many characters' love for the Mississippi and adventure. Clemens' interest in pirates, caves, and even "Becky Thatcher" were developed for his writings from his life. This book follows his life from a young child in Hannibal, Missouri, through many different jobs—a cub printer, a river boat pilot, a reporter in Nevada—until he became one of the world's most famous and beloved writers. Originally published in 1942.

21.25   Myers, Walter Dean. **Malcolm X: By Any Means Necessary.** Scholastic, 1993. 192 pp. ISBN 0-590-46484-1.

Malcolm Little was a man of two lives. His first was that of a street hustler named Detroit Red; his second, that of a civil rights activist known as Malcolm X. Sent to prison for six years after being convicted of armed robbery, Malcolm became interested in Elijah Mohammed's Nation of Islam. After his release from prison, Malcolm left behind his days as a hoodlum and took up the role of a Muslim preacher, striving for equal rights for African Americans. But before his dream could be fully achieved, Malcolm was gunned down in the Audubon Ballroom in New York City in 1965. Photographs and bibliography included.

21.26 Otfinoski, Steven. **Nelson Mandela: The Fight Against Apartheid.** Millbrook Press, 1992. 128 pp. ISBN 1-56294-067-8.

This biography explores the life and career of Nelson Mandela, the South African civil rights leader. Readers will learn exactly what apartheid is and how it affects the people of South Africa. Readers will also learn how Mandela has struggled to change race relations in a country where a minority race rules a majority one. Black-and-white photographs and a map of South Africa aid in understanding.

21.27 Parks, Rosa, with Jim Haskins. **Rosa Parks: My Story.** Dial Books, 1992. 192 pp. ISBN 0-8037-0673-1.

In 1965, on a segregated bus in Montgomery, Alabama, a simple but dramatic event occurred that changed laws and attitudes: Rosa Parks refused to give up her seat to a white man. She rebelled against racism. Ultimately, her action led to the passage of a federal law against segregation on buses, established Dr. Martin Luther King as a national figure, and launched the civil rights movement into popularity. This autobiography looks at the life of this American heroine.

21.28 Peck, Richard. **Anonymously Yours.** Julian Messner, 1991. 117 pp. ISBN 0-671-74162-4.

At the age of thirty-seven, Richard Peck turned in his plan book, quit his teaching job, and set out to be a writer. In this autobiography, Peck traces his life experiences (especially those of growing up in a small town in America) as actual preparation for that fateful day. And his first trip to England as a college student, his service as a chaplain's assistant in the army in Germany (at the same time as Elvis), his work for a major textbook publisher, and his teaching experiences were all preparation and subject matter for his work as an author. These experiences have given Peck events and characters used in his eighteen published books to date.

21.29 Pious, Richard M. **Richard Nixon: A Political Life.** Julian Messner, 1991. 113 pp. ISBN 0-671-72852-0.

This book paints a disturbing picture of a politician whose ambition and hard work made him President, but whose basic dishonesty brought about his downfall. Richard Nixon was elected the thirty-seventh President in 1969, but after one year and seven months into his second term, he resigned the office in August of 1974. At that time, Congress was giving consideration to putting him on trial for covering up a burglary his election staff committed. The break-in at Democratic headquarters—a crime that came to be known as Watergate— brought to an end the political career of Richard Nixon, one of America's most intriguing public figures.

21.30   Richmond, Robin. **Introducing Michelangelo.** Little, Brown and Company, 1992. 32 pp. ISBN 0-316-74440-9.

Introducing Michelangelo does just that. This is a biography of the Renaissance artist, complete with color illustrations of his works. It emphasizes his early years as an apprentice, his sculptures such as the *Pietàs* and *David,* and of course, the magnificent ceiling of the Sistine Chapel.

21.31   St. George, Judith. **Dear Dr. Bell . . . Your Friend, Helen Keller.** G. P. Putnam's Sons, 1992. 95 pp. ISBN 0-399-22337-1.

This biography follows the parallel lives of Helen Keller and Alexander Graham Bell, who continued to encounter and support each other from that eventful meeting when Bell recommended Helen be given a teacher, thus leading her to Annie Sullivan. Through excerpts from Helen's letters and photographs of both Helen and Bell, the reader can experience the devotion these two legendary people felt for each other.

21.32   Seymour, Flora Warren. **Sacagawea: American Pathfinder.** Illustrated by Robert Doremus. Aladdin Books, 1991. 192 pp. ISBN 0-689-71482-3.

Sacagawea was the Native American girl who became "Bird Woman" to and guide for the Lewis and Clark expedition in the early 1800s. While following Sacagawea's amazing life, the reader will learn about the daily lives of the Shoshani Indians of the Northwest, their dependence on the buffalo,

Sacagawea's capture by the Minitarees, her marriage to a "tabba bone" (as the white men were called), and her aid in opening up the West to settlers. Part of the Famous Americans series, originally published in 1945.

21.33 Simon, Sheridan. **Stephen Hawking: Unlocking the Universe.** Dillon Press, 1991. 112 pp. ISBN 0-87518-455-3.

"My goal is simple. It is the complete understanding of the universe." These are the words of Stephen Hawking, renowned British theoretical physicist, and this is the story of his quest to reach his goal while battling Lou Gehrig's disease. Despite his need for a wheelchair and computer to move and communicate, Hawking has taken the study of cosmology further than anyone else in the field. Photographs and illustrations included.

21.34 Stefoff, Rebecca. **George H. W. Bush: 41st President of the United States.** Garrett Educational Corporation, 1990. 138 pp. ISBN 1-56074-033-7.

George Bush became the first wartime President in almost two decades when he oversaw the American military operation in the Persian Gulf. From his days as the youngest pilot in the U.S. Navy during World War II to his days as vice president under Ronald Reagan to his term as forty-first President of the United States, this book provides an overview of the man who looked at American and saw "a thousand points of light."

21.35 Stevens, Bryna. **Frank Thompson: Her Civil War Story.** Macmillan, 1992. 149 pp. ISBN 0-02-788185-7.

Frank Thompson was born Sarah Emma Edmondson in 1841, a time when women were subservient to father or husband. She began wearing men's clothes at first to hide from her father's wrath, but it did not take long for her to learn that men enjoyed freedom and independence women would never know. At the beginning of the Civil War, she joined the army and served for two years, mostly as postmaster, nurse, and spy for the Union forces. Some twenty years later, Congress voted that she have veterans' benefits, even though she was a woman. She is buried in a military cemetery in Texas under her married name of Seelye. Bibliography and index included.

21.36   Stevenson, Augusta. **Buffalo Bill: Frontier Daredevil.** Illustrated by E. Joseph Dreany. Aladdin Books, 1991. 192 pp. ISBN 0-689-71479-3.

William F. Cody, better known as Buffalo Bill, was indeed a "Frontier Daredevil." By the age of twenty-one, he had worked on wagon trains, worked as a fur trapper, was one of the first riders for the famous Pony Express, and had supplied the railroads with fresh buffalo meat. He went on to establish the first of the "Wild West Shows," which did much to educate the people of the world about the settling of the West. Originally published in 1948.

21.37   Terkel, Studs, with Milly Hawk Daniel. **Giants of Jazz.** HarperCollins, 1975. 210 pp. ISBN 0-690-00998-4.

Louis Armstrong, Count Basie, Billie Holiday, Benny Goodman, and Dizzy Gillespie. These names conjure up images of trumpets, swing bands, and throaty voices singing the blues. Beginning with "Papa Joe" Oliver, the father of jazz, the stories behind these artists reveal the lives behind the performers, some of whom played strictly from the heart without ever learning to read music; others were highly educated and classically trained. Through the performers' lives, we see the development of jazz in all its forms—blues, swing, and be-bop—and we watch this musical art form earn its place in music history. Photographs included.

21.38   Uchida, Yoshiko. **The Invisible Thread.** Julian Messner, 1991. 136 pp. ISBN 0-671-74164-0.

Japanese American Yoshiko Uchida is a second generation citizen born in the 1930s, four years after her older sister. The family faces prejudice in Berkeley, California, yet ball games, dances, and hot dogs make life good in the American way. Then comes Pearl Harbor and the moment of truth. One hundred and twenty thousand West Coast Japanese Americans are sent to interment camps all over the country; the Uchida family is sent to Topaz in Utah. From Topaz, Yoshiko begins her search for freedom of body as well as for her soul.

21.39 Wadsworth, Ginger. **John Muir: Wilderness Protector.** Lerner Publications Company, 1992. 144 pp. ISBN 0-8225-4912-3.

This biography of John Muir describes a man of vision, whose reverence for nature bordered on the sentimental, yet who also had a strong core of practicality. Through exploring woods and fields, farming, walking tours, and mountaineering, John Muir developed an unshakable respect for the land. Torn between his contentment as a husband and father and his desire to leave society to live in and study remote regions, he nevertheless managed to succeed in both areas. Crusading tirelessly for national parks, he never lost sight of the importance of his family ties, though he compromised by living alone in the wilderness several months each year. Bibliography and index included.

21.40 Wadsworth, Ginger. **Rachel Carson: Voice for the Earth.** Lerner Publications Company, 1992. 128 pp. ISBN 0-8225-4907-7.

This biography discusses the many accomplishments of Rachel Carson, eminent naturalist and bestselling author. She began a lifetime of publishing at age eleven, was one of the few women of her generation to obtain a graduate degree in science, and wrote a controversial book condemning pesticides. Many black-and-white photographs show Rachel at all ages. The book includes many of Rachel's own quotes, an index, a bibliography, and a list of environmental organizations the reader can contact for further information.

21.41 Yep, Laurence. **The Lost Garden.** Julian Messner, 1991. 117 pp. ISBN 0-671-74160-8.

For much of his life, Laurence Yep did not appreciate his Chinese heritage. In fact, he had little to do with it at all—he occasionally visited his grandmother in San Francisco's Chinatown, but the Chinese culture did not interest him. After all, the sweets at Christmas were much superior to those at the Chinese New Year. It wasn't until Yep experienced culture shock as he began to attend school in the Midwest that he began to see the significance and majesty of his Chinese background. In this autobiography, Yep describes how he came to use his heritage in his writings and how he came to be one of America's emerging minority authors.

21.42   Zindel, Paul. **The Pigman & Me.** HarperCollins/Charlotte Zolotow Books, 1992. 168 pp. ISBN 0-06-020857-0.

"He'll want you to be his friend, to follow him, and in his eyes you'll see angels and monsters. Your pigman will come to you when you need him most." So wrote Paul Zindel, author of the acclaimed young adult book, *The Pigman.* This autobiography of Zindel details his teenage years on Staten Island when he found his own personal pigman, or mentor, living in the apartment downstairs. Fans of Zindel will read how this pigman, whose name was Nonno Frankie, influenced Zindel to become one of the best known young adult authors today. Black-and-white photographs and maps included.

Series

21.43   **Sports Immortals.** Crestwood House.

The Sports Immortals series explores the greatest moments in the careers of some of sports' greatest participants. From Jesse Owens, the black track star who broke records at the 1936 Berlin Olympics, to Babe Ruth, home-run hitter for baseball's New York Yankees, these books introduce readers to some of the legends whose records still stand today. Each book contains a trivia quiz about its featured immortal, and all the books contain bibliographies to lead young readers to more works about these sports legends.

21.44   **Wizards of Business.** Garrett Educational Corporation.

How does an ordinary person become wildly successful? The authors of this series cover amazing stories of business success in a variety of fields, ranging from rock music to computer science. One of the superstars, Helen Gurley Brown, held seventeen jobs in just a few years, before discovering her talent for editing. Another, Debbi Fields, was not particularly intelligent or academically successful. All, however, share a willingness to take risks, the ability to spend much more time working than the average person, and great enthusiasm for their chosen professions. That's what makes them wizards of business.

Collected Biographies

21.45   Faber, Doris, and Harold Faber. **Nature and the Environment.** Charles Scribner's Sons, 1991. 284 pp. ISBN 0-684-19047-8.

This book explores the lives of famous people who loved nature and devoted their lives to the study and preservation of it. A cross-section of people whose lives are an inspiration to others is presented, including Luther Burbank, George Washington Carver, Clifford Pinchot, John James Audubon, Charles Darwin, Theodore Roosevelt, Henry David Thoreau, Rachel Carson, and Jacques Cousteau. A Great Lives book.

21.46   Haskins, Jim. **Against All Opposition: Black Explorers in America.** Walker and Company, 1992. 128 pp. ISBN 0-8027-3138-1.

Though no one knows for sure how many black explorers passed into history without recognition for their accomplishments, this book focuses on nine adventurers whose bravery has not been overlooked. Each of these nine black men were instrumental in discovering new worlds, and this book details their individual lives, as well as their discoveries in geography. Includes bibliographical references and index.

21.47   Haskins, Jim. **Outward Dreams: Black Inventors and Their Inventions.** Bantam Books, 1991. 85 pp. ISBN 0-553-29480-6.

History tends to forget some of the significant people who have contributed to our civilization and our heritage. In this collection of stories about African American inventors and their inventions, the reader will meet brave, courageous people who overcame great odds to believe in their dreams and hopes. These are the people who made important discoveries that will be useful forever. Contains an appendix of significant inventions by African Americans.

21.48   Hoobler, Dorothy, and Thomas Hoobler. **Vanished!** Walker and Company, 1991. 201 pp. ISBN 0-8027-8148-9.

This book examines the controversies surrounding such famous disappearances as those of Judge Crater, hijacker D. B. Cooper, and the inhabitants of the Lost Colony, allowing readers to make up their own minds as to what actually happened. The book also contains some excellent photographs of the missing people. From the Fact or Fiction Files series.

21.49   Johnson, James E. **The Scots and Scotch Irish in America.** Lerner Publications Company, 1991. 71 pp. ISBN 0-8225-1038-3.

This is a brief history of the Scots and Scotch-Irish and their immigration to and settlement in the United States. Since their appearance in the new nation, members of this ethnic group have made substantial contributions to American life and culture. The book provides thumbnail sketches of how people of Scottish and Scotch-Irish descent have influenced American life.

21.50   Morey, Janet Nomura, and Wendy Dunn. **Famous Asian Americans.** Cobblehill Books, 1992. 170 pp. ISBN 0-525-65080-6.

In this book, the authors explore the personality traits that helped many well-known Asian Americans succeed in their chosen professions. Many of the subjects took risks, worked laboriously, and were willing to defy convention. Among the noted Asian Americans are a children's book illustrator, a world-class tennis player, a musician, a senator, and a physician/actor, as well as many others. Each chapter includes photos of the famous Asian Americans at various ages. Includes a bibliography and index.

21.51 Olsen, Frank H. **Inventors Who Left Their Brands on America.** Bantam Books, 1991. 191 pp. ISBN 0-553-29211-0.

Here are the stories of the men and women who founded Hallmark Cards, Wrigley's Chewing Gum, Levi's Jeans, J. C. Penney, Kraft Cheese, and Kellogg's Cereals, among others. Their stories are as different as the products themselves; some of these people became famous as teenagers while others declared bankruptcy before creating a famous product, and still others created their businesses out of a deep religious faith. Whatever the reason for their creativity, these inventors added their products to our world, making their names household names.

21.52 Pollard, Michael. **Absolute Rulers.** Garrett Educational Corporation, 1992. 48 pp. ISBN 1-56074-034-5.

From Charlemagne to Idi Amin, there have always been rulers who sought to lead their people with an iron fist. In this book, nineteen of history's most famous—and infamous—rulers are examined. What brings men like Adolf Hitler to power? How did Napoleon finally tumble from his emperor's throne in France? A Pioneers in History book.

21.53 Pollard, Michael. **People Who Care.** Garrett Educational Corporation, 1992. 48 pp. ISBN 1-56074-035-3.

Poverty, disease, mental illness, and hunger make the lives of many people all over the world miserable. However, there have been people throughout history who have cared enough to devote their lives to helping the unfortunate ones. In this book, nineteen short biographies are presented about these benevolent people and their contributions towards making our society a better place to live. A Pioneers in History book.

21.54 Pollard, Michael. **Thinkers.** Garrett Educational Corporation, 1992. 48 pp. ISBN 1-56074-036-1.

From the great philosopher Plato to the famed civil rights leader Nelson Mandela, history is dotted with great thinkers who shaped the way we see the world. Nineteen such thinkers are included in this anthology, from St. Thomas Aquinas to Mary Wollstonecraft. A time chart is included to indicate these thinkers' relationships to their eras and to each other. A Pioneers in History book.

21.55   Rappaport, Doreen. **Escape from Slavery: Five Journeys to Freedom.** Illustrated by Charles Lilly. HarperCollins, 1991. 117 pp. ISBN 0-06-021631-X.

In this book, the author historically documents five accounts of African Americans who risked all for freedom from pre-Civil War slavery. Readers follow the stories of Eliza, the historical prototype for the heroine of *Uncle Tom's Cabin;* Dosha, who helps his sisters Camelia and Selena outsmart the sheriff; Henry Brown, who mails himself to freedom; Jane and her sons, aided by freedman William Still, who challenges the laws of slavery; and Ellen and William, whose love for each other binds stronger than any chain of slavery.

21.56   Rappaport, Doreen. **Living Dangerously: American Women Who Risked Their Lives for Adventure.** HarperCollins, 1991. 117 pp. ISBN 0-06-025108-5.

This book presents six stories of American women who dared to defy convention to undertake dangerous adventures. Sketches include a woman who went over Niagara Falls in a barrel; a woman mountain climber in Peru; the first black woman pilot; an expedition to the Belgian Congo led by women; and a physically challenged woman competing in the New York City Marathon.

21.57   Sloate, Susan. **Hotshots: Baseball Greats of the Game When They Were Kids.** A Sports Illustrated for Kids Book, 1991. 116 pp. ISBN 0-316-79853-3.

This anthology includes mini-biographies of over twenty baseball heroes, from Babe Ruth to Bo Jackson. The three to four page summaries emphasize that each hero wasn't born a star;

each had to work hard and overcome obstacles to achieve his greatness. The summaries are enhanced by baseball statistics and numerous photographs including childhood photos of the stars.

22 Careers

22.1 Blumenthal, Howard J. **Careers in Baseball.** Little, Brown and Company, 1993. 163 pp. ISBN 0-316-10095-1.

Have you ever dreamed of having a job in baseball? After reading this book, it will be easy for you to picture yourself on the baseball field! Seventeen baseball professionals provide information on the kinds of careers that are possible in professional baseball, each giving specific advice on how to make your dream a reality.

22.2 Blumenthal, Howard J. **You Can Do It! Careers in Television.** Little, Brown and Company, 1992. 162 pp. ISBN 0-316-10076-5.

How many different careers are available in the field of television? This book provides a firsthand look at the wide variety of jobs in television—some in front of cameras, some behind the scenes. The reader meets twenty people who work in television. All of these people explain what they did to get where they are, provide details about the work they do and give advice for readers who are interested in TV careers.

22.3 Briggs, Carol S. **At the Controls: Women in Aviation.** Lerner Publications Company, 1991. 72 pp. ISBN 0-8225-1593-8.

The skies are not restricted to men alone; many women have been pioneers in the field of aviation over the past six decades. This book profiles four female aviators—Jackie Cochran, Sheila Scott, Jerrie Cobb, and Bonnie Tiburzi—and sketches the amazing careers and record-setting flights of such greats as Amelia Earhart and Beryl Markham.

22.4   Crisman, Ruth. **Hot Off the Press: Getting the News into Print.** Lerner Publications Company, 1991. 87 pp. ISBN 0-8225-1625-X.

Consider the hundreds of thousands of newspapers which are printed around the world each day. How are those newspapers produced? This book examines the process of newspaper production, from the journalists writing their stories to distributors sending their finished product around the world. The future of the printed media, the history of newspapers, and possible careers in journalism are also considered.

22.5   Ferrell, Nancy Warren. **The U.S. Air Force.** Lerner Publications Company, 1990. 72 pp. ISBN 0-8225-1433-8.

From its beginnings in 1907 with only three men flying bi-planes, the U.S. Air Force has grown to more than one million people flying sound-breaking jets. The text includes a description of the organization and structure of the Air Force, the enlistment requirements, the Air Force Academy, educational benefits, and much more.

22.6   Jaspersohn, William. **A Week in the Life of an Airline Pilot.** Little, Brown and Company, 1991. 96 pp. ISBN 0-316-45822-8.

Is it hard to be a pilot? Join one for a week and find out! This book provides a detailed account of seven days in the life of a commercial airline pilot on a trip from New York City to New Delhi, India, and home again. Black-and-white photographs highlight the duties and responsibilities of the job, as well as offer insight into the history of flight.

22.7   Krementz, Jill. **A Very Young Musician.** Photographs by Jill Krementz. Simon & Schuster, 1991. 48 pp. ISBN 0-671-72687-0.

Through photographs and words, this book details the trials and tribulations of striving to master a musical instrument. Study and practice—and strict devotion—are the keys to success as a young boy struggles to play the trumpet in this unusually told story.

22.8 Lantz, Fran. **Rock, Rap, and Rad: How to Be a Rock or Rap Star.** Avon, 1992. 215 pp. ISBN 0-380-76793-7.

"All of today's music stars started out just like you—with big dreams and no experience." By talking to dozens of people, going to rehearsals, and tracking down leads to managers, agents, promoters, and publicists, the author has assembled a "how to" for becoming a musician. Advice on dealing with auditions, your first gig, managers, and money are all provided. Readers will also find photos and helpful hints from the stars.

22.9 Lindblom, Steven. **Fly the Hot Ones.** Houghton Mifflin Company, 1991. 102 pp. ISBN 0-395-51075-9.

The eight aircraft represented in this book are the "radical extremes of flying," according to the author, who has flown many of the planes described. With the aid of definitions of unfamiliar terms, photographs, and simple diagrams, the author is able to put the reader in the pilot's seat from boarding to landing.

22.10 Morgan, Terri, and Shmuel Thaler. **Photography: Take Your Best Shot.** Lerner Publications Company, 1991. 72 pp. ISBN 0-8225-2302-7.

This book explains basic and advanced techniques of photography to help the amateur photographer improve picture-taking skills. The reader will learn how to see the way a camera "sees," set up shots, adjust for light, capture action, and take portraits. The book even explains how to develop black-and-white film and how to print photographs.

22.11 Schwartz, Perry. **How to Make Your Own Video.** Lerner Publications Company, 1991. 72 pp. ISBN 0-8225-2301-9.

How to Make Your Own Video provides helpful advice for the reader, including what kind of camera to buy, how to light scenes, and how to tell a story on tape. The book covers all of the technical basics behind making a home video and is illustrated with full-color and black-and-white photographs. This book is ideal for someone with a new camcorder or for someone who is deciding which camcorder will best suit their particular needs.

22.12 Warner, J. F. **The U.S. Marine Corps.** Lerner Publications Company, 1991. 88 pp. ISBN 0-8225-1432-X.

Do you think you want to join the Marines? This book is both informative and interesting, with details about how to enlist and how to become an officer. A retired Marine Corps officer describes the history of the U.S. Marine Corps, examines its struggles to remain a separate military branch, and offers details about life in the modern-day Marine Corps. The author makes use of many full-color and black-and-white photographs in this book about one of the smallest United States military services.

22.13 Wurmfeld, Hope Herman. **Trucker.** Photographs by Hope Herman Wurmfeld. Macmillan, 1990. 64 pp. ISBN 0-02-793581-7.

If you think you might want to be a trucker, you will want to read this account of a trucker's duties and responsibilities. This detailed story of one trucker's route and experiences is informative and written in an easy-to-understand language. The reader will learn that there is much more to a trucker's life than driving down the open highway listening to the radio.

Series

22.14 **Choices.** The Millbrook Press.

Through interviews and photographs, this series introduces readers to a variety of careers available to individuals with broad interests. Do you love animals but aren't sure what careers will allow you to work with them? Are you an expert in a foreign language but can't figure how to apply your skills?

This series has the answer. From people who love to perform to people who just like people, this series is bound to have something for you!

22.15   A Day in the Life of. . . . Troll Associates.

This series explores a full day in the life of men and women in a variety of professions. From the physical demands of an F.B.I. agent to the thrills of a professional baseball player, these books take the reader along on a day's labors and the failures and successes these men and women experience in their chosen careers.

22.16   Fashion World. Crestwood House.

Each book in this series explores a different realm in the fascinating world of fashion. Fame, fortune, fashion, and beauty—are these what being a model is all about? Welcome to the *real* world of modeling. In *Fashion Model,* we find out what it is to get started in modeling and what hard work it really can be. *Fashion Designer* and *Fashion Photographer* take us behind the scenes of the fashion world, and *Street Fashion* examines the clothes we wear every day and what those clothes say about us.

23 Physical and Emotional Health

23.1 Ackerman, Karen. **The Broken Boy.** Philomel Books, 1991. 160 pp. ISBN 0-399-22254-5.

When the Ferris family moves in next door to Solly and his family, Solly becomes friends with Daniel Ferris, who has been hospitalized for "temper tantrums." Their friendship is strengthened when they discover an old set of diaries left behind in the Ferris house and realize that Daniel's life parallels that of Martin Sawyer, the subject of those secret diaries. And throughout the two boys' friendship, Daniel seems to move closer and closer towards a serious tragedy.

23.2 Auch, Mary Jane. **Seven Long Years Until College.** Holiday House, 1991. 169 pp. ISBN 0-8234-0901-5.

Natalie takes her unorganized, scatterbrained mother's remarriage in stride. Even her sister's departure for college is not that upsetting. Then Natalie's new stepfather begins to organize Natalie's life. Her best friend is moving away, and her step-grandmother wants to redecorate the house. It's too much, and Natalie runs away to be with her sister at college. It will take cooperation from everyone for Natalie to work out her problems.

23.3 Cannon, A. E. **Amazing Gracie.** Delacorte Press, 1991. ISBN 0-385-30487-0.

Her mother is divorced, she has very few friends, and she's very unhappy. Gracie and her mother are like sisters, but then Gracie learns that she will have a stepfather and a little brother. Just how much can a girl take? Gracie's big problem becomes even bigger; her mother is so depressed that she takes too many pills. What can Gracie do? Where can she go? To whom can she turn for help? Can Amazing Gracie find a solution to her ever-growing collection of problems?

23.4   Cooper, Ilene. **The New, Improved Gretchen Hubbard.** Morrow Junior Books, 1992. 204 pp. ISBN 0-688-08432-X.

Gretchen, who had been called "Hippo Hubbard" by her middle school class, has slimmed down and definitely shaped up; the most obvious change is in the way her classmates now treat her. But being slim and popular doesn't solve all of Gretchen's problems, the biggest of which is her mother's planned move to Santa Fe from Illinois to pursue her career and to "find herself." Gretchen worries that her mother may stay in California permanently. Can Tim, a teenage movie star, take Gretchen's mind off of her problems? A Kids from Kennedy Middle School book.

23.5   Degens, T. **On the Third Ward.** Harper & Row, 1990. 243 pp. ISBN 0-06-021428-7.

At the end of World War II, Wanda is taken to the Hessian State Hospital for Children with Tuberculosis. Her world is filled with x-rays, pills, shots, dull gray pajamas, pain, and the personalities of the other sick children on the third ward. Among them are PB, in a cast from her neck down; Carla, whose hours are spent in endless romantic fantasies; and the Empress of China, a delicate girl whose wondrous stories blend fantasy and reality so that Wanda can hardly tell the difference. In this bleak existence, the children defy the rules, create diversions, and live for the moment of escape.

23.6   Durant, Penny Raife. **When Heroes Die.** Macmillan, 1992. 136 pp. ISBN 0-689-31764-6.

To twelve-year-old Gary, his Uncle Rob is a hero, a surrogate father, and a best friend. Then Uncle Rob becomes very, very sick. When Gary learns his uncle has AIDS, he worries that maybe he himself is gay, too, and that's why he gets tongue-tied when he talks to girls. Gary suddenly finds himself with many questions and fears, but he finds answers and comfort in Uncle Rob himself.

23.7 Geras, Adèle. **Watching the Roses.** Harcourt Brace Jovanovich, 1992. 152 pp. ISBN 0-15-294816-3.

Why has Alice stopped talking and withdrawn into her room? Through Alice's diary entries, she reveals that she was recently raped at her eighteenth birthday party, and now all she can do is sit, think, and watch the neglected roses die. No one—not her family, not her two best friends—can reach her in this modern version of the Sleeping Beauty fairy tale.

23.8 Holland, Isabelle. **The House in the Woods.** Little, Brown and Company, 1991. 194 pp. ISBN 0-316-37178-5.

Feeling overweight and unattractive, Bridget resents her adoptive father and wants to find her real father. She discovers an old house in the woods and is drawn to it. Intrigued enough to investigate, she soon finds clues to her past. What she learns offers a new insight and appreciation for her adopted family.

23.9 Johnson, Julie Tallard. **Celebrate You! Building Your Self-Esteem.** Lerner Publications Company, 1991. 67 pp. ISBN 0-8225-0046-9.

This book will help adolescents learn about the importance of self-esteem and about ways to boost their self-esteem. One important suggestion shows the reader how to replace negative thoughts of oneself with positive, esteem-building ideas. Readers should be sure to take the quiz in chapter one to determine the strength of their own self-esteem.

23.10 Kelleher, Victor. **Del-Del.** Illustrated by Peter Clarke. Walker and Company, 1992. 180 pp. ISBN 0-8027-8154-3.

Beth's sister has been dead one year exactly when her gifted seven-year-old brother Sam is suddenly possessed by an evil presence he calls Del-Del. Who is Del-Del? Is it a demon or a cunning being from another galaxy? Or is it something else? With her parents deep in the middle of marital problems, Beth may be the only one able to solve this mystery.

23.11   Kittredge, Mary. **Teens with AIDS Speak Out.** Julian Messner, 1991. 119 pp. ISBN 0-671-74542-5.

Teens who have contracted AIDS tell how having a fatal disease has changed their lives. They urge young people to avoid getting AIDS by using condoms or by having no sex until they are ready for the responsibility. They stress that it only takes one sexual act with an infected person or one time sharing a needle for intravenous drugs to contract the disease.

23.12   Langone, John. **Growing Older: What Young People Should Know About Aging.** Little, Brown and Company, 1991. 163 pp. ISBN 0-316-51459-4.

This is a provocative approach to the process of growing old, a process that teenagers need to think about. Objectively, the author presents the myths, realities, and problems of the aging process. While addressing how scientists are trying to slow down the aging process, the author also challenges the readers to project their own conceptions of what they will be like as an older adult. This is one in a series of books by John Langone that provides understanding and guidance to teenagers as they try to cope with adult issues.

23.13   Lipsyte, Robert. **The Chemo Kid.** HarperCollins, 1992. 167 pp. ISBN 0-06-020284-X.

The lump that Fred's girlfriend Mara finds on the back of Fred's neck is cancerous. But what might be a tragedy for someone else turns into a blessing for Fred when the drugs that he takes as part of his chemotherapy suddenly transform him from a wimp to a superhero. Are his superpowers enough to help him fight this personal battle?

23.14   Little, Jean. **Listen for the Singing.** HarperCollins, 1991. 262 pp. ISBN 0-06-023910-7.

Anna Golden and her family move from Germany to Canada in the 1930s. Anna faces many problems because her vision is so poor; she is often teased because of her thick glasses. Once World War II breaks out, she and her family must face resentment from people around them for their German heritage. Through her courage and perseverance, Anna helps others to cope with the tragedy of war, especially her brother, who is blinded during a battle.

23.15 Mayfield, Sue. **I Carried You on Eagles' Wings.** Lothrop, Lee & Shepard Books, 1991. 128 pp. ISBN 0-688-10597-1.

Tony feels his life is doubly hard as a minister's son with an invalid mother. Because he hates being teased, pitied, or ignored, he spends much of his time alone. Then, while walking along the beach one day, Tony finds a gull with a broken wing. Watching as the bird grows stronger and his mother grows weaker, Tony discovers the true meaning of his mother's favorite Bible passage, "He gives strength to the weary . . . They will soar on wings like eagles, they will run and not grow weary, they will walk and not grow faint. . . ."

23.16 McDaniel, Lurlene. **A Time to Die.** Bantam Books, 1992. 154 pp. ISBN 0-553-29809-7.

Kara Fischer is a sixteen-year-old junior in high school, and she has cystic fibrosis, a fatal genetic condition. The people closest to her, after her parents, are Vince, another CF victim, and Christy, their physical therapist. Kara does not see Vince as more than a friend who understands the illness that afflicts them both. When Christy's brother Eric moves from Houston to live with her, he is attracted to Kara, but avoids a relationship because he does not understand her illness. At Kara's last school activity, she and Eric overcome the barrier between them. Only after her last wish gift helps him realize a goal does Eric come to understand what a special person Kara was. Second in the *One Last Wish* series.

23.17 McDaniel, Lurlene. **Mother, Help Me Live.** Bantam Books, 1992. 136 pp. ISBN 0-553-29811-9.

Fifteen-year-old Sarah McGreggor needs a bone marrow transplant as a last chance to beat her leukemia. It is only then, when a donor is needed, that she learns she was adopted when she was only three days old. Her birth mother swore her adoptive parents to secrecy as a condition of the adoption. Now Sarah is caught between hurting her adoptive parents and finding her birth mother for a possible match, which would allow the transplant. When she is given $100,000 by a last wish foundation, Sarah must decide which road to take. Third in the *One Last Wish* series.

23.18 Perl, Lila. **Fat Glenda Turns Fourteen.** Clarion Books, 1991. 168 pp. ISBN 0-395-53341-4.

This is the story of a broken and mended friendship, of family and teenage relationships, and of Glenda's search for making sense of herself. Becoming a "plus-size" teen fashion model and making friends with the newest and fattest girl in town, Giselle, leads to self-acceptance for Glenda, who must remain fat to model, even if being overweight makes her unhappy.

23.19 The Scott Newman Center, with Beth Anne Munger. **Straight Talk with Kids: Improving Communication, Building Trust and Keeping Your Child Drug Free.** Bantam Books, 1991. 146 pp. ISBN 0-553-29352-4.

An introduction by Paul Newman and Joanne Woodward presents this book as a source of useful guidelines to help parents relax a little and "to raise kids that grow up and remain drug free." The book is divided into two parts: prevention and intervention. Some of this book's many suggestions include keeping communication open, confronting the child, and seeking professional treatment. An appendix documents commonly used illicit drugs and their effects.

23.20 Silverstein, Alvin, and Virginia B. Silverstein with Robert Silverstein. **So You Think You're Fat? All about Obesity, Anorexia Nervosa, Bulimia Nervosa, and Other Eating Disorders.** HarperCollins, 1991. 205 pp. ISBN 0-06-021641-7.

Why are some of us heavier than others? What are the causes behind "binging and purging"? This book focuses on eating disorders and the causes behind them. Tips on dieting, appreciation of self-image, consideration of fat intake, and the need for exercise are all stressed.

23.21 Sinykin, Sheri Cooper. **Next Thing to Strangers.** Lothrop, Lee & Shepard Books, 1991. 147 pp. ISBN 0-688-10694-3.

Overweight Cass McFerren finds herself spending the Christmas holidays with grandparents she has seen only one other time in her life. When she meets young Jordy Sondel, who is also visiting family in the trailer park, she decides the time may pass quickly. When Jordy and Cass take a long hike to the mountains, Jordy, a diabetic, passes out. Cass must get help for him, knowing that with every passing minute, Jordy's life becomes more endangered.

23.22 Taylor, Theodore. **The Weirdo.** Harcourt Brace Jovanovich, 1991. 289 pp. ISBN 0-15-294952-6.

The Powhatan National Wildlife Refuge is the setting for this story of a young man, his face disfigured as a result of an airplane crash, and a young woman who is an eyewitness to a murder. Samantha Sanders and Chip Clewt become fast friends as they try to solve the disappearance of Chips' friend and mentor, Thomas Telford, an environmentalist who specialized in the study of bears.

23.23 Wilson, Johnniece Marshall. **Poor Girl, Rich Girl.** Scholastic, 1992. 179 pp. ISBN 0-590-44732-7.

Miranda lives with a great family; everyone gets along most of the time and all do their part to share the chores. They love each other very much, but when it comes to buying contacts to replace thick lenses, Miranda is told they are not affordable and she will have to go without them. Not to be discouraged, Miranda spends the summer in various jobs, all the while thinking how much better she will look without her ugly old glasses. She is bound and determined to earn the money for her contacts herself.

23.24 Wood, June Rae. **The Man Who Loved Clowns.** G. P. Putnam's Sons, 1992. 224 pp. ISBN 0-399-21888-2.

Thirteen-year-old Delrita's goal is to be invisible in her new town's school. In the country, where she and her family once lived, she did not have to hide. Of course, Delrita was younger then and not so embarrassed by Uncle Punky, her mother's brother who has Down's syndrome. To avoid any further embarrassment, Delrita keeps her Uncle Punky a secret. Then Avanelle Shackleford's family moves to town, and Avanelle has an even bigger secret. Can the two teenagers share secrets and become friends? Avanelle seems to think so, and Delrita finds herself becoming more open about her life—until tragedy strikes.

24 Beyond Our Borders: People Outside the United States

24.1   Blair, David Nelson. **Fear the Condor.** Lodestar Books, 1992. 137 pp. ISBN 0-525-67381-4.

Bartolina, an Amarya Indian living in South America, might be ignorant, but she is not unintelligent. Though she has never even heard of reading or writing as her story begins, she knows enough about the world to distrust Fortunato, the man forcing her family to work someone else's land, for someone else's gain. When Amarya men are conscripted into the Bolivian army, Bartolina mourns the loss of her father, but even worse, she is forced to work for no wages cleaning house. When both of her grandparents die, Bartolina leaves home to seek a twin the village has ostracized. With her twin's help, Bartolina at last finds the courage to learn to read.

24.2   Brennan, J. H. **Shiva's Challenge: An Adventure of the Ice Age.** HarperCollins, 1992. 209 pp. ISBN 0-06-020826-0.

Shiva is awakened to face a trial of the six bowls. Five contain poison; the sixth does not. She must choose and drink. With spirit powers from her dead mother, Shiva makes the correct choice but is drugged and carried to a far-off cave. In this cave, other trials await her, as she learns she is being tested to become the next Crone, or shaman, of her tribe. Alone, with the snows of winter coming and a power struggle in a nearby clan beginning, Shiva does not find an easy path to success and safety. Sequel to *Shiva* and *Shiva Accused.*

24.3   Choi, Sook Nyul. **Year of Impossible Goodbyes.** Houghton Mifflin Company, 1991. 169 pp. ISBN 0-395-57419-6.

Living in Pyongyang, Korea, during the days of the Japanese occupation, a young girl relates her family's struggle to survive. Her mother is forced to operate a sock factory until the war with Japan is over, and liberation only brings the Russians and a new kind of terror. Learning that her father and three elder brothers have somehow survived Japanese prison camps and made it south of the 38th parallel, the mother, younger brother, and sister face more obstacles to join them in the American-occupied South Korea.

24.4 Drucker, Olga Levy. **Kindertransport.** Henry Holt, 1992. 146 pp. ISBN 0-8050-1711-9.

From December 1938 until August 1939, some ten thousand Jewish children between the ages of four and seventeen were sent to safety in England. Of that number, only one thousand ever saw their families again. Olga Levy was one of the lucky ones. Arriving in England at eleven, she spent six years—the war years—in various homes. Her older brother, Hans, who had arrived before her, worked or was imprisoned with other Germans, both Jewish and non-Jewish, after the war began on September 1, 1939. Olga's parents obtained a visa to the U.S. one day before the consulate was closed in Stuttgart, but it was not until 1946 that the entire family was reunited in New York.

24.5 Farley, Carol. **Korea: Land of the Morning Calm.** Dillon Press, 1991. 127 pp. ISBN 0-87518-464-2.

Emphasizing the political rift between North and South Korea, the author explores everything from ancient history, major religions such as Confucianism and Buddhism, to current politics and daily life. Emphasis is also placed on Korean arts, including dance, poetry, sculpture, and painting, discussing the similarities and differences between North and South Korea. Color photographs, glossary, bibliography, index, and list of addresses where readers can obtain further information are included.

24.6 Gee, Maurice. **The Fire-Raiser.** Houghton Mifflin Company, 1992. 172 pp. ISBN 0-395-62428-2.

Set in a small New Zealand town in 1915, this is the tale of four friends who pool their ideas and push their limits as they attempt to learn the identity of the arsonist who is burning their town and terrifying their neighbors. Can Kitty Wix and her friends stop the arsonist? Or will the arsonist corner them in the bell tower and stop them?

24.7 Hiçyilmaz, Gaye. **Against the Storm.** Little, Brown and Company, 1992. 200 pp. ISBN 0-316-36078-3.

Mehmet, a young boy from a rural Turkish village, does not believe that life will be easier in the city. Haryi, Mehmet's former best friend and village genius, left to study in the city, and no one has heard from him since. Once settled in the city of Ankara, Mehmet's worst fears are realized. Ankara is crowded, dirty, and even poorer than the rural village. However, Mehmet's new friend, Muhlis, a streetwise orphan, makes life bearable with his steady humor and generosity. When the two boys see Haryi at last, apparently driven insane by poverty, they decide to do what they can to help, with surprising results.

24.8 Ho, Minfong. **The Clay Marble.** Farrar, Straus and Giroux, 1991. 160 pp. ISBN 0-374-31340-7.

Twelve-year-old Dara and her family flee their war-torn Cambodia for a refugee camp on the border with Thailand. She makes friends with Juntee, whose family shares food with them and teaches them the way to survive. Juntee keeps faith in the promise of the future and encourages Dara to do the same, even if hope is only made of clay.

24.9 Hotze, Sollace. **Summer Endings.** Clarion Books, 1991. 165 pp. ISBN 0-395-56197-3.

Christine is excited that World War II is ending, and she longs for word about her father, who has been a political prisoner in Poland for many years. Along with endings are beginnings in Christine's life, as she fills in as a soda jerk at a drugstore and as her sister gets married. Will her father rejoin the family that had to leave him behind? Will the waiting ever end?

24.10 Houston, James. **Drifting Snow: An Arctic Search.** Margaret K. McElderry Books, 1992. 150 pp. ISBN 0-689-50563-9.

At the age of two, Apoutee, now Elizabeth Queen, was taken south from her Inuit home on Nisok Island. Her life was saved from the threatening tuberculosis, but the records and identification of her family were all lost. Now, some twelve years later, Elizabeth has returned to search out her identity and to learn the language and life of her nomadic people. With those who have accepted her into their clan, Elizabeth travels from the winter home to the summer hunting grounds and shares the risks and perils of life in the Arctic wilderness.

24.11 Kordon, Klaus. **Brothers Like Friends.** Translated from the German by Elizabeth D. Crawford. Philomel Books, 1992. 206 pp. ISBN 0-399-22137-9.

Frank idolizes his older brother, Burkie, a talented soccer player. Both boys idolize their mother, until she remarries. She and "Uncle Willi" seem happy at first, though Frank and Burkie resent the new, harsh discipline Uncle Willi insists upon. Frank works hard to accept his new stepfather, wanting to please both Burkie and his mother. Their family life seems stable until Burkie swears Frank to secrecy after Burkie receives a soccer injury; it is then that Frank learns the harm that can result from listening to a beloved brother rather than to your own common sense. Originally published in 1978.

24.12 Laird, Elizabeth. **Kiss the Dust.** Dutton Children's Books, 1991. 281 pp. ISBN 0-525-44893-4.

Thirteen-year-old Tara is a Kurd living a normal teenage life in Iraq when Iraqi soldiers and secret police begin to terrorize the Kurdish people. Tara and her family must leave their home and hide in the mountains of northern Iraq, where they live in the filth and poverty of refugee camps to avoid being killed. This fictional but realistic struggle of one family gives insights into Middle Eastern problems and their effects on family life.

24.13 Leathers, Noel L. **The Japanese in America.** Lerner Publications Company, 1991. 64 pp. ISBN 0-8225-1042-1.

Tracing the history of Japanese immigration to the U.S., the author discusses both the hardships Japanese-Americans have faced, as well as contributions they have made to American life. Many Japanese emigrated to the U.S. in the hopes of a higher standard of living, and in these hopes they were usually disappointed. In spite of economic and social problems, many Japanese-Americans have made significant contributions to American society, becoming astronauts, senators, and leaders in business, medicine, the arts, entertainment, and literature.

24.14 Lutzeier, Elizabeth. **The Coldest Winter.** Holiday House, 1991. 153 pp. ISBN 0-8234-0899-X.

In this tale of one family's struggle to stay alive after the potato blight in Ireland in 1846, English soldiers drive Eamonn and his family from their home, which is then torn down. With nowhere to go and little hope for the future, Eamonn and his family struggle to survive during the coldest winter Ireland has ever known.

24.15 Macdonald, Caroline. **Speaking to Miranda.** HarperCollins/Willa Perlman Books, 1990. 251 pp. ISBN 0-06-021102-4.

When Ruby was only a toddler, her mother, Emma, died in a swimming accident. Her stepfather tried unsuccessfully to find Emma's relatives after her death, finally deciding to adopt Ruby and bring her up as his own daughter. Now, at eighteen, Ruby decides she must know more about her mother's puzzling past. Her quest for answers leads her to uncover startling things about herself.

24.16 Matas, Carol. **Sworn Enemies.** Bantam Books, 1993. 144 pp. ISBN 0-553-08326-0.

From 1827 to 1856, young Jewish boys were conscripted into the Russian army. Because many were taken at ages eight or nine, most had forgotten their Jewish heritage by the time they became adults. Zev and Aaron both love Miriam. Aaron has evaded the Russian army because his father has paid to keep him out of it so that he can attend school to become a rabbi;

Zev has evaded the army because he works each year as a khapper, one who captures young boys for the army—thus saving his own skin. These two bitter enemies begin a journey which will eventually lead to one of them living with Miriam in England, free of the Russian army altogether.

24.17   Merino, José María. **The Gold of Dreams.** Translated by Helen Lane. Farrar, Straus and Giroux, 1991. 217 pp. ISBN 0-374-52692.

Miguel Villace is taken on a trip of discovery in post-Cortez New Spain by his godfather, his dead father's best friend. Proud to be included in this important search for gold, Miguel is still confused by his Indian grandfather's warning to him the night before the expedition departs. Miguel sees his world with the Spanish eyes of his father but questions with the Indian heart of his mother, and he makes discoveries which will only hurt those left behind and yet prove him to be a man. He must grow up fast as his two worlds pull him in opposite directions.

24.18   Nixon, Joan Lowery. **Land of Hope.** Bantam Books, 1992. 171 pp. ISBN 0-553-08110-1.

Rebekah Levinsky and her family flee Russia in 1902 because life has become unsafe for Jews. Along with her family, Rebekah boards a ship in Germany, bound for New York City and the promise Uncle Avir has made for a good future. Upon landing, the family learns that life is not going to be what they had dreamed; but instead, it will be hard work and will require much sacrifice. However, Rebekah's dream of an education is not an impossibility for a girl in this new land. With hope, even the sweatshop her family must run does not seem so harsh. First in the Ellis Island trilogy.

24.19   Orlev, Uri. **The Man from the Other Side.** Translated from the Hebrew by Hillel Halkin. Houghton Mifflin Company, 1991. 186 pp. ISBN 0-395-53808-4.

What was the Warsaw Ghetto like for children who lived in it and for those who lived near it? What was it like to be on the other side? This is the story of Marek, an eleven-year-old boy who helps his stepfather smuggle food to sell in the Ghetto. When he becomes involved in the Ghetto uprising, Marek begins to see the world differently. After doubting the existence of God, he comes to feel the vastness of God within himself. Originally published in 1989.

24.20 Pfeiffer, Christine. **Poland: Land of Freedom Fighters.** Dillon Press, 1991. 143 pp. ISBN 0-87518-464-2.

Poland's geography, history, culture, and religion are covered in this text, which is enhanced by numerous color photographs, a pronunciation guide, glossary, bibliography, index, and maps. The reader learns about famous Poles such as Chopin, Joseph Conrad, Copernicus, and Pope John Paul II. The vast history of Poland's struggle for independence and the wars with Sweden, Turkey, and Russia are covered, as are facts about its kings, queens, legends, holiday customs, educational system, and typical family life. Even recipes for a traditional Polish meal are provided.

24.21 Schlein, Miriam. **I Sailed with Columbus.** Illustrated by Tom Newsom. HarperCollins, 1991. 136 pp. ISBN 0-06-022513-0.

"My name is Julio . . . I am twelve and . . . the Franciscan Brothers have taught me to write. At first I thought it was for this reason the ship's master took me on. . . . Later I found out there was another reason." So says Julio, an orphan who is in town to sell canaries for the monastery when he sees the three ships in port. He helps load the boats, singing as he works. His singing results in his chance to sail on the Santa Maria with the great Cristobal Colon!

24.22 Schlein, Miriam. **The Year of the Panda.** Illustrated by Kam Mak. Thomas Y. Crowell, 1990. 83 pp. ISBN 0-690-04864-5.

Set in China, this fictional book concerns a young boy who finds a baby giant panda and tries to save its life. Behind the fiction of the story are woven true situations and facts about the problems facing the daxiong mao—giant panda—an animal that is nearing extinction.

24.23 Sender, Ruth Minsky. **The Holocaust Lady.** Macmillan, 1992.
192 pp. ISBN 0-02-781832-2.

The Holocaust Lady, an English teacher, recounts to her students her story of survival during WWII in a concentration
camp in Poland. Because she survived while all of her family
died, she feels a responsibility to tell the story of her family
and her survival, so that no one will ever forget the ordeal
millions of people went through at that time in history. The
story teller is "doomed" to relive the nightmare of fear in her
dreams, and can only hope and pray that all of her family now
will remain safe and secure.

24.24 Strasser, Todd. **The Diving Bell.** Scholastic, 1992. 159 pp.
ISBN 0-590-44620-7.

The women in Culca's village weave, cook, and do other
"womanly" things while the men and boys dive for pearl oys-
ters and mother-of-pearl. Culca cannot understand why she
must weave when she would rather dive. Then the Spanish
occupiers of her land enslave the divers in an attempt to sal-
vage sunken ships loaded with gold for Spain. In a desperate
attempt to save her brother Tulore from certain death, Culca
convinces the governor she knows a way to dive deep enough
to rescue the gold, and she unveils her invention—a diving
bell. Can she save Tulore?

24.25 Sutcliff, Rosemary. **The Shining Company.** Farrar, Straus and
Giroux, 1992. 296 pp. ISBN 0-374-46616-5.

Britain in 600 A.D. is about to be invaded by the Saxons. At
first, young Prosper, who tells the story, is unaware of the
threat and continues to enjoy his life with his servant, Conn,
and his beautiful friend, Luned. Then, as a shieldbearer, he
faces many great dangers fighting alongside the three hundred
select, trained warriors to stop the Saxon invasion. Includes a
guide to pronunciation.

24.26 Thomson, Peggy. **City Kids in China.** Photographs by Paul S.
Conklin. HarperCollins, 1991. 114 pp. ISBN 0-06-021654-9.

In this depiction of life for the Chinese children who live in the city of Changsha, a collection of interesting photographs display the Chinese way of life, their various customs, beliefs, and upbringings, many of which are very different from the American culture. How different can it be? You might be surprised.

24.27 Vogel, Ilse-Margaret. **Bad Times, Good Friends: A Personal Memoir.** Harcourt Brace Jovanovich, 1992. 239 pp. ISBN 0-15-205528-2.

Ilse Vogel, a German, lived in Berlin during Hitler's rule of Germany. She describes how she and her friends defied Hitler to try to hasten his downfall. These ordinary people lived in constant fear of air raids, of being turned in by Hitler sympathizers, and of starving because of a constant lack of food. Her narrative reveals everyday problems that history books do not contain, such as the struggle to save pieces of German culture which Hitler wanted destroyed, the dangerous effort to hide Jews, the endless hunt for necessities on the black market, and the neverending battle to maintain sanity amidst the destruction and death.

24.28 Vos, Ida. **Hide and Seek.** Translated by Terese Edelstein and Inez Smidt. Houghton Mifflin Company, 1991. 132 pp. ISBN 0-395-56470-0.

Rachel is growing up during a difficult time: the Germans have occupied her native Holland. First they make her wear a gold star; then she's forbidden to go to school, play outside, or keep her toys. Finally, she and her family must go into hiding, and she even has to give up her name. She and her sister are often separated from their parents as they're hidden by one courageous Christian family after another. This survival story tells of endurance and the bravery shown by people of many faiths confronting a common enemy.

24.29 Weaver-Gelzer, Charlotte. **In the Time of Trouble.** Dutton Children's Books, 1993. 267 pp. ISBN 0-525-44973-6.

Twins Jessie and Joshua Howells attend a missionary boarding school with their younger sister, Cassie. The political upheaval in Cameroun in the late 1950s seems unimportant next to the excitement Jessie feels as she plans to attend school the next year in Egypt. Then the telegram comes announcing the children's parents are missing; they have been caught between the opposing forces as Cameroun struggles to rid itself of the colonial power of France. As the days wear on, the children begin to consider plans for returning to the United States while trying to accept the fact that they may now be orphans.

24.30   Yue, Charlotte, and David Yue. **Christopher Columbus: How He Did It.** Houghton Mifflin Company, 1992. 136 pp. ISBN 0-395-52100-9.

Why would Columbus dare to sail into uncharted waters? How could he be sure his calculations regarding the type of boats, amounts of food, and length of passage required were correct? Why would sailors tolerate cramped quarters, worm-infested food, and dangerous weather on three ships bound for adventure? This book discusses the motives and desires of Columbus and his men and reveals the dangers of their journey.

25 Against an American Backdrop: Realistic Books Set in the United States

25.1 Avi. **The True Confessions of Charlotte Doyle.** Illustrated by Ruth E. Murray. Avon, 1992. 232 pp. ISBN 0-380-71475-2.

In the summer of 1832, Charlotte Doyle sails on her father's company ship the *Seahawk,* bound for America from England. Even as the only passenger, she soon learns that the crew is afraid of Captain Jaggary because he caused the death of a shipmate on an earlier voyage. Siding with the Captain because he is a gentleman, Charlotte reports a planned mutiny of the crew. Suddenly, the tables are turned and Charlotte, despite all of her good intentions, is accused of the murder of the first mate!

25.2 Avi. **"Who Was That Masked Man, Anyway?"** Orchard Books, 1992. 170 pp. ISBN 0-531-05457-8.

Franklin D. Wattleson would much rather listen to the radio, with its heroes like the Lone Ranger, the Green Hornet, and Buck Rogers, than do school work. His parents think just the opposite. Beyond Frankie's world of fantasy, the real world of World War II has Frankie's brother Tom in the army, both of Frankie's parents working, and a medical student boarding in Tom's room. When Tom comes home wounded and will not leave the house, Frankie enlists his friend Mario, and together they use all of their secret spy talents learned from radio to help get everyone back to normal.

25.3 Beatty, Patricia. **Jayhawker.** Morrow Junior Books, 1991. 224 pp. ISBN 0-688-09850-9.

Lije Tulley's parents are abolitionists and friends of the famous John Brown himself. Wanting to personally help the cause of the abolitionists, Lije hires himself out as a spy for the Kansas militia. He is sent to live with Lotta, whose farmhouse is a stopover for Kansas Redlegs and bushwackers. Her friends include two men named Frank and Jesse James and a fearful man who calls himself Charley Quantrill.

25.4   Beatty, Patricia. **Who Comes with Cannons?** Morrow Junior Books, 1992. 186 pp. ISBN 0-688-11028-2.

Truth Hopkins has been sent to live with her uncle's family in North Carolina just prior to the Civil War. Because they are Quakers, the entire family is scorned by most of their neighbors, who are strongly in favor of secession and war. Truth learns by accident that the farmhouse is a station on the Underground Railroad. When Truth is sent on an important mercy mission, she finds herself sneaking behind enemy lines and into a Union prisoner-of-war camp in New York state.

25.5   Branscum, Robbie. **Old Blue Tilley.** Macmillan, 1991. 90 pp. ISBN 0-02-711931-9.

Hambone, fourteen, lives with Old Blue Tilley, a circuit-riding preacher, until he's old enough to reclaim the land his parents left to him. In the spring, he and Tilley ride up in the Ozark mountains to visit the mountain folks and attend the revival meeting, discovering as they go that Oxalee, Old Blue's sworn enemy, has been everywhere before them. This year, on the eve of World War II, they meet a variety of unusual people on what may well be their last trip together.

25.6   Collier, James Lincoln, and Christopher Collier. **The Clock.** Illustrated by Kelly Maddox. Delacorte Press, 1992. 161 pp. ISBN 0-385-30037-9.

Anne's father signs his daughter on to a year at the mill, never mind that she always wanted to be a teacher. Frustrated and resentful, Anne hates working at the mill, even though she sees more of Robert, the boy she hopes to marry someday. The overseer of the mill, Mr. Hoggart, is a cruel thief; worst of all, he seems jealous of Robert. Mr. Hoggart tries to coerce Anne into a relationship, insisting he will ensure her better working conditions if she cooperates. No one believes Anne when she reveals this; her father obviously does not *want* to believe, since he needs the money so desperately. When Anne and Robert catch Mr. Hoggart stealing wool, he responds by punishing Robert, with tragic results.

25.7 Cormier, Robert. **Tunes for Bears to Dance To.** Delacorte Press, 1992. 101 pp. ISBN 0-385-30818-3.

Henry's family has moved to a new town in an effort to overcome the death of Henry's brother, but Henry's father only sinks deeper into depression as Henry and his mother struggle to provide food and shelter. At the craft center, Henry's only refuge from his troubles, Henry is drawn to Mr. Levine, a concentration camp survivor of World War II, who works on a model village that re-creates the real one which was destroyed in the war. When Henry is manipulated into doing something which betrays Mr. Levine and his friendship with Henry, Henry comes to know true evil and learns something important about grief and anger.

25.8 Davis, Ossie. **Just Like Martin.** Simon & Schuster, 1992. 215 pp. ISBN 0-671-73202-1.

In Alabama in the 1960s, members of Holy Oak Baptist Church are planning their trip to the great civil rights march in Washington, D.C. Little Stone will not be attending the march, in spite of being the youth leader of the church. He is needed at home: his father has returned to the U.S. from the Korean War and has to deal with the death of Little's mother. Little's father is angry and bitter with man and God, and Little doesn't wish to upset his father further. Then a bomb goes off in the church killing two of Little Stone's friends and outraging Little. Against his father's wishes, Little, with the support of Martin Luther King, Jr., organizes a youth march in honor of his friends.

25.9 Dillon, Eilís. **Children of Bach.** Charles Scribner's Sons, 1992. 164 pp. ISBN 0-684-19440-6.

Pali, Suzy, and Peter come home from school one day during World War II to find their musician parents missing. Even Aunt

Eva, who kept house for the family, is gone. Joined by their friend David, whose parents are also missing, the children learn that the Germans have taken away their parents. Neighbors piece together a story of arrests in the Jewish community all over Budapest. When Aunt Eva eventually returns after outwitting the Nazis, it is clear that the family must leave Hungary—possibly forever.

25.10   Forman, James D. **Becca's Story.** Charles Scribner's Sons, 1992. 180 pp. ISBN 0-684-19332-9.

Becca Case is a delightful young girl living in Indiana before, during, and after the Civil War. At fifteen, she is courted by two charmers, Alex, who is shy and serious, and Charlie, who is impulsive and funny. The war makes it possible for her to avoid choosing immediately between the two when they both enlist. But tragedy strikes, and Becca finds that the horrors of war have denied her a chance to choose; one of her charming suitors is killed. This book is constructed from actual journals that are a part of the author's family heritage.

25.11   Green, Connie Jordan. **Emmy.** Macmillan, 1992. 152 pp. ISBN 0-689-50556-6.

Eleven-year-old Emmy Morfield must assume responsibilities early when her father is injured in a coal-mining accident in the 1920s. To help her mother, brothers, and sisters survive, Emmy cooks for boarders, helps raise the children, and aids Pa, who cannot cope with his injury. And while Emmy struggles to keep the family's home together, her fourteen-year-old brother takes their father's place in the mine where Pa was injured.

25.12   Gregory, Kristiana. **Earthquake at Dawn.** Gulliver Books, 1992. 187 pp. ISBN 0-15-200446-7.

On April 18, 1906, when the great earthquake rocked San Francisco, two young ladies, one of whom was the famous photographer Edith Irvine, risked their lives to get forbidden photographs of the death and devastation that resulted from the disaster. In this historical novel, their adventures together provide an exciting account of what really happened when the earth shook in California.

25.13 Hamm, Diane Johnston. **Bunkhouse Journal.** Charles Scribner's Sons, 1990. 89 pp. ISBN 0-684-19206-3.

It is the winter of 1911 when seventeen-year-old Sandy Mannix runs away from his drunk and abusive father and their dismal Denver boarding house to his cousin Karen's Wyoming sheep ranch. After the summer hands leave, he stays alone in the bunkhouse and helps Karen's husband John with chores. He befriends Joanne, a girl at a nearby ranch, and learns to reach out to others. But Sandy is often lonely, and the work is cold and hard. Telling the story through his journal, Sandy grows into manhood, overcomes hardships, and takes charge of his future.

25.14 Henry, Marguerite. **King of the Wind: The Story of the Godolphin Arabian.** Illustrated by Wesley Dennis. Aladdin Books, 1991. 173 pp. ISBN 0-689-71486-6.

This Newbery Medal book is the remarkable story of a young, mute, Moroccan horse-boy and his love for the beautiful bay stallion, Sham. Their adventures from the time they leave the Sultan's palace to be a gift for the French boy-king Louis XV to their life of destitution in the street markets of Paris, false imprisonment in London, and Sham's eventual recognition as the sire of world-famous race horses, is a tribute to their dedication to one another. Based on a true story.

25.15 Keehn, Sally M. **I Am Regina.** Philomel Books, 1991. 240 pp. ISBN 0-399-21797-5.

Regina is only eleven when Indians kill her father and brother. She and her sister, Barbara, are adopted into different tribes. Separated from everyone she knows, Regina at first feels only hatred for the Indians. Gradually, however, she realized that they have been just as badly hurt by the settlers, and as the years pass, Regina begins to forget her life before the capture. She takes an Indian name, learns the ways of the tribe, and even learns their language. When most of the tribe—her family, Regina now feels—is lost to smallpox or war, Regina mourns. Eventually, however, she is reunited with her birth mother, a woman she no longer recognizes. Based on a true story.

25.16 Koller, Jackie French. **Nothing to Fear.** Gulliver Books, 1991. 288 pp. ISBN 0-15-200544-7.

In this story about the Garvey family during the Depression, Danny's father must leave home to find work to support his family. At thirteen, Danny must take on new responsibilities. And though he is forced to beg for food, he has a strong sense of family pride and commitment, which grows stronger when his mother becomes ill.

25.17 Koller, Jackie French. **The Primrose Way.** Harcourt Brace Jovanovich, 1992. 271 pp. ISBN 0-15-256745-3.

In 1633, sixteen-year-old Rebekah Hall sails from England with her friend Eliza Walker to join Rebekah's father and other Puritan settlers. When Rebekah is chosen to learn the language of the local tribe in the New World, she invites an Indian girl to live with her and to share learning each other's language. Rebekah soon begins to question the wisdom of the elders in her own community, who consider the natives to be savage heathens, something Rebekah knows they are not. As she learns the language and begins to understand the culture and gentle nature of Qunnequawise and her people, Rebekah is torn between the two worlds. Bibliography included.

25.18 Lawson, Robert. **The Great Wheel.** Illustrated by Robert Lawson. Walker and Company, 1993. 192 pp. ISBN 0-8027-7392-3.

At eighteen, Conn answers the desperate plea of his Uncle Michael in New York to travel from Ireland to help Michael in his business. On board the ship to America, Conn meets Trudy, whose family is going to be with relatives in Wisconsin. After only nine months in New York, Conn finds himself spirited away by another uncle, Patrick, an iron worker who is building Mr. Ferris's giant wheel for the 1893 fair. Even after that technical marvel is completed, Conn stays on to help operate it—all the while dreaming of Trudy and a farm life with her. Originally published in 1957.

25.19 Lyons, Mary E. **Letters from a Slave Girl: The Story of Harriet Jacobs.** Charles Scribner's Sons, 1992. 142 pp. ISBN 0-684-19446-5.

Harriet Jacobs, born into slavery, was owned by a Miss Horniblow, who taught her to read. On Horniblow's death, rather than being set free as she had hoped, Harriet became the property of James Norcom. Avoiding his sexual advances, Harriet finally faked an escape to the North by hiding for seven years in the attic of her grandmother's house until safe escape became possible. This book, written in the form of letters to various Jacobs family members, is based on the actual autobiography Harriet Jacobs wrote. That autobiography was important in the abolition movement for exposing sexual abuse slave women encountered from white males. Black-and-white photographs, bibliography, and drawings are included.

25.20 Markle, Sandra. **The Fledglings.** Bantam Books, 1992. 162 pp. ISBN 0-553-07729-5.

Aunt Mildred has two small daughters and is eight months pregnant with her third child. Kate recoils at the idea of becoming a built-in babysitter for her two cousins, but what choice is left after her mother's death in an auto accident? Then she overhears neighbors discussing her grandfather, a grandfather she always thought was dead. Kate scrapes together enough money to buy a bus ticket to Cherokee in the Qualla Boundary, where she has learned her grandfather, Tsan, lives. When she arrives, Tsan, who lives close to nature, alone with his dog, will not allow himself to love her for fear of losing her as he once did her long-dead father. Yet when Kate rescues an eagle fledgling whose parents poachers have stolen, Tsan sees himself and his love of nature in Kate.

25.21 Matas, Carol. **Code Name Kris.** Charles Scribner's Sons, 1990. 152 pp. ISBN 0-684-19208-X.

During World War II, hundreds of Danish teenagers joined secret resistance movements against the Nazis. Jesper, one such teenager, is alone in a prison cell when the book opens. As he waits for death, he looks back on the events that brought him to the cell. At first, Jesper (code name Kris) participates in sabotage missions; later, he works for an underground newspaper, falling in love with Janicke, another writer. When Janicke is killed, Jesper grows even more desperate, until he is willing to risk everything for revenge. Sequel to *Lisa's War.*

25.22   Meyer, Carolyn. **Where the Broken Heart Still Beats: The Story of Cynthia Ann Parker.** Gulliver Books, 1992. 194 pp. ISBN 0-15-295602-6.

When raiding other tribes and white settlements, many Native American tribes carried away children to adopt and to replace those of their own who had died. Cynthia Ann Parker was taken by Comanches on May 19, 1836, and recaptured by Texas Rangers on December 18, 1860. This story details the four years of Cynthia Ann's life after she rejoined her white family. It was not a happy time; Cynthia Ann, or Naduah, as she was called by the Comanches, had been the wife of a Comanche chief, Peta Nocona. One of her two sons by Nacona, Quanah, became one of the last Native Americans to accept defeat by the whites. This retelling of her story builds on historical fact and tribal lore to explain what might have been.

25.23   Moore, Robin. **Maggie among the Seneca.** J. B. Lippincott, 1990. 104 pp. ISBN 0-397-32455-3.

After her mother dies, sixteen-year-old Maggie sets out west across Pennsylvania to find her Aunt Franny. When she is captured by a band of Seneca warriors, she joins them and learns to appreciate the beauty of the natural rhythms of Seneca Indian life. But nature has its dangerous power, too, and once again Maggie faces tragedy and loss and must draw on her courage to survive.

25.24 Moore, Yvette. **Freedom Songs.** Puffin Books, 1991. 168 pp. ISBN 0-14-036017-4.

It's Easter of 1963, and Sheryl's family heads to North Carolina from Brooklyn to visit Shery's grandmother. Faced with Jim Crow laws and attitudes unfamiliar to her life in New York, Sheryl watches freedom schools emerge and cautious but determined relatives struggle for equal rights. Returning to New York, Sheryl and her friends organize a gospel concert to raise money for the freedom movement in the South. When tragedy strikes, the reality of the struggle becomes even more personal to Sheryl and her family. For Sheryl, hatred and bigotry fought with nonviolence gives new meaning to the lyrics, "Ain't gonna let nobody turn me 'round!"

25.25 Rinaldi, Ann. **A Ride into Morning: The Story of Tempe Wick.** Gulliver Books, 1991. 304 pp. ISBN 0-15-200573-0.

The American Revolution against the British is in full swing, and the Pennsylvania line is stationed on Tempe Wick's farm. The hardships and suffering of the soldiers are real; many have little food or clothing but are expected to fight the British. Tempe may be the only person who can thwart the mutinous conspiracy to steal Tempe's horse, a prize the soldiers desperately want. Many of the characters in this book were based on real people of that era.

25.26 van Raven, Pieter. **A Time of Troubles.** Charles Scribner's Sons, 1990. 180 pp. ISBN 0-684-19212-8.

Roy Purdy is a fourteen-year-old boy who suffers the pain of being an adult as he withstands the hardships of poverty, separation, and exploitation during the Depression. After his father is released from prison, Roy abandons his security and "rides the rails" to California with his father. As they travel, Roy discovers that his father is a shiftless man who believes the world "owes him." Eventually, Roy finds himself on the opposite side of his father during a citrus pickers' strike.

25.27 Voigt, Cynthia. **David and Jonathan.** Scholastic, 1992. 249 pp. ISBN 0-590-45165-0.

Henry Marr comes from an established New England family, but his best friend Jonathan is Jewish and excluded from many exclusive clubs. This has not hurt their friendship; maybe it has even strengthened it. Then Jonathan's cousin, David, a survivor of the Holocaust, comes to live with Jonathan's family. He has had psychological problems, been hospitalized, and is considered suicidal. David seems to enjoy disrupting Jon and Henry's friendship and even Jonathan's family life. The question is: just how far will David go?

25.28   Wallace, Bill. **Buffalo Gal.** Holiday House, 1992. 185 pp. ISBN 0-8234-0943-0.

Spunky fifteen-year-old Amanda Guthridge is horrified when her liberated mother plans a trip to Texas to "save the buffalo." Amanda much prefers the refinements of turn-of-the-century San Francisco society to the rigors of life on the trail. Therefore, she is quite surprised that she enjoys her adventures and actually falls in love with the handsome, but arrogant, David Talltree.

25.29   Wilton Katz, Welwin. **Whalesinger.** Margaret K. McElderry Books, 1990. 212 pp. ISBN 0-689-50511-6.

Nick, seventeen, gets a summer job on the coast of California for what he thinks is a mere conservation project. Many different things suddenly come together at once: A mother gray whale with a sick baby; Marty, a girl who can communicate with the whales; and the hunt for a sunken treasure ship from Sir Francis Drake's expedition. All of these combine to make Nick's summer far from ordinary or safe.

25.30   Woodson, Jacqueline. **The Dear One.** Laurel-Leaf Books, 1991. 145 pp. ISBN 0-440-21420-3.

Catherine and Claire were best friends at Spelman College. Claire became pregnant and left to live in Harlem and have more children; Catherine became a lawyer, married, drank, had Afani, divorced, and joined AA. Now the circle of the college friends closes as Rebecca, Claire's fifteen-year-old daughter, comes to the suburbs to live with Catherine and Afani and to have her own daughter. Afani is only twelve, unable to come to terms with her grandmother's death, and now obligated to share her life and room with Rebecca. Can Rebecca and Afani re-create the friendship of the previous generation?

25.31 Wyman, Andrea. **Red Sky at Morning.** Holiday House, 1991. 230 pp. ISBN 0-8234-0903-1.

In Indiana in 1909, Papa has gone to Oregon to find a new life for the Common family: Callie, Katherine, grandfather Opa, and Mama. A letter comes telling them that all is not going well. Mama, who is expecting a baby, goes into labor, and before the day ends, both Mama and the baby are dead. Katherine goes off to work in a boarding house to help pay for the funeral and Callie is left with Opa. Can Callie endure alone on the farm with ailing Opa?

26 Self-Improvement

26.1 Andersen, Yvonne. **Make Your Own Animated Movies and Videotapes.** Little, Brown and Company, 1991. 163 pp. ISBN 0-316-03941-1.

In this book, Yvonne Andersen explains with illustrations and examples how to create animation. She includes various types of animation, and also offers tips on how to create special effects, edit, and create sound tracks. Many examples of students' works are included, as well as lists of equipment and supplies needed. The book serves as a guide to show beginning animators how to create imaginative films for school or for pleasure. Updated from original release in 1970.

26.2 Gilbert, Sara. **You Can Speak Up in Class.** Illustrated by Roy Doty. Morrow Junior Books, 1991. 64 pp. ISBN 0-688-10304-9.

Are you afraid to hear your own voice in class? Learn techniques for overcoming such fears and feel comfortable joining in class discussions and giving speeches in front of a class. This book lists problems which may cause a speaker discomfort and then provides solutions for conquering these problems. Shyness, fear, boredom, and other hurdles are carefully addressed.

26.3 LeShan, Eda. **What Makes You So Special?** Dial Books, 1992. 145 pp. ISBN 0-8037-1155-7.

You have inherited fifty thousand genes from your parents which combine to make the special human you are. Your uniqueness is also the result of your mother's habits and health during her pregnancy, your school experiences, your family habits and relationships, and your environment. According to

Eda LeShan, understanding all that makes you special is "becoming your own best friend."

26.4 Levinson, Nancy, and Joanne Rocklin. **Getting High in Natural Ways: An Infobook for Young People of All Ages.** Hunter House, 1986. 103 pp. ISBN 0-89793-036-3.

It doesn't take a drug to make someone feel high—sometimes all it takes is a good laugh. Watching movies, dancing, exercising, even crying can make us feel good, thus achieving an emotional high. In easy-to-follow examples, this book leads the reader to an understanding of how to be more in control of emotions, how to be productive, and how to be content with life.

26.5 Levy, Barbara. **How to Draw Clowns.** Illustrated by Barbara Levy. Watermill Press, 1992. 32 pp. ISBN 0-8167-2477-6.

Clowns make people laugh when they perform in the circus, in shows, and at parties. Drawing clowns can be simple by following the four simple steps in this book. Learn how to position, shape, and detail clowns while having fun at the same time. After all, fun is what clowns are all about!

26.6 Martinez, Alicia. **Feeling Fit.** Troll Associates, 1991. 116 pp. ISBN 0-8167-2141-6.

Physical fitness and self-confidence are especially important for girls ages ten to fourteen. But having a "perfect body" is possible for any girl because it simply means having a body that is satisfactory to the individual. This book offers exercise hints; suggests food for fitness; establishes routines for various kinds of activities, like walking, skating, and cycling; and stresses the importance of setting goals, all to achieve a fit body. As the author emphasizes, "Perfection means being the best that you can be." A Smart Talk book.

26.7 Newman, Susan. **Don't Be S.A.D.: A Teenage Guide to Handling Stress, Anxiety & Depression.** Julian Messner, 1991. 121 pp. ISBN 0-671-72611-0.

Stress, anxiety and depression are a part of life, especially during the teen years. Sometimes stress can help people be alert and do their best; however, too much stress may lead to anxiety or depression. This book helps teenagers learn to recognize the effects of stress, to take charge and control a stressful situation, and to know how and where to get help if the stress becomes too much to handle alone.

Appendix of Suggested Readings

Any list of "150 Books for Suggested Reading," all originally published prior to 1990, can hardly be considered comprehensive to meet the needs and tastes of all students. In compiling this list, I included only one title by an author. This does not mean that other books by this person are not noteworthy. In some cases, I listed a title that I thought was worthy of recognition, but which did not seem to get the attention other books by this author received. (Some good books fall between the cracks.) Some titles might be out of print. Support your local library, and request a particular title through its services. This bibliography does include titles that reflect cultural diversity and a variety of literary genres—poetry, mystery, biography/autobiography, fantasy, science fiction, general nonfiction, short stories, historical fiction, humor, and much more.

The list is subjective. I confess I had a good time selecting these, and I hope many students will discover something here to whet their literary, intellectual appetites.

Adoff, Arnold, ed. *Black Out Loud: An Anthology of Modern Poems by Black Americans.*

Aiken, Joan. *The Wolves of Willoughby Chase.*

Alexander, Lloyd. *Westmark.*

Armstrong, William H. *Sounder.*

Arrick, Fran. *Chernowitz!*

Asher, Sandy. *Daughter of the Law.*

Avi. *The Fighting Ground.*

Babbitt, Natalie. *Tuck Everlasting.*

Bellairs, John. *The House with a Clock in its Walls.*

Bennett, Jay. *The Executioner.*

Bierhorst, John, ed. *In the Trail of the Wind: American Indian Poems and Ritual Orations.*

Blos, Joan. *Brothers of the Heart.*

Blume, Judy. *Tiger Eyes.*

Bond, Nancy. *A String in the Harp.*

Boyd, Candy Dawson. *Charlie Pippin.*

Bradford, Richard. *Red Sky at Morning.*

Bridgers, Sue Ellen. *All Together Now.*

Brooks, Bruce. *The Moves Make the Man.*

Bunting, Eve. *Someone is Hiding on Alcatraz Island.*

Byars, Betsy. *The Pinballs.*

Cameron, Eleanor. *The Court of the Stone Children.*

Childress, Alice. *A Hero Ain't Nothin' But a Sandwich.*

Clapp, Patricia. *Dr. Elizabeth: The First Woman Doctor.*

Cleaver, Vera. *Trial Valley.*

Clements, Bruce. *I Tell a Lie Every So Often.*

Cohen, Barbara. *Tell Us Your Secret.*

Cole, Brock. *The Goats.*

Collier, James Lincoln, and Christopher Collier. *The Bloody Country.*

Conford, Ellen. *The Alfred G. Graebner Memorial High School Handbook of Rules and Regulations.*

Conrad, Pam. *Prairie Songs.*

Cooney, Caroline B. *Among Friends.*

Cormier, Robert. *I Am the Chesse.*

Cresswell, Helen. *Ordinary Jack.*

Cunningham, Julia. *Dorp Dead.*

Dahl, Roald. *Boy: Tales of Childhood.*

Danziger, Paula. *The Cat Ate My Gymsuit.*

Davis, Ossie. *Escape to Freedom: A Play about Young Frederick Douglass.*

Dickinson, Peter. *The Changes.*

Duncan, Lois. *Don't Look Behind You.*

Erdoes, Richard, ed. *The Sound of Flutes and Other Indian Legends.*

Evslin, Bernard. *Greeks Bearing Gifts: The Epics of Achilles and Ulysses.*

Fitzhugh, Louise. *Nobody's Family is Going to Change.*

Fleming, Alice. *Trials That Made Headlines.*

Fox, Paula. *One-Eyed Cat.*

Freedman, Russell. *Indian Chiefs.*

French, Michael. *Us Against Them.*

Fritz, Jean. *Homecoming: My Own Story.*

Gallo, Donald R., ed. *Visions: Nineteen Short Stories by Outstanding Writers for Young Adults.*

George, Jean Craighead. *My Side of the Mountain.*

Gilson, Jamie. *Can't Catch Me, I'm the Gingerbread Man.*

Giovanni, Nikki. *Ego-Tripping and Other Poems for Young People.*

Glenn, Mel. *Class Dismissed!*

Greenberg, Jan. *Bye, Bye, Miss American Pie.*

Greene, Bette. *Philip Hall Likes Me, I Reckon Maybe.*

Greenwald, Sheila. *It All Began with Jane Eyre: Or, The Secret Life of Franny Dillman.*

Guy, Rosa. *The Disappearance.*

Hamilton, Virginia. *The Magical Adventures of Pretty Pearl.*

Hansen, Joyce. *Out From This Place.*

Haskins, James. *Fighting Shirley Chisholm.*

Hautzig, Esther. *The Endless Steppe: Growing Up in Siberia.*

Hentoff, Nat. *The Day They Came to Arrest the Book.*

Hermes, Patricia. *You Shouldn't Have to Say Goodbye.*

Hinton, S. E. *The Outsiders.*

Holland, Isabelle. *Of Love and Death and Other Journeys.*

Holman, Felice. *Slake's Limbo.*

Hughes, Monica. *Devil On My Back.*

Hunter, Kristin. *Guests in the Promised Land.*

Hunter, Mollie. *The Stronghold.*

Janeczko, Paul, ed. *Don't Forget to Fly: A Cycle of Modern Poems.*

Johnston, Norma. *Strangers Dark and Gold.*

Jones, Ron. *The Acorn People.*

Kerr, M. E. *Gentlehands.*

Keisel, Stanley. *The War Between the Pitiful Teachers and the Splendid Kids.*

Klein, Norma. *Mom, the Wolf Man and Me.*

Koehn, Ilse. *Mischling, Second Degree: My Childhood in Nazi Germany.*

Konigsburg, E. L. *Journey to an 800 Number.*

Korman, Gordon. *Don't Care High.*

Langton, Jane. *The Fragile Flag.*

Larrick, Nancy, ed. *Crazy to be Alive in Such a Strange World: Poems About People.*

Lasky, Kathryn. *Pageant.*

Lee, Mildred. *The Skating Rink.*

LeGuin, Ursula K. *Very Far Away from Anywhere Else.*

L'Engle, Madeleine. *A Wrinkle in Time.*

Lester, Julius. *To be a Slave.*

Levitin, Sonia. *The Mark of Conte.*

Levoy, Myron. *Alan and Naomi.*

Levy, Elizabeth. *Lawyers for the People: A New Breed of Defenders and Their Work.*

Lipsyte, Robert. *One Fat Summer.*

Livingston, Myra Cohn, ed. *O Frabjous Day! Poetry for Holidays and Special Occasions.*

Lowry, Lois. *Autumn Street.*

Lund, Doris H. *Eric.*

Macauley, David. *Castle.*

MacLachlin, Patricia. *Sarah, Plain and Tall.*

Mathis, Sharon Bell. *Listen for the Fig Tree.*

Mazer, Harry. *Guy Lenny.*

Mazer, Norma Fox. *Dear Bill, Remember Me? And Other Stories.*

McCaffrey, Anne. *Dragonsinger.*

McKinley, Robin. *Beauty: A Retelling of the Story of Beauty & the Beast.*

Meltzer, Milton. *Rescue: The Story of How Gentiles Saved Jews in the Holocaust.*

Miklowitz, Gloria D. *The War Between the Classes.*

Miles, Betty. *Maudie and Me and the Dirty Book.*

Mohr, Nicholasa. *Nilda.*

Myers, Walter Dean. *Fast Sam, Cool Clyde, and Stuff.*

Naylor, Phyllis Reynolds. *Alice in Rapture, Sort Of.*

Newton, Suzanne. *I Will Call It Georgie's Blues.*

Nhuong, Quang Nhuong. *The Land I Lost: Adventures of a Boy in Vietnam.*

Nixon, Joan Lowery. *The Seance.*

O'Dell, Scott. *Child of Fire.*

Patent, Dorothy Hinshaw. *Evolution Goes on Every Day.*

Paterson, Katherine. *Park's Quest.*

Paulsen, Gary. *Hatchet.*

Peck, Richard. *The Dreadful Future of Blossom Culp.*

Peck, Robert Newton. *A Day No Pigs Would Die.*

Peet, Bill. *Bill Peet, An Autobiography.*

Pfeffer, Susan Beth. *The Year Without Michael.*

Pierce, Tamora. *Alanna: The First Adventure.*

Plotz, Helen, ed. *The Gift Outright: America to Her Poets.*

Prelutsky, Jack. *Nightmares: Poems to Trouble Your Sleep.*

Pullman, Philip. *The Ruby in the Smoke.*

Raskin, Ellen. *The Westing Game.*

Rawls, Wilson. *Where the Red Fern Grows.*

Rinaldi, Ann. *The Last Silk Dress.*

Rodgers, Mary. *Freaky Friday.*

Rodowsky, Colby. *The Gathering Room.*

Rylant, Cynthia. *A Fine White Dust.*

St. George, Judith. *The Mount Rushmore Story.*

Silverstein, Shel. *Where the Sidewalk Ends: Poems and Drawings.*

Simon, Seymour. *Poisonous Snakes.*

Singer, Isaac Bashevis. *Naftali the Storyteller and His Horse, Sus and Other Stories.*

Sleator, William. *House of Stairs.*

Smith, Doris Buchanan. *A Taste of Blackberries.*

Snyder, Anne. *My Name Is Davey: I'm an Alcoholic.*

Snyder, Carol. *Memo to Myself When I Have a Teenage Kid.*

Soto, Gary. *Living Up the Street.*

Spinelli, Jerry. *Space Station Seventh Grade.*

Staples, Suzanne Fisher. *Shabanu: Daughter of the Wind.*

Stine, R. L. *Twisted.*

Strasser, Todd. *Friends Till the End.*

Sullivan, George. *How the White House Really Works.*

Talbert, Marc. *Dead Birds Singing.*

Taylor, Mildred D. *Roll of Thunder, Hear My Cry.*

Townsend, John Rowe. *Noah's Castle.*

Voigt, Cynthia. *Izzy, Willy-Nilly.*

Westall, Robert. *The Machine Gunners.*

Whitney, Phyllis A. *Mystery of the Golden Horn.*

Wolkstein, Diane, ed. *The Magic Orange Tree and Other Haitian Folktales.*

Yep, Laurence. *Child of the Owl.*

Yolen, Jane. *The Girl Who Cried Flowers and Other Tales.*
Zindel, Paul. *A Begonia for Miss Applebaum.*

M. Jerry Weiss
Jersey City State College

Directory of Publishers

Harry N. Abrams. Subsidiary of Times Mirror Company, 100 Fifth Avenue, New York, NY 10011. 800-345-1359.

Ace Books. Division of Berkley Publishing Group. Orders to: P. O. Box 506, East Rutherford, NJ 07073. 800-631-8571.

Aladdin Books. Imprint of Macmillan. Orders to: 100 Front Street, Riverside, NJ 08075. 800-257-5755.

Atheneum. Division of Macmillan. Orders to: 100 Front Street, Riverside, NJ 08075. 800-257-5755.

Atheneum/Jean Karl Books. See Atheneum.

Avon. Orders to: P. O. Box 767, Dresden, TN 38225. 800-762-0779.

Ballantine Books. Division of Random House. Orders to: 400 Hahn Road, Westminster, MD 21157. 800-733-3000.

Bantam Books. Division of Bantam Doubleday Dell, 666 Fifth Avenue, New York, NY 10103. 800-223-6834.

Bradbury Press. Imprint of Macmillan. Orders to: 100 Front Street, Riverside, NJ 08075. 800-257-5755.

Bullseye Books. Imprint of Knopf, a division of Random House. Orders to: 400 Hahn Road, Westminster, MD 21157. 800-733-3000.

Carolrhoda Books. 241 First Avenue, N., Minneapolis, MN 55401. 800-328-4929.

Clarion Books. Divison of Houghton Mifflin. Orders to: Wayside Road, Burlington, MA 01803. 800-225-3362. Call for school ordering information.

Cobblehill Books. Division of Penguin USA. Orders to: 120 Woodbine Street, Bergenfield, NJ 07621. 800-253-6476.

Collier Books. Division of Macmillan. Orders to: 100 Front Street, Riverside, NJ 08075. 800-257-5755.

Commission on Voluntary Service and Action. P. O. Box 117, New York, NY 10009. 212-974-2405.

Crestwood House. Imprint of Macmillan. Orders to: 100 Front Street, Riverside, NJ 08075. 800-257-5755.

Crown. Division of Random House. Orders to: 400 Hahn Road, Westminster, ND 21157. 800-733-3000.

Thomas Y. Crowell. Distributed by HarperCollins. Orders to: 1000 Keystone Industrial Park, Scranton, PA 18512. 800-242-7737.

Delacorte Press. Division of Bantam Doubleday Dell. Orders to: 666 Fifth Avenue, New York, NY 10103. 800-223-6834.

Dial Books. Division of Penguin USA. Orders to: 120 Woodbine Street, Bergenfield, NJ 07621. 800-253-6476.

Dillon Press. Imprint of Macmillan. Orders to: 100 Front Street, Riverside, NJ 08075. 800-257-5755.

Doubleday. Division of Bantam Doubleday Dell. Orders to: 666 Fifth Avenue, New York, NY 10103. 800-223-6834.

Dutton Children's Books. Division of Penguin USA. Orders to: 120 Woodbine Street, Bergenfield, NJ 07621. 800-253-6476.

Eakin Press. Division of Sunbelt Media. P. O. Drawer 90159, Austin, TX 78709-0159. 512-288-1771.

Farrar, Straus and Giroux. 390 Murray Hill Parkway, East Rutherford, NJ 07073. ATTN: Dept. B. 800-631-8571.

Four Winds Press. Imprint of Macmillan. Orders to: 100 Front Street, Riverside, NJ 08075. 800-257-5755.

Garrett Educational Corporation. P. O. Box 1588, Ada, OK 74820. 800-654-9366.

Greenwillow Books. Division of William Morrow. Orders to: 39 Plymouth Street, Fairfield, NJ 07004. 800-843-9389.

Gulliver Books. Imprint of Harcourt Brace Jovanovich, 6277 Sea Harbor Drive, Orlando, FL 32887. 800-225-5425.

Harcourt Brace Jovanovich. 6277 Sea Harbor Drive, Orlando, FL 32887. 800-225-5425.

Harper & Row. Division of HarperCollins. Orders to: 1000 Keystone Industrial Park, Scranton, PA 18512. 800-242-7737.

HarperCollins. Orders to: 1000 Keystone Industrial Park, Scranton, PA 18512. 800-242-7737.

HarperCollins/Charlotte Zolotow Books. See HarperCollins.

HarperCollins/Laura Geringer Books. See HarperCollins.

HarperCollins/Willa Perlman Books. See HarperCollins.

HarperKeypoint. See HarperCollins.

Holiday House. 425 Madison Avenue, New York, NY 10017. 212-688-0085.

Henry Holt. Orders to: 4375 W. 1980 S., Salt Lake City, UT 84104. 800-488-5233.

Houghton Mifflin Company. Orders to: Wayside Road, Burlington, MA 01803. 800-225-3362.

Hunter House. P. O. Box 2914, Alameda, CA 94501. 510-865-5282.

Ivy Books. Division of Ballantine Books. Orders to: 400 Hahn Road, Westminster, MD 21157. 800-733-3000.

Laurel-Leaf Books. Imprint of Bantam Doubleday Dell, 666 Fifth Avenue, New York, NY 10103. 800-223-6834.

Lerner Publications Company. 241 First Avenue, N., Minneapolis, MN 55401. 800-328-4929.

J. B. Lippincott. 227 E. Washington Square, Philadelphia, PA 19106-3780. 800-638-3030.

Little, Brown and Company. Division of Time Warner Publishing. Orders to: 200 West Street, Waltham, MA 02254. 800-343-9204.

Little Simon. Imprint of Simon & Schuster. Orders to: 200 Old Tappan Road, Old Tappan, NJ 07675. 800-223-2336.

Lodestar Books. Division of Dutton Children's Books. Orders to: Penguin USA, 120 Woodbine Street, Bergenfield, NJ 07621. 800-253-6476.

Lothrop, Lee & Shepard Books. Division of William Morrow. Orders to: 39 Plymouth Street, Fairfield, NJ 07004. 800-843-9389.

Macmillan. Orders to: 100 Front Street, Riverside, NJ 08075. 800-257-5755.

Margaret K. McElderry Books. Division of Macmillan Children's Books Group. See Macmillan.

Julian Messner. Division of Silver Burdett Press. Orders to: P. O. Box 1226, Westwood, NJ 07675-1226. 800-843-3464.

Millbrook Press. 2 Old New Milford Road, Brookfield, CT 06804. 203-740-2220.

William Morrow. Orders to: 39 Plymouth Street, Fairfield, NJ 07004. 800-843-9389.

New Discovery Books. Imprint of Macmillan. Orders to: 100 Front Street, Riverside, NJ 08075. 800-257-5755.

Orchard Books. Division of Franklin Watts, 387 Park Avenue, S., New York, NY 10016. 800-672-6672.

Philomel Books. Imprint of The Putnam Berkley Group. Orders to: 390 Murray Hill Parkway, East Rutherford, NJ 07073. 800-631-8571.

Pocket Books. Division of Simon & Schuster. Orders to: 200 Old Tappan Road, Old Tappan, NJ 07675. 800-223-2336.

Puffin Books. Division of Penguin USA. Orders to: 120 Woodbine Street, Bergenfield, NJ 07621.

G. P. Putnam's Sons. Imprint of The Putnam Berkley Group. Orders to: 390 Murray Hill Parkway, East Rutherford, NJ 07073. 800-631-8571.

Scholastic. Orders to: 2931 E. McCarty Street, Jefferson City, MO 65102. 800-325-6149.

Charles Scribner's Sons. Division of Macmillan. Orders to: 100 Front Street, Riverside, NJ 08075. 800-257-5755.

Sierra Club Books. Orders to: 400 Hahn Road, Westminster, MD 21157. 800-733-3000.

Simon & Schuster. Orders to: 200 Old Tappan Road, Old Tappan, NJ 07675. 800-223-2336.

Skylark Books. Imprint of Bantam Doubleday Dell, 666 Fifth Avenue, New York, NY 10103. 800-223-6834.

Sports Illustrated for Kids Books. Distributed by Little, Brown and Company. Orders to: 200 West Street, Waltham, MA 02254. 800-343-9204.

Sterling Publishing. 387 Park Avenue, S., New York, NY 10016-8810. 800-367-9692.

Tambourine Books. Division of Morrow. Orders to: 39 Plymouth Street, Fairfield, NJ 07004. 800-843-9389.

Tern Enterprise Books. Imprint of M. Friedman Publishing Group, 15 W. 26th Street, New York, NY 10010. 212-685-6610.

Troll Associates. Subsidiary of Educational Reading Services, 100 Corporate Drive, Mahwah, NJ 07430. 800-526-5289.

Viking. Division of Penguin USA. Orders to: 120 Woodbine Street, Bergenfield, NJ 07621. 800-253-6476.

Viking/Reinhardt Books. See Viking.

Walker and Company. Division of Walker Publishing, 720 Fifth Avenue, New York, NY 10019. 800-289-2553.

Watermill Press. Imprint of Troll Associates, subsidiary of Educational Reading Series, 100 Corporate Drive, Mahwah, NJ 07430. 800-526-5289.

Franklin Watts. Subsidiary of Grolier, Inc. Orders to: 5450 N. Cumberland Avenue, Chicago, IL 60656. 800-672-6672.

Yearling Books. Imprint of Bantam Doubleday Dell, 666 Fifth Avenue, New York, NY 10103. 800-223-6834.

Jane Yolen Books. Imprint of Harcourt Brace Jovanovich, Inc. Orders to: 465 South Lincoln Drive, Troy, MO 63379. 800-225-5425.

Author Index

Title Index

Subject Index

Abolition, 25.3
Abortion, 13.8, 13.19
Actors and acting, 14.13, 15.3, 15.42, 16.22, 18.8, 19.4, 19.8, 19.21, 22.2
Adolescence, 2.15, 13.13, 13.22, 14.29, 26.7
Adoption, 15.40, 15.44, 15.54, 23.8, 24.15
Africa, 6.3, 7.15, 16.24, 20.4, 21.26
African Americans, 9.5, 10.8, 10.12, 15.19, 15.45, 16.7, 16.25, 18.28, 19.9, 21.4, 21.9, 21.11, 21.19, 21.21, 21.23, 21.25–27, 21.46, 21.47, 25.8, 25.19, 25.24
Aging, 23.12
AIDS, 19.2, 21.19, 23.6, 23.11
Airplanes, 15.8, 21.16, 22.5, 22.9
Alcoholism, 3.8, 25.30
Aliens, 6.2, 6.4, 6.16
American Revolution, 25.25
Ancient civilizations, 10.21, 24.25
Animal rights, 21.22
Animals (see also specific animals), 1.1–7, 2.9, 2.14, 2.15, 3.13, 3.40, 4.7, 7.5, 7.12, 11.3–6, 11.9–11, 11.13, 11.17, 11.29, 11.32, 11.33, 11.35, 11.37, 11.38, 11.41, 14.8, 14.11, 14.27, 15.11, 18.14, 19.5, 19.14, 20.8, 24.22, 25.14, 25.25
Animals, extinct, 14.5, 24.22, 25.20, 25.29
Animation, 12.7, 26.1
Anteaters, 11.37
Apartheid, 7.15, 16.24, 21.26
Archeology, 3.10, 6.3, 11.24, 12.6
Architecture and construction, 10.2, 11.26, 21.14
Arson, 24.6
Art and artists, 9.1, 9.5, 14.2, 15.41, 18.9, 18.21, 21.15, 21.30, 26.5

Asian Americans, 7.18, 16.5, 16.9, 16.13, 16.26, 21.38, 21.41, 21.50, 24.13
Astronomy, 12.4, 12.9
Atlantis, 6.17
Australia, 7.8, 11.6, 11.37, 11.38, 16.14
Auto racing, 18.18
Autobiographies, 21.27, 21.28, 21.41, 21.42

Baseball, 8.3, 8.4, 8.10, 8.12, 8.14, 18.20, 19.13, 21.4, 21.11, 21.57, 22.1
Basketball, 8.11, 21.19
Bats, 11.32
Berlin Wall, 13.9
Bible, and Bible stories, 4.1
Biking, 6.18
Biographical fiction, 21.10
Biographies, 21.1–9, 21.11–26, 21.29–40, 21.43–57
Biology, 11.2, 11.5, 11.6, 11.9, 11.17, 11.19–21, 11.25, 11.30, 11.39, 11.41, 11.43
Birds, 14.5, 17.9, 25.20
Boxing, 16.6, 21.9
Buried treasure, 3.7, 3.26, 14.4, 14.17, 24.24, 25.29
Business, 21.44

Cambodia, 24.8
Cancer, 23.13
Captivity, 3.1, 25.15, 25.23
Careers, 21.44, 22.1–10, 22.12–15
Cats, 2.9, 3.40, 4.7, 14.8
Celts, 2.32
Chemical warfare, 3.38
China, 16.11, 24.22, 24.26
Chinese Americans, 7.18, 16.26, 21.41
Christmas, 16.20
Civil rights, 10.8, 10.12, 21.25–27, 25.8, 25.24

About the Committee

Paul Hirth and C. Anne Webb. *Photo: Kenneth S. Lane.*

Editor **C. Anne Webb** discovered young adult literature in 1968, served as president for the Assembly on Literature for Adolescents in 1988, and after thirty years retired from full-time teaching in 1993. She now freelances, substitutes, and consults.

Paul Hirth, associate editor, is the English department chair at Lafayette Senior High School. Paul served as president of the Greater St. Louis English Teachers Association and is current chair of the Assembly of Science and Humanities.

Julie Aikens teaches at Royster Junior High School in Chanute, Kansas. She edits *Young Kansas Writers* for KATE (Kansas Association of Teachers of English).

Betty David is a reading teacher at Clary Middle School in Syracuse, New York, and is a state Whole Language participant.

Martha Eise, librarian at St. Mary's Grade School in Bridgeton, Missouri, is working on a degree in management and supervision.

RoseMarie Fleming teaches eighth-grade language arts at Wydown Middle School in Clayton, Missouri. She has received grants to develop units using adolescent literature with multicultural influences.

Barbara Gunkel, a former English teacher, is now a librarian at Desert Spring High School in the Paradise Valley School District in Arizona.

Linda Hayes teaches English/language arts at McGrath Elementary School in Brentwood, Missouri.

Penny Longnecker, an avid YA reader, teaches at Nipher Middle School in the Kirkwood District in Missouri.

Lydia Martin is district leader for the Marquette area of the Illinois Association of Teachers of English. She teaches at Roxana Junior-Senior High School in Roxana, Illinois.

Susan Morice has served many years on the board of the Greater St. Louis English Teachers Association (GSLETA). She presently teaches at Wydown Middle School in Clayton, Missouri.

Susan Rakow contributed to the eighth edition of *Your Reading,* as well as to this ninth edition. She completed her degree work teaching full time at Beachwood Middle School in Cleveland, Ohio.

Linda Reaves teaches at Chattanooga State Technical Community College in Chattanooga, Tennessee. She is a regular participant in the ALAN workshop.

Betsy Simmons graduated from the school of library science at the University of South Florida, Tampa. She is now a librarian at Richmond Heights Public Library in St. Louis County.

Clifford E. Stratton retired after forty years in education, as both an English teacher and a principal. He is now a lay minister for the United Methodist Church and conducts book talks in his former school to promote reading.

Elaine Weatherford serves as elementary librarian at two schools in the Fox School District in Arnold, Missouri.